Volume 7

Industrial Organization & Regulation Reading Lists

Economics Reading Lists,
Course Outlines, Exams,
Puzzles & Problems

Compiled by Edward Tower, *Duke University*, August 1990

NOTES TO USERS AND POTENTIAL CONTRIBUTORS

These teaching materials are drawn from both undergraduate and graduate programs at 93 major colleges and universities. They are designed to widen the horizons of individual professors and curriculum committees. Some include suggestions for term-paper topics, and many of the lists are useful guides for students seeking both topics and references for term papers and theses. Thus, they should enable faculty members to advise students more effectively and efficiently. They will also be useful to prospective graduate students seeking more detailed information about various graduate programs; to those currently enrolled in programs who are preparing for field examinations; and to librarians responsible for acquisitions in economics. Finally, they may interest researchers and administrators who wish to know more about how their own work and the work of their department is being received by the profession.

The exams, puzzles and problems include both undergraduate and graduate exams contributed by economics departments and individual professors. They should be especially useful to professors making up exams and problem sets and to students studying for comprehensive exams. They may also serve as the focus for study groups.

From time to time we will reprint updated and expanded versions. Therefore, we would welcome new or updated teaching materials, especially those which compliment material in this collection or cover areas we missed. Potential contributors should contact Ed Tower, Economics Department, Duke University, Durham, North Carolina 27706, U.S.A.

While Eno River Press has copyrighted the entire collection, authors of the various parts retain the right to reproduce and assign the reproduction of their own materials as they choose. Thus, anyone wishing to reproduce particular materials should contact the author of them. Similarly, those wishing to make verbatim use of department-wide examinations, except as teaching materials for one's own class, should contact the department chairperson concerned.

Acknowledgement

The associate compilers for this series are Cliff Carrubba, Maia Sisk, and Ron Temple. Cliff is a senior at Duke, majoring in Economics and Political Science. Maia is a senior at Duke, majoring in Economics and Computer Science. Ron is a graduate student at Harvard's John F. Kennedy School of Government. Andy Seamons, Kathy Shelley, and Geoff Somes also provided important help with production of the volumes. The cover was designed by the Division of Audiovisual Education, Duke University, and the volumes were printed by Multiprint, Inc., New York.

Eno River Press, Inc.©1990. All rights reserved. No part of this publication may be reproduced, stored in a retrieval system, or transmitted, in any form or by any means, electronic, mechanical, photocopying, recording or otherwise, without the prior permission of Eno River Press.

Eno River Press
Box 4900, Duke Station
Durham, North Carolina 27706 U.S.A.

ISBN for this volume: 0-88024-135-7
ISBN Eno River Press for this series: 0-88024-128-4
Library of Congress Catalog Number: 90-082701

INDUSTRIAL ORGANIZATION READING LISTS

Contents

RICHARD J. ARNOULD, *University of Illinois*	
Antitrust Economics, G	5
WILLIAM J. BAUMOL AND ROBERT WILLIG, *Princeton University*	
Industrial Organization and Public Policy, G	15
SEVERIN BORENSTEIN, *University of Michigan*	
Government Regulation of Industry, R&E, U	18
Economics of Government Regulation, R&E, G	26
DENNIS W. CARLTON AND ROBERT H. GERTNER, *University of Chicago, Graduate School of Business*	
Advanced Industrial Organization I, G	39
Advanced Industrial Organization II, G	43
H. E. FRECH III, *University of California at Santa Barbara*	
Industrial Organization, R&E, G	48
HENRY GRABOWSKI, *Duke University*	
Regulation and Industrial Economics, R&E, U	68
Industrial Organization II, G	77
PAUL L. JOSKOW, *Massachusetts Institute of Technology*	
Government Regulation of Industry, U	84
Industrial Organization II, G	88
AVERY KATZ, *University of Michigan*	
Government Regulation of Industry, R&E, U	99
RICHARD A. MILLER, *Wesleyan University*	
Antitrust Economics, U	108
Industrial Organization, U	113
SAM PELTZMAN, *University of Chicago, Graduate School of Business*	
Industrial Organization, R&E, G	122
Economics of Regulation, R&E, G	137
ROBERT S. PINDYCK, *Massachusetts Institute of Technology, Sloan School of Management*	
Industrial Economics for Strategic Decisions, R&E, G	164
STEVE POLASKY, *Boston College*	
Industrial Organization, R&E, U	174
Industrial Organization, R&E, G	183
ROBERT PORTER, *Northwestern University*	
The Structure of American Industry, R&E, U	202
Industrial Organization, R&E, G	211

ANDREW POSTLEWAITE, *University of Pennsylvania*
    Industrial Organization, U   228

STEPHEN W. SALANT, *University of Michigan*
    Industrial Organization, R&E, G   230

FREDERIC M. SCHERER, *Harvard University, John F. Kennedy School of Government*
    The Economics of Industry, U   259
    (taught at Swarthmore College)

PETER SWAN, *University of New South Wales*
    Economics of Regulation, G   263
    Industrial Organization, R&E, G   268

LESTER TELSER, *University of Chicago*
    Theories of Competition and Their Applications, G   283

M. A. UTTON AND MICHAEL WATERSON, *University of Reading*
    Business Economics, U&G   287

OLIVER E. WILLIAMSON, *University of California at Berkeley*
    The Economics of Institutions, G   292

* * *

U = Undergraduate   **G** = Graduate
R&E = Reading Lists & Exams and/or Problems

UNIVERSITY OF ILLINOIS
DEPARTMENT OF ECONOMICS

R.J. ARNOULD
SPRING 1989

Antitrust Economics
Economics 481

This reading list is to provide a survey of a number of antitrust topics. Do not panic as a result of its length. Not all topics will be covered. An attempt is made to provide balance among theoretical and empirical issues. Also, after many topics readings are provided that contain detailed analyses of particular (recent) cases. Most of these are taken from Kwoka and White, The Antitrust Revolution, (Scott, Foresman and Co., 1989). Sometimes these cases will provide a basis for class discussions.

I strongly suggest that you read chapters 19-21 in Scherer, Industrial Markets Structure and Economic Performance and Chapter 3 in Posner, Antitrust Law: An Economic Perspective during the first week to get an overall perspective of antitrust issues. Citations that refer to Posner are from the same book; those referring to Tirole are found in The Theory of Industrial Organization, 1988; citations that refer to Singer are in E. M. Singer, Antitrust Economics and Legal Analysis, Grid Publishing, Columbus, OH, 1981; those referring to New Developments are from J. Stiglitz and G. Mathewson, New Developments in The Analysis of Market Structure, MIT Press, and those referring to Spulber are in Regulation and Markets. Readings with an asterisk are more important and are on reserve in the Commerce Library.

I. Antitrust Policy: Introduction and Overview

   *Posner, Ch. 1-3
   *Scherer, Ch. 18.
   *R. Schmalensee, "Antitrust and the New Industrial Economics" American Economic Review, May 1982.
   *R. Posner, "Chicago School of Antitrust Enforcement," U. Pa. Law Review, April 1979.

II. Relevant Market Determination

   *Posner, pp. 125-134.
   *Stigler, George and Robert A. Sherwin, "The Extent of the Market," Journal of Law and Economics, 28 (3) (October 1985), pp. 555-587.
   Horowitz, Ira, "Market Definition in antitrust Analysis: A Regression-Based Approach," Southern Economic Journal, Vol. 48, No. 1, July 1981, pp. 1-16.
   *Elzinga, K., and T. Hogarty, "The Problem of Geographic Market Delineation in Antimerger Suits," Antitrust Bulletin, Spring 1973, pp. 45-81.

*Scheffman, David and P. Spiller, "Geographic Market Definition under U.S. Department of Justice Merger Guidelines," J. of Law & Economics, 30 (1), (April 1987), pp. 123-128.

III Collusion (Sherman act, Section 1 and 2)

A. STRAIGHT-FORWARD PRICE FIXING

1) Theory

Posner, Ch. 4, 7.
Tirole, Ch. 6.
*G. J. Stigler, "A Theory of Oligopoly," Journal of Political Economy, February 1964.
*Osborne, D. K., "Cartel Problems," AER, Dec. 1976.
*d'Aspremont, C., and J. Gabszewitlz, "On The Stability of Collusion," in New Developments.
*Salop, S. "Practices That (Credibly) Facilitate Oligopoly Co-ordination," in New Developments.

2) Empirical Studies

*Sjostrom, W., "Collusion in Ocean Shipping: A Test of Monopoly and Empty Core Models, JPE (Oct 1989) pp. 1160-1179.
Ash, P. and J. Seneca, "Is Collusion Profitable?" RESTAT, Feb. 1976, pp. 1-12.
Posner, R. A., "A Statistical Study of Antitrust Enforcement," JLE, Oct. 1970, pp. 365-420.
*Hay, G. and D. Kelley, "An Empirical Survey of Price Fixing and Collusion," JLE, April 1974, pp. 13-38.
*Porter, Robert, "A Study of Cartel Stability: The Joint Economic Committee, 1880-1886," Bell Journal of Economics, 14 (1983) pp. 301-314.
Lee, L. F. and R. Porter, "Switching Regression Models --- With Application to Cartel Stability," Econometrica, Vol. 52 (Jan. 1984)

3) Case studies

Case 7. "Practices That Facilitate Cooperation: The Ethyl Case (1984)," George Hay.
Kwoka and White
Grether, D. M. and C. Plott, "The Effect of Market -- Practices in Oligopoly Markets: An Experimental Examination of the Ethyl Case," Economic Inquiry, 22 (1984): 479-507.

B. Tacit Collution -- Conscious Parallelism

1) Theory

*Schmalensee, R., "Entry Deterence in the Ready-To-Eat Breakfast Cereal Industry," Bell Journal, Autumn 1978, pp. 407-414.

Scherer, F. M., "The Welfare Economics of Product Variety: An Application to The Ready To Eat Cereals Industry, " *Journal of Industrial Economics*, 28 (Dec. 1979), pp. 113-134.

*Gisser, Micha, "Price Leadership and Welfare Losses in U.S. Manufacturing," *AER* 76 (4) Sept. 1986, pp. 756-67.

_____, "Price Leadership and Dynamic Aspects of Oligopoly in U.S. Manufacturing," *JPE*, 92 (Dec. 1984), 1035-1048.

Haddock, D., "Base-Point Pricing: Competitive vs. Collusive Theories," *AER* 72 (June 1982), pp. 289-306.

2) Empirical Studies

*Sumner, D., 1981, "Measurement of Monopoly Behavior: An Application to the Cigarette Industry," *Journal of Political Economy*, 89:1010-1019.

Bresnahan, T., 1981, "The Relationship between Price and Marginal Cost in the U.S. Automobile Industry," *Journal of Econometrics*, 17:201-227.

* _____, 1987a, "Competition and Collusion in the American Automobile Industry: The 1955 Price War," *Journal of Industrial Economics*, 35:457-482.

3) Case Studies

Nicholls, W. H., "The Tobacco Case of 1946," *AER*, Vol. 39, (1949), pp. 284-96.

IV. Monopolization -- Indsutry Behavior
(Sherman Act, Section 2; FTCA, Section 5)

A. Definitions of Predation

*Areeda, P. and D. Turner, "Predatory Pricing and Related Practices under Section 2 of the Sherman Act," *Harvard Law Review*, 1975, p. 697.

_____, "Scherer on Predatory Pricing: A Reply," *Harvard Law Review*, 1976, p. 891.

_____, "Williamson on Predatory Pricing," *Yale Law Journal*, 1978, p. 1337.

Telser, L. G., "Cutthroat Competition and the Long Purse," *JLE*, Oct. 1966, p. 259.

Scherer, F. M., "Predatory Pricing and the Sherman Act: A Comment," *Harvard Law Review*, 1976, p 869.

_____, "Some Last Words on Predatory Pricing," *Harvard Law Review*, 1976, p. 901.

*Williamson, O. E., "Predatory Pricing: A Strategic and Welfare Analysis," *Yale Law Journal*, 1977, p. 284.

_____, "A Preliminary Response," *Yale Law Journal*, 1978, p. 1353.

_____, "Williamson on Predatory Pricing II," *Yale Law Journal*, May 1979, p. 1183.

Joskow, P. and A. K. Klevorick, "A Framework for Analyzing Predatory Pricing Policy," Yale Law Journal, 1979, p. 213.
*Ordover, J. And R. Willig, "An Economic Definition of Predation," Yale Law Journal, Vol. 91 (Nov. 1981)

B. Theories of Predation

Posner, pp. 184-196.

McGee, J., "Predatory Price Cutting: The Standard Oil (N.J.) Case," JLE, Oct. 1958.
*_____, "Predatory Pricing Revisited, " JLE, Oct. 1980, pp. 289-300.
*Burns, M., "Predatory Pricing and The Acquisition Cost of Competitors," JPE, 94 (April 1986) pp. 266-296.
Fudenberg, D. and J. Tirole, "A 'Signal-Jamming' Theory of Predation," Rand, 17 (Autumn 1986), pp. 366-376.
Gilbert, R., "Premptive Competition," New Developments, pp. 90-124.
J. Miller III and Paul Pautler, "Predation: The Changing View In Economics and the Law," JLE 28 (1985)
Krattenmaher, T.and S. Salop, "Anticompetitive Exculsion: Raising Rivals' Costs to Achieve Power over Price," Yale Law Journal, 96 (Dec. 1986), 209-293.
*Salop, S. and D. Scheffman, "Raising Rival's Cost," AER, Vol. 73, (May 1983), pp. 267-172.

C. Case Studies

Case 8: "Nonprice Predation and Attempted Monopolization: The Coffee (General Foods) Case (1984)," John Hillce and Phillip B. Nelson.
Case 9: "Collusion Predation: Matsushita v. Zenith (1986)," Kenneth Elzinger
Case 6: "Dominant Firm Response to Competition Challenge: Peripheral Equipment Manufacturings: Suits against IBM (1979-1983)," Gerald W. Brock.

V. Vertical Arrangements

A. Theory of Vertical Integration

Tirole, Ch. 4.

1) Transaction Costs

Posner, pp. 196-201.
*Williamson, "Vertical Integration of Production: Market Failure Consideration," AER, May 1971, pp. 112-123.
New Developments, part III.
*Williamson, O. E., "Assessing Vertical Market Restrictions: Antitrust Ramifications of the Transactions Cost Approach," U. Pa Law Review, Vol. 127, (April 1979).

2) Monopoly Power

*Vernon & Graham, "Profitability of Monopolization by Vertical Integration," *JPE*, July-August 1971, pp. 924-25.

Hay, "An Economic Analysis of Vertical Integration," *Ind. Org. Review*, 1973, pp. 188-198.

*Warren-Boulton, F., "Vertical Control with Variable Proportions," *JPE*, Vol. 82, No. 4, pp. 783-802, July 1974.

Mallela, and Nahata, "Theory of Vertical Control with Variable Proportions," *JPE* (95) (1980), pp. 1009-1025.

*Westfield, F., "Vertical Integration: Does Product Price Rise or Fall?" *AER*, Vol 71, No. 3, pp. 334-346, June 1981.

*Dixit, A. K., "Vertical Integration in a Monopolistically Competitive Industry," *International Journal of Industrial Organization*, 1 (March 1983), 63-78.

Gallini, N. and R. W. Winter, "On Vertical Control in Monopolistic Competition," *International Journal of Industrial Organization*, 1 (August 1983), 275-86.

Greenhut, M. L. and H. Ohta, "Vertical Integration of Successive Oligopolists," *AER*, March 1979.

B Vertical Mergers

1) Theory

*Fisher, A. A. and R. Sciacca, "An Economic Analysis of Vertical Merger Enforcement Policy in R. O Zerbe," *Research in Law & Economics*, (1984)

Ordover, J., G. Saloner and S. Salop, "Equilibrium Vertical Foreclosure," mimeo.

2) Empirical Studies

*Perry, M. K., "Forward Integration by Alcoa: 1888-1930," 29. *J. Ind. Econ.*, 1980.

Lafferty, Ronald N., Robert H. Lande and John B. Kirkwood, "Impact Evaluation of Federal Trade Commission Vertical Restraints Cases," Bereau of Competition, Federal Trade Commission, Washington, August 1984.

Allen, T., "Vertical Integration and Market Foreclosure: Case of Cement," *Journal of Law and Economics*, April 1971, Comments, Oct. 1972.

3) Case Studies

Case 12 "Vertical Integration as a Threat to Competition: Airline Computer Reservation Systems," Margaret E. Guerin-Calvert.

C. Vertical Restraints

*Rey P. and J. Tirole, "The Logic of Vertical Restraints,"
    AER 76 (5) Dec. 1986, pp. 921-939.
*Mathewson, G. F., and R. A. Winter, "An Economic Theory
    of Vertical Restraints," Rand Journal of Economics,
    15:Spring (1984), pp. 27-38.
Contemporary policy Issues 3 (Sep. 1985) pp. 1-43.
Spulber, Ch. 16.4.

1) Resale Price Maintenance

*Holohan, W., "A Theoretical Analysis of Resale Price
    Maintenance,:" JET, Dec. 1979, pp. 411-420.
*Marvel H. P. and S. McCaffety, "Resale Price
    Maintenance and Quality Certification," Rand
    Journal of Ecnomics, Autumn 1984.
    *_____, "The Welfare
    Effects of Resale Price Maintenance," JLE 28 (May
    1985), pp. 363-380.
Telser, L., "Why Should Manufacturers Want Fair Trade?"
    JLE, Vol. 3 (Oct. 1960), pp. 86-105.

2) Case Study

*T.W. Gilligan, "The Competitive Effects of R.P.M.,"
    Rand Journal, 17 (Winter 1986), 544-556.
Case 13: Resale Price Maintenance Reexamined: Monsante,
    Frederick Warren-Boulton

3) Exclusive Dealing and Territorial Restrictions

*Marvel, Howard P., "Exclusive Dealing," Journal of Law
    and Economics, Vol. 25 (April 1982), pp. 1-25.
*Easterbrook, Frank, H., "Vertical Arrangements and the
    Rule of Reason," Antitrust Law Journal, Vol. 53,
    p135, 1984.
Katz, B., "Territorial Exclusivity in the Soft Drink
    Industry," J. Ind. Econ., Sept. 1978, pp. 85-96.
Posner, R. A., "The Rule of Reason and the Economic
    Approach," Univ. Chicago Law Rev., Fall 1977.
_____, "Exclusionary Practices and Antitrust
    Laws," Univ. Chicago Law Rev., March 1974, p. 506.
Rubin, P., "The Theory of the Firm and the Structure of
    the Franchise Contract," JLE, April 1978.
Inaba, F. S., "Franchising: Monopoly by Contract,"
    SEJ, July 1980, p. 65.

4) Case Studies

Case 10: Territorial Restraints: GTE Sylvania (1977),
    Lee Preston.

5) Tying Arrangements and Two Part Tarrifs

Singer, Ch. 3

*Blair, R. D. and D. L. Kaserman, "Vertical Integration, Tying, and Antitrust Policy," <u>AER</u>, June 1978.
Oi, W. Y., "A Disneyland Dilemma: Two-Part Tariffs for a Mickey Mouse Monopoly," <u>Quarterly Journal of Economics</u>, February 1971.
*Schmalensee, R., "Monopolistic Two-Part Pricing Arrangements, <u>Bell Journal</u>, Autumn 1981.
Adams, W. J., and J. L. Yellen, "Commodity Bundling and the Burden of Monopoly," <u>Quarterly Journal of Economics</u>, August 1976.
Hansen, R. and R. Roberts, "Metered Tying Arrangements, Allocative Efficiency, and Price Discrimination," <u>SEJ</u>, July 1980, pp. 73-83.
*Stockdale, "An Economic and Legal Analysis of Physical Tie-Ins," <u>Yale Law Journal</u>, March 1980, p.769.
Klein, B. and Lester F. Saft, "The Law and Economics of Franchise Tying Contracts," <u>JLE</u> 28 (May 1985), pp. 345-362.

VI. Price Discrimination

Tirole, Chapter 3.

Spulber, Ch. 18.
*Katz, M., "The Welfare Effects of Third Degree Price Discrimination in Intermediate Good Markets," <u>AER</u>, 77 (March 1987), pp. 154-167.
*Schmalensee, R., "Output and Welfare Implications of Monopolistic Third-Degree Price Discrimination," <u>AER</u>, 71, (March 1981), pp. 242-247.
*Varion, H., "Price Discrimination and Social Welfare," <u>AER</u>, 75 (Sept. 1985), pp. 870-875.
*Ross, T., "Winners and Losers Under The Robinson-Patman Act.," <u>JLE</u>, 27 (Oct. 1984), pp. 243-272.

VII. Mergers (Clayton Act, Section 7)

A. Overview

U.S. Department of Justice Merger Guidelines.
Posner, pp. 96-134, Ch. 6.
Singer, Chs. 2, 10.
<u>Contemporary Policy Issues</u>, 4 (July 1986), pp. 1-46.
<u>Journal of Economic Perspectives</u>, 1 (Fall 1987), pp. 3-55.
Spulber, Ch. 17.

B. Horizontal

1) Structural Approach

*Demsetz, Harold, "Two Systems of Belief About Monoply," in *Industrial Concentration: The New Learning*, 1974, pp. 164-183.
*Bothwell, James, Thomas Cooley, and Thomas Hall, "A New View of the Market Structure-Performance Debate," *Journal of Industrial Economics (JLE)*, June 1984.
Weiss, Leonard, "The Concentration-Profits Relationship and Antitrust," in *Industrial Concentration: The New Learning*, 1974.
Ravenscraft, David, "Structure-Profit Relationships at the Line of Business and Industry Level," *RESTAT*, Vol. 65, (Feb. 1983), pp. 22-31.
Geroski, Paul, "Simultaneous Equations Models of the Structure-Performance Paradigm," *European Economic Review (EER)*, October, 1982.
*Eckbo, B. and Peggy Wier "Antimerger Policy Under the Hart-Scott-Rodino Act: A Reexamination of the Market Power Hypothesis," *JLE*, 28 (April 1985), pp. 119-150.
Peltzman, S., "The Gains and Losses from Industrial Concentration," *JLE*, Vol. 20 (Oct. 1977), pp. 229-64.
*Shrighart, W. F. II and R. Tollison, "The Random Character of Merger Activity," *Rand Journal of Economics*, 15:4 (Winter 1984), pp. 500-510.

2) Issues Related to Exit

Fudenberg, D. and J. Tirole, "A Theory of Exit in Duopoly," *Econometrica*, 54 (1986), pp. 143-960.
Ghemawat, P. and B. Nalbuff, "Exit," *RAND*, 16 (Summer 1985), pp. 184-194.
Dowell, R. "Asset Salvageability and the Potential for Trade Restraint Through Mergers," 15:4, *The Rand Journal of Economics*, (Winter 1984), pp. 537-546.

3) Case Studies

Case 1: Merger in the Petroleum Industry: The Modil-Marathon Case (1981), F.M. Schere.
Case 3: Application of the Merger Guidelines: The Proposed Merger of Coca-Cola and Dr Pepper (1986), Lawrence J. White.
Case 4: The Importance of Entry Conditions: Texas Air's Acquisition of Eastern Airlines (1986), George W. Douglas

C. Joint Ventures

1) Theory and Empirical Evidence

*Kalish, L., M. Cassidy, and J. Hertzog, "Potential Competition: The Probability of Entry with Mutually Aware Potential Entrants," *Southern Economic Journal*, Jan. 1978, pp. 542-555.

Reynolds, R., and B. Reeves, "The Economic of Potential Competition," in Masson and Qualls, <u>Essays on Industrial Organization in Honor of Joe S. Bain</u>, Ballinger, 1976.

*Stiglitz, J. E., "Potential Competition May Reduce Welfare," <u>AER</u>, May 1981.

Brodley, J. F., "Potential Competition Mergers: A Structural Synthesis," <u>Yale Law Journal</u>, Nov. 1977.

Reynolds, Robert and Bruce Snapp, "The Economic Effects of Partial Equity Interests and Joint Ventures," <u>International Journal of Organizatyion</u>, 4(1986), pp. 141-153.

*Bresnahan, Timothy and Steven Salop, "Quantifying the Competitive Effects of Production Joint Ventures," <u>International Journal of Industrial Organization</u>, 4(1986), pp. 155-175.

Brodley, Joseph, "Joint Ventures and Antitrust Policy," <u>Harvard Law Review</u>, 95 (May 1982), pp. 1521-1590.

Ordover, J. A. and R. D. Willig, "Antitrust for High-Technology Indsutries: Assessing Research Joint Ventures and Mergers," <u>JLE</u>, 28:2 (May 1985), pp. 311-334.

2) Case Studies

Case 2: International Joint Venture: General Motors and Toyota (1983), John E. Kwoka, Jr.

D. Conglomerate Mergers

Turner, D. F., "Conglomerate Merges and Section 7 of the Clayton Act," How, L. R., May 1965.

*Allen, B. T., "Industrial Reciprocity: A Statistical Analysis" 18, <u>JLE</u>, 537 (Oct. 1975).

*Amihud, Y. and B. Lev, "Risk Reduction as a Managerial Motive for Conglomerate Mergers," <u>Bell Journal of Economics</u>, Autumn 1971.

Mueller, "A Theory of Conglomerate Mergers," <u>QJE</u>, Nov. 1969, Vol. 84, pp. 643-659.

Berry, C. H., "Corporate Diversification and Market Structure," <u>BJ</u>, Spring 1974.

Gort, M., "An Economic Disturbance Theory of Mergers," <u>QJE</u>, 11/69.

Rhoades, S., "Effect of Diversification on Industry Profit Performance in 241 Manufacturing Industries," <u>RESTAT</u>, 5/73, Vol. 55, pp. 146-155 and 11/74, Vol. 55, pp. 279-289.

Goldberg, L., "The Effect of Conglomerate Mergers on Competition," <u>Journal of Law and Economics</u>, 4/73.

Berry, C. H., "Corporate Growth and Industrial Diversification," <u>JLE</u>, 10/71.

Meyer, R., "Risk Efficient Monopoly Pricing for Multiproduct Firms," <u>QJE</u>, Vol. 90, pp. 461-474.

Baumol, Panzer, and Willig, <u>Contestable Markets and the Theory of Industry Structure</u>, Ch. 9.

VIII. Antitrust Enforcement

Smith, W. and M. Vaughan, "Economic Welfare, Price and Profit: The Deterrent Effect of Alternative Antitrust Regimes," *Economic Inquiry*, 24 ()ct. 1986), pp. 615-630.

Elzinga, K., and W. Breit, *The Antitrust Penalties: A Study in Law and Economics*, New Haven, 1976.

Block, M., and F. Nold, "The Deterrent Effect of Antitrust Enforcement," *JPE*, June 1981, 89 (3), pp. 429-45.

Easterbrook, F., "Detrebiling Antitrust Damages," *JLE*, 28 (May 1985), pp. 445-468.

Snyder, E., "Efficient Assignment of Rights to Sue for Antitrust Damages," *JLE*, 28 (May 1985), pp. 469-482.

Peterson, L., "Comment on Antitrust Remedies," *JLE*, (May 1985), pp. 483-488.

Spiller, P. "Comments on Easterbrook and Snyder," *JLE*, (May 1985), pp. 489-494.

Polinsky, A. M. and S. Shavell, "The Optimal Tradeoff between the Probability and Magnitude of Fines," *AER*, Dec. 1979, pp. 880-891.

Breit, W., and K. Elzinga, "Antitrust Enforcement and Economic Efficiency: The Uneasy Case of the Treble Damages," *JLE*, Oct. 1974, p. 329.

Long, W., R. Scharam, and R. Tollison, "The Economic Determinants of Antitrust Activity," *JLE*, Oct. 1973, p. 351.

Siegfreid, J., "The Determinants of Antitrust Activity," *JLE*, Oct. 1975, p. 559.

Asch, P., "The Determinants and Effects of Antitrust Activity," *JLE*, Oct. 1975, p. 575.

VIII. Private Antitrust Enforcement

Breit, W. and K. Elzinga, "Private Antitrust Enforcement: The New Learning," *JLE*, 28 (May 1985), pp. 405-444.

White, L., *Private Antitrust Enforcement*, (MIT Press, Cambridge), 1988.

PRINCETON UNIVERSITY   G
Department of Economics

Econ 541: Industrial Organization and Public Policy

Fall Term 1985   William Baumol
                                          Robert Willig

                          Readings

Books:

Scherer, F. M., <u>Industrial Market Structure and Economic Performance</u>, second edition, Rand McNally, 1980. (henceforth, "Scherer")

Baumol, W. J., J. C. Panzar, and R. D. Willig, <u>Contestable Markets and the Theory of Industry Structure</u>, Harcourt Brace Jovanovich, 1982. (henceforth, "BPW")

I. Ramsey Pricing

Baumol, W. J. and D. F. Bradford, "Optimal Departures from Marginal Cost Pricing," <u>American Economic Review</u>, Vol. 60, June 1970, pp. 265-83.

Baumol, W. J., E. E. Bailey, and R. D. Willig, "Weak Invisible Hand Theorems on the Sustainability of Prices in a Multiproduct Monopoly," <u>American Economic Review</u>, Vol. 67, June 1977, pp. 350-365.

Boiteux, M., "Sur la question des monopoles publiques astreints à l'èquilibre budgétaire," <u>Econometrica</u>, Vol. 24, Jan. 1956, pp. 22-40.

Diamond, P. A. and J. A. Mirrlees, "Optimal Taxation and Public Production: II," <u>American Economic Review</u>, Vol. 61, June 1971, pp. 261-78.

Hicks, Ursula, <u>Public Finance</u>, New York: 1947.

Hotelling, H., "The General Welfare in Relation to Problems of Taxation and of Railway and Utility Rates," <u>Econometrica</u>, Vol. 6, July 1938, pp. 642-69.

Pigou, A. C., <u>A Study of Public Finance</u>, London: 1928.

Ramsey, Frank, "A Contribution to the Theory of Taxation," <u>Economic Journal</u>, Vol. 37, March 1927, pp. 47-61.

Samuelson, P. A., "Theory of Optimal Taxation," 1951 (unpublished).

II. Peak-Load Pricing

* Kahn, I, Ch. 4.

Steiner, Peter O., "Peak Loads and Efficient Pricing," QJE, November 1957, pp. 585-610.

Hirshleifer, Jack, "Peak Loads and Efficient Pricing: Comment," QJE, August 1958, pp. 451-62.

*Williamson, Oliver E., "Peak-Load Pricing and Optimal Capacity Under Indivisibility Constraints," AER, September 1966, pp. 810-27.

Wilson, George W., "The Theory of Peak-Load Pricing: A Final Note," BJ, Spring 1972, pp. 307-10.

Williamson, Oliver E., "Peak-Load Pricing: Some Further Remarks," BJ, Spring 1974, pp. 223-28.

Boiteau, Marcel, "Peak-Load Pricing," Journal of Business, April 1960, pp. 157-79 (Translated from Revue Generale de L'Electricité, August 1949).

Turvey, Ralph, "Peak-Load Pricing," JPE, January/February 1968, pp. 101-14.

Crew, Michael and Paul Kleindorfer, "Marshall and Turvey on Peak-Load or Joint Product Pricing," JPE, November/December 1971, pp. 1369-77.

Panzar, John C., "A Neoclassical Approach to Peak-Load Pricing," BJ, Autumn 1976, pp. 521-30.

Mohring, Herbert, "The Peak-Load Problem with Increasing Returns and Pricing Constraints," AER, September 1970, pp. 693-705.

Bailey, Elizabeth E. and Lawrence J. White, "Reversals in Peak and Off Peak Prices," BJ, Spring 1974, pp. 75-92.

Pressman, Israel, "A Mathematical Formulation of the Peak-Load Pricing Problem," BJ, Autumn 1970, pp. 304-25.

Escarraz, D. R., "The Peak-Load Problem: Davidson's Solution Reconsidered," Quarterly Review of Economics and Business, Summer 1970, pp. 85-90.

Littlechild, Stephen C., "Peak-Load Pricing of Telephone Calls," BJ, Autumn 1970, pp. 191-210.

Symposium on Peak-Load Pricing: Articles by Joskow, Crew and Kleindorfer, Wenders, and Nguyen, in BJ, Spring 1976, pp. 197-218.

*Bailey, Elizabeth E. and Eric Lindenberg, "Peak-Load Pricing Principles: Past and Present," pp. 9-31, in Harry M. Trebing, editor, <u>New Dimensions in Public Utility Pricing</u>, 1976.

Meyer, Robert A., "Comment," pp. 32-37 in Trebing, 1976.

Steiner, Peter O., "Comment" pp. 37-43 in Trebing, 1976.

Greene, Robert L., "Peak-Load Pricing: An Application," <u>Quarterly Review of Business and Economics</u>, Autumn 1973, pp. 105-14.

Vardi, Joseph, Jacob Zahavi, and Benjamin Avi-Itzhak, "Variable Load Pricing in the Face of Loss of Load Probability," <u>BJ</u>, Spring 1977, pp. 270-88.

*Faulhaber, G. R., "Peak-Load Pricing and Regulatory Accountability," Rutgers Conference on Public Utility Regulation, October, 1978 (mimeo).

III. Optimal Depreciation Policy

Baumol, "Optimal Depreciation Policy: Pricing the Products of Durable Assets," <u>BJ</u>, Autumn 1971, pp. 365-76.

* denotes required reading

Economics 432 – Government Regulation of Industry
The University of Michigan
Winter 1988   Prof. Severin Borenstein

Office: 412 Lorch Hall, 746-6133. Office hours: Monday 11:15-Noon, Wednesday 11:15-Noon, Friday 1:30-3:00.

Readings: There are three required books and a coursepack of required readings.

1. *Government and Business* by D. Gujarati (McGraw-Hill, 1984)

2. *The Political Economy of Deregulation: Interest Groups in the Regulatory Process* by R. Noll and B. Owen (A.E.I., 1983)

3. *Regulatory Reform: What Actually Happened*, L. Weiss and M. Klass, eds. (Little, Brown, 1986)

The coursepack is available from Dollar Bill Copying on Church St. All readings not listed under Gujarati, Noll & Owen (N & O), or Weiss & Klass (W & K) are in the coursepack.

Exams: Grades will be based on two midterm exams and the final exam.
First Midterm Exam, February 10 in class.
Second Midterm Exam, March 25 in class.
Final Exam for 9 a.m. section, April 27, 10:30-12:30.
Final Exam for 10 a.m. section, April 26, 1:30-3:30.

NOTE!: Midterm exams must be taken with the section in which you are registered. Final exam may be taken at either exam time.

Grading: Your grade will be calculated from the greater of
a) 0.25 X 1st Midterm + 0.25 X 2nd Midterm + 0.5 X Final, or
b) 0.25 X Highest Midterm Grade + 0.75 X Final Exam Grade.

Course Description: This course studies government policies toward business. Government intervention in private business in the U.S. takes three forms: direct regulation of prices and outputs in an industry, safety and information regulation, and antitrust enforcement. After an extended introduction, the course proceeds accordingly.

The order of topics and associated reading assignments are:

I. INTRODUCTION

1. **The Role of Government Regulation**

    Gujarati, Ch. 1 and 2

    N & O, Ch. 1-3

2. **History and Philosophy of Regulation**

Greer, *Business, Government and Society*, (Macmillan, 1983), Ch.4.

II. OVERVIEW OF GOVERNMENT INTERVENTION – THE AIRLINE INDUSTRY

1. History of the Industry and Its Regulation

Gujarati, Ch. 12

Kahn, "Deregulation and Vested Interests: The Case of Airlines," in N & O.

"Deregulation Raises Prices, Cuts Service in Many Rural Areas," *Wall Street Journal*, 10/5/87.

2. Airline Deregulation and the Role of Antitrust

Gujarati, Ch. 10.

Kaplan, "The Changing Airline Industry," in W & K.

Borenstein, "High Air Fares: Don't Blame Deregulation," *Washington Post*, 8/25/87.

Levine, "Airline Competition in Deregulated Markets: Theory, Firm Strategy, and Public Policy," *Yale Journal on Regulation*, July 1987, pp. 408-423.

"Climbing Air Fares Increase Worries of Price-Setting," *New York Times*, 9/9/87.

3. Airline Safety and Consumer Protection

Gray, "Aviation Safety: Fact or Fiction," *Technology Review*, August/September 1987, pp. 33-40.

Chalk, "Market Outperforms FAA as Air-Safety Enforcer," *Wall Street Journal*, 9/1/87.

"Complaint Department: Airlines Find New Ways to Enrage Fliers," *Wall Street Journal*, 6/1/87.

"Bad Air Service Prompts Call for Changes," *Wall Street Journal*, 11/9/87.

"Airlines Come to the Aid of Consumers – Sort of," *Wall Street Journal*, 11/9/87.

"Price of Reform: Fliers May Find Re-Regulation Adds to Problems," *Wall Street Journal*, 11/12/87.

"Gluttons for Punishment? Fliers Continue Using Airlines They Hate," *Wall Street Journal*, 11/19/87.

"Delay Data: Airlines' Figures Hold Surprises – and Spark Controversy," *Wall Street Journal*, 11/11/87.

"New Data on Airline Performance May End Up Misleading Travelers," *Wall Street Journal*, 11/23/87.

III. DIRECT ECONOMIC REGULATION

1. The Methods and Impacts of Regulation

Gujarati, Ch. 4 and 5

Goldfarb, "Compensating Victims of Policy Change," *Regulation*, September/October 1980.

Schelling, "Economic Reasoning and the Ethics of Policy," *Public Interest*, Spring 1981.

2. Public Utility Regulation

Weiss, "State Regulation of Public Utilities and Marginal-cost Pricing," in W & K

Navarro, "Save Now, Freeze Later: The Real Price of Cheap Electricity," *Regulation* September/October, 1983.

Detroit Edison, "Important Notice to Residential Customers" February, 1987.

Kahn, "Who Should Pay for Power-Plant Duds?" *Wall Street Journal*, 8/15/85.

"Middle South Pressured by Grand Gulf Costs," *Wall Street Journal*, 8/29/85.

3. Natural Gas - Gujarati, Ch. 13, pp. 333-348

Braeutigam & Hubbard, "Natural Gas: The Regulatory Transition," in W & K.

"Table 17: Total Gas Proved Reserves ..."

4. Regulating Insurance and Statistical Discrimination

"Insurance and the Price of Sex," *Fortune*, 2/21/83.

"Insurers to Limit Policies of Buyers Refusing AIDS Test," *New York Times*, 6/5/87.

Chamberlin, "Assessing the Fairness of Insurance Classifications," *Research in Law And Economics*, 1985.

5. Cable Television Regulation - Gujarati, pp. 412-426.

Owen and Gottlieb, "The Rise and Fall and Rise of Cable Television Regulstion," in W & K.

"Those Catchwords of Cable," *Wall Street Journal*, 4/25/86.

"Cable Tackles the "Must-Carry" Rules," *Regulation*, May/June 1984.

6. Franchise Licensing

Gujarati, Ch. 14

Stoll, "Revolution in the Regulation of Securities: An Examination of the Effects of Increased Competition" in Weiss & Klass eds., *Case Studies in Regulation: Revolution and Reform*, (Little, Brown, 1981).

"NYC looks at Taxi Regulation," *Regulation*, March/April, 1982.

"Koch Taxi Plan #3," *New York Times*, 4/19/85.

Kirp and Soffer, "Taking California to the Cleaners," *Regulation*, September/October 1985.

IV. INFORMATION AND SAFETY REGULATION

1. Product Standardization and Disclosure

Greer, Ch. 12

Beales, Craswell, and Salop, "The Efficient Regulation of Consumer Information," *Journal of Law and Economics*, December, 1981.

"Car Buyers Discover 'Lemon Laws' Often Fail to Prevent Court Trip," *Wall Street Journal*, 10/21/86.

2. Safety and Health Regulation

Gujarati, Ch. 4

Viscusi, "Reforming OSHA Regulation of Workplace Risks" in W & K.

"Job-Safety Agency Is Firing Buckshot Again, And Industry Runs for Cover as Penalties Fly," *Wall Street Journal*, 4/22/87.

Huber, "The Market for Risk," *Regulation*, March/April 1984.

"Motorcycles, Safety, and Freedom," *Regulation*, July/August 1980.

"Serfdom and Seatbelts," *New Republic*, 6/3/85.

"Despite Recent Laws, Many Motorists Are Still Casual About Wearing Seat Belts," *Wall Street Journal*, 3/7/86.

"How Much Is Your Life Worth?", *Fortune*, 3/3/86.

3. Environmental Protection - Gujarati, Ch. 17

Crandall, "Air Pollution, Environmentalists, and The Coal Lobby," in N & O.

Tietenberg, "Uncommon Sense: The Program to Reform Pollution Control Policy" in W & K.

Levin, "Building a Better Bubble at EPA," *Regulation*, March/April, 1985.

"Clean Water: Apocalypse Later," *Regulation*, July/August, 1983.

V. ANTITRUST

1. Introduction to Antitrust Policy - Gujarati, Ch. 6 and 7

2. Collusion Among Firms - Gujarati, Ch. 8

"Auto Dealers' Hours Are Legal," *Detroit News*, 7/22/87.

3. Monopolization - Gujarati, Ch. 6

4. Vertical Restrictions - Gujarati, Ch. 9

"Round and 'Round on RPM" 4 articles from *Regulation*, Jan/Feb 1984.

"The Noisy War Over Discounting," *New York Times*, 9/25/83.

Economics 432
First Mid-Semester Exam

February 10, 1988   Prof. Borenstein

Please try to write legibly. Use ink, not pencil.   **Univ. Michigan**
(Points = Suggested Minutes in parentheses)

True/False/Maybe – Explain

(6) 1. If a monopolist's limit price is above its unconstrained monopoly price already, an increase in the excess capacity it holds will not cause it to raise price.

(8) 2. Stigler's economic theory of regulation predicts that regulation is more likely to be found in industries with few firms than industries with many firms.

Short Answer

(12) 3. If a regulated electric power company does not have a fuel adjustment clause, it may be months between the time that fuel prices increase and the time that the firm is allowed to increase the price of electricity to cover the higher fuel costs. Explain how this may cause deadweight loss from *overconsumption* of electricity in the short run. Explain how this may cause the firm to use an inefficient input mix in the long run.

(8) 4. In 1974, the Civil Aeronautics Board started setting fares based on a "target" load factor of 55%. How did this help to eliminate the "ratcher effect"?

(8) 5. Some critics of airline deregulation argue that firms that are near bankruptcy may not have the right incentive to take safety precautions. What is the economic logic behind this assertion?

(8) 6. To enter a new city, an airline must pay for $1 million in advertising, buy gates and facilities that cost $2 million, and lease some airplanes for $5 million per year. If the airline decides not to stay in the market, the gates and facilities can be resold at the same price the airline paid. The leases, however, have a $100,000 cancellation penalty that must be paid to cancel the leases. What are the sunk costs of entering this route? Explain how you treat each expenditure in this question.

22

Economics 432
Second Mid-Semester Exam

March 25, 1988

Prof. Borenstein
Univ. Michigan

Please try to write legibly. Use ink, not pencil.
(Points = Suggested Minutes in parentheses)

True/False/Maybe – Explain

(7) 1. Nuclear power is a more efficiently used to produce base load power (which operates most of the time), while oil-burning plants are more efficiently used to produce power needed only during peak periods.

(8) 2. If insurance companies were allowed to determine risk categories based only on factors that people could *control*, they would able to limit adverse selection, but moral hazard problems would persist.

(7) 3. Ramsey pricing usually imposes more deadweight loss than a two-part tariff (entry-fee plus a marginal charge) when each plan is used so that the regulated firm breaks even.

(10) 4. Without copyright protection, television producers have a suboptimal incentive to create a new show, but with full copyright protection, the producers have an incentive to produce too many new shows.

Short Answer

(8) 5. If federal regulation of natural gas prices had applied to intrastate (Texas) sales as well as interstate (U.S.) sales, would interstate consumers have benefitted more from the regulation than they did under the actual regulation that excluded intrastate buyers?

(10) 6. What are incomplete contracts? Why does incompleteness of contracts limit the usefulness of franchise bidding as a way to solve the problem of natural monopoly?

Economics 432
Final Examination #1

April 26, 1988

Prof. Borenstein
University of Michigan

Please try to write legibly. Use ink, not pencil.
(Points = Suggested Minutes in parentheses)

True/False/Maybe – Explain

(8) **1.** It is inefficient for worker safety levels (*i.e.*, the probability of being hurt on the job) to differ among employees in the same industry; this indicates that some Pareto improving trades have not yet been made.

(8) **2.** If pollution is controlled with tradeable pollution rights, then the marginal profitability of pollution will be equal across firms, but if pollution is controlled with taxes, marginal profitability of pollution will vary across firms.

(7) **3.** Rent-seeking behavior may cause the social losses from monopoly to be greater than the traditional deadweight loss "triangle."

(6) **4.** An extremely narrow market definition (*e.g.*, ethnic frozen dinners) in an antitrust case is likely to lead to overestimates of a firm's market power.

Short Answer

(8) **5.** In the 1960's, air fares in the U.S. were set as a linear function of trip distance (*e.g.*, $Fare = Miles * 20¢$). Which travelers benefitted from this approach? Which travelers tended to pay more than the cost of serving them?

(12) **6.** If New York City increased the number of taxi medallions (licenses) available in the city, would the total value of all medallions decrease? Would consumer surplus of New York City taxi users increase if they bought back all taxi medallions at their current values and then allowed free entry into the market? (Assume that the regulated price is unchanged.)

(9) **7.** Explain the deadweight loss caused when the government prohibits insurance companies from charging different rates based on where the buyer lives? How might insurance companies be able to get around this prohibition.

(11) **8.** Define the Minimum Efficient Scale of Production (MES). If monopoly is found to exist in an industry, explain how the MES would enter into the determining whether the problem should be dealt with through antitrust laws or economic regulation.

(7) **9.** How might the demise of fixed stock broker commission rates in 1975 have led brokers to do less than the optimal amount of research into which stocks are "good buys"?

(12) **10.** What inefficiency is likely to result if consumers do not have to pay any costs of a cancelled nuclear power plant? What inefficiency is likely to result if consumers have to pay all costs of a cancelled nuclear power plant?

(12) **11.** Why did the Natural Gas Policy Act differentiate between "old" and "new" gas? Explain two *different* inefficiencies caused by the lower regulated price set for "old" gas.

Economics 432
Final Examination #2
University of Michigan
Prof. Borenstein

April 27, 1988

Please try to write legibly. Use ink, not pencil. (Points = Suggested Minutes in parentheses)

True/False/Maybe – Explain

(6) **1.** Prohibiting life insurance companies from testing for the HIV virus that causes AIDS would probably cause adverse selection, but is unlikely to result in moral hazard.

(8) **2.** If the marginal social cost of pollution is fairly constant, then the optimal pollution tax will vary depending on the marginal benefit (marginal profit) functions of firms in the area, but the optimal quantity of pollution will be fairly constant.

(6) **3.** Trademarks are more important conveyors of information for search goods than for experience goods.

(6) **4.** The Areeda-Turner rule for detection of predatory pricing ($P < AVC$) is more likely to falsely accuse firms of this activity (false positives) than to fail to detect predatory pricing when it actually is occuring (false negatives).

Short Answer

(10) **5.** State and explain two *different* ways in which government regulation of airlines resulted in a subsidy to people living in rural areas.

(8) **6.** Could an increase in the regulated price for taxis lower the value of a taxi medallion? Is so, how? If not, why not?

(12) **7.** Explain why Huber argues that safety standards lead to less efficient accident prevention than a "market for risk." Would an injury tax – a tax on the employer depending on the severity of the employee's injury – allow efficient operation of such a risk market?

(10) **8.** Could it increase efficiency to break up a natural monopoly into 2 firms of equal size? Could such a move harm consumers?

(9) **9.** Over the year, would you expect to see the price of air travel fluctuate more or less than the price of blue jeans? Explain why.

(10) **10.** How might vertical mergers be used by firms to avoid government imposed price controls? Would mergers in response to these controls generally be efficient?

(15) **11.** Assume that an electric utility faces a daytime demand and a nighttime demand of equal length time periods. The company has analyzed its problem with constant fuel costs and constant marginal capital costs and has set the optimal capacity and peak load prices. Capacity is no longer adjustable. Now a very small additional fixed cost (say, $100 per year) – unrelated to the capital or fuel costs – becomes necessary.

   a. If there is no requirement that the company break even, does the additional fixed cost change the optimal prices? If so, how? If not, why not?

   b. Now assume that there is a break even requirement and that the additional revenue must be raised by increasing the price of peak (P_p) or off-peak (P_{o-p}) electricity. Will increasing P_p slightly to raise the additional revenue create more or less deadweight loss than the small increase in P_{o-p} that would be necessary.

THE UNIVERSITY OF MICHIGAN
DEPARTMENT OF ECONOMICS
ECON 632 - Economics of Government Regulation

Winter 1988

Professor Severin Borenstein

Course Description: This course explores economic theories of government intervention in and regulation of business practices. It is divided up into three broad sections, reflecting the major areas of government policies towards business: Antitrust Law, Direct Economic Regulation, and Social Regulation.

Office: 412 Lorch Hall. 764-6133. Office hours: Monday 11:15-Noon, Wednesday 11:15-Noon, Friday 1:30-3:00.

Grading: Grades will be based one midterm exam and the final exam according to the higher of two formulae: (1) 0.3 X Midterm + 0.7 X Final, or (2) 1.0 X Final.

Starred items on the reading list are required reading.

1. ANTITRUST I: Introduction

*R.H. Bork, *The Antitrust Paradox: A Policy at War with Itself*, New York: Basic Books, 1978. Ch. 1.

*R. Schmalensee, "Antitrust and the New Industrial Organization," *American Economic Review*, 72(May 1982).

*G.J. Stigler, "The Economic Effects of the Antitrust Laws," *Journal of Law and Economics*, 9(October 1966).

R.A. Posner, *Antitrust Law: An Economic Perspective*. Chicago: University of Chicago Press, 1976.

J.J. Sigfried, "The Determinants of Antitrust Activity," *Journal of Law and Economics*, 18(October 1975).

R.D. Tollison, "Antitrust in the Reagan Administration: A Report from the Belly of the Beast," *International Journal of Industrial Organization*, 1(August 1983).

2. ANTITRUST II: Market Power through Collusion

*P. Areeda, *Antitrust Analysis*, 2nd ed., Boston: Little, Brown, 1974. Ch. 3, pp. 261-268, 322-342.

*M.K. Block, F.C. Nold, and J.G. Sidak, "The Deterrent Effect of Antitrust Enforcement," *Journal of Political Economy*, 89(June 1981).

*G. Hay and D. Kelley, "An Empirical Survey of Price-Fixing Conspiracies," *Journal of Law and Economics*, 17(April 1974).

*S.W. Salant, "Treble Damage Awards in Private Lawsuits for Price Fixing," *Journal of Political Economy*, 95(December 1987).

*F.M. Scherer, *Industrial Market Structure and Economic Performance*, 2nd ed., Chicago: Rand McNally, 1980. Ch. 19.

*R. Schmalensee, "Another Look at Market Power," *Harvard Law Review*, 95(June 1982).

P. Asch and J. Seneca, "Is Collusion Profitable?", *Review of Economics and Statistics*, 58(February 1976).

R.H. Bork, "The Rule of Reason and the Per Se Concept: Price Fixing and Market Division," *Yale Law Journal*, 74(April 1965) and 75(January 1966).

R.M. Feinberg, "Antitrust Enforcement and Subsequent Price Behavior," *Review of Economics and Statistics*, 62(November 1980).

W.M. Landes and R.A. Posner, "Market Power in Antitrust Cases," *Harvard Law Review*, 94(March 1981).

J. Palmer, "Some Economic Conditions Conducive to Collusion," *Journal of Economic Issues*, 6(September 1972).

G.J. Stigler, "A Theory of Oligopoly," *Journal of Political Economy*, 72(February 1964).

3. ANTITRUST III: Market Power Through Monopolization

*P. Areeda, *Antitrust Analysis*, 2nd ed., Boston: Little, Brown & Co., 1974. Ch. 2, pp.133-153, 195-219.

*M.R. Burns, "Predatory Pricing and the Acquisition Cost of Competitors," *Journal of Political Economy*, 94(April 1986).

*F.M. Fisher and J.J. McGowan "On the Misuse of Accounting Rates of Return to Infer Monopoly Profits," *American Economic Review*, 73(March 1983).

*P. Joskow and A.K. Klevorick, "A Framework for Predatory Pricing Policy," *Yale Law Journal*, 89(December 1979).

*F.M. Scherer, *Industrial Market Structure and Economic Performance*, 2nd ed., Chicago: Rand McNally, 1980. Ch. 20.

P. Areeda and D.F. Turner, "Predatory Pricing and Related Practices Under Section 2 of the Sherman Act," *Harvard Law Review*, 88(February 1975).

M.R. Burns, "The Competitive Effects of Trust-Busting: A Portfolio Analysis," *Journal of Political Economy*, 85(August 1977).

F.M. Fisher "Diagnosing Monopoly," *Quarterly Review of Economics and Business*, (Summer 1979).

D. Gaskins, "Alcoa Revisited: The Welfare Economics of a Second Hand Market," *Journal of Economic Theory*, 7(March 1974).

J. Ordover and R. Willig, "An Economic Definition of Predation," *Yale Law Journal*, 91(November 1981).

R. Schmalensee, "Entry Deterrence in the Ready-to-Eat Breakfast Cereal Industry," *Bell Journal of Economics*, 9(Autumn 1979).

R. Schmalensee, "On the Use of Economic Models in Antitrust: The ReaLemon Case," *University of Pennsylvania Law Review*, 127(April 1979).

R. Schmalensee, "Do Markets Differ Much?", *American Economic Review*, 75(June, 1985).

V. Suslow, "Estimating Monopoly Behavior with Competitive Recycling: An Application to Alcoa," *Rand Journal of Economics*, 17(Autumn 1986).

L.W. Weiss, "The Structure-Conduct-Performance Paradigm and Antitrust," *University of Penn-

sylvania Law Review, **127**(April 1979).

4. ANTITRUST IV: Market Power Through Mergers

*R.H. Bork, *The Antitrust Paradox: A Policy at War with Itself*, New York: Basic Books, 1978. pp. 201-262.

*O.E. Williamson, "Economies as an Antitrust Defense: the Welfare Tradeoffs," *American Economic Review*, **58**(March 1968).(Also see discussions of this paper in *AER*, **58**(December 1968) and **59**(December 1969).

W.S. Comanor, "Vertical Mergers, Market Power, and the Antitrust Laws," *American Economic Review*, **57**(May 1967).

A.K. Dixit, "Vertical Integration in a Monopolistically Competitive Industry," *International Journal of Industrial Organization*, **1**(August 1983).

K. Elzinga, "The Antimerger Law: Pyrrhic Victories?" *Journal of Law and Economics*, **12**(April 1969).

D.L. Kayserman, "Theories of Vertical Integration: Implications for Antitrust Policy," *Antitrust Bulletin*, **23**(Fall 1978).

J.L. Peterman, "The *Brown Shoe* Case," *Journal of Law and Economics*, **18**(April 1975).

G.W. Stocking and W.F. Mueller, "The Cellophane Case and the New Competition," *American Economic Review*, **45**(March 1955).

U.S. Department of Justice, *Merger Guidelines*, (1982).

A. Werden, "Market Delineation and the Justice Department's Merger Guidelines," Department of Justice Working Paper, (December 1982).

5. ANTITRUST V: Vertical Restrictions

*F. Easterbrook, "Restricted Dealing is a Way to Compete," *Regulation*, **8**(Jan/Feb, 1984).

*H.P. Marvel and S. McCafferty, "The Political Economy of Resale Price Maintenance," *Journal of Political Economy*, **94**(October 1986).

*G.F. Mathewson and R.A. Winter "An Economic Thoery of Vertical Restraints," *Rand Journal of Economics*, **15**(Spring 1984).

*J.C. Miller III, "An Analytical Framework," *Regulation*, **8**(Jan/Feb, 1984).

*R. Pitofsky, "Why *Dr. Miles* was Right," *Regulation*. **8**(Jan/Feb, 1984).

*F.M. Scherer, *Industrial Market Structure and Economic Performance*, 2nd ed., Chicago: Rand McNally, 1980. Ch. 21.

N. Gallini and R.A. Winter "On Vertical Control in Monopolistic Competition," *International Journal of Industrial Organization*, **1**(August 1983).

T.W. Gilligan, "The Competitive Effects of Resale Price Maintenance," *Rand Journal of Economics*, **17**(Winter 1986).

P. Rey and J. Tirole, "The Logic of Vertical Restraints," *American Economic Review*, **76**(December 1986).

O.E. Williamson, "Assessing Vertical Market Restrictions: Antitrust Ramifications of the Transaction Cost Approach," *University of Pennsylvania Law Review*, **127**(April 1979).

6. Theories of Economic Regulation

*R.A. Posner. "Theories of Economic Regulation," *Bell Journal of Economics and Management Science*, **5**(Autumn 1974).

*P. Joskow and R. Noll, "Regulation in Theory and Practice: An Overview," ch. 1 in G. Fromm. ed., *Studies of Public Regulation*, Cambridge: MIT Press, 1981.

*G.W. Schwert. "Using Financial Data to Measure Effects of Regulation." *Journal of Law and Economics*. **24**(April 1981).

J.P. Kalt and M.A. Zupan. "Capture and Ideology in the Economic Theory of Politics," *American Economic Review*, **74**(June 1984).

S. Peltzman, "Toward a More General Theory of Regulation." *Journal of Law and Economics*, **20**(October 1977).

R.A. Posner. "Taxation by Regulation," *Bell Journal of Economics and Management Science*, **2**(Spring 1971).

F.M. Scherer, *Industrial Market Structure and Economic Performance*, 2nd ed., Chicago: Rand McNally, 1980. Ch. 18.

G.J. Stigler. "The Theory of Economic Regulation," *Bell Journal of Economics and Management Science*, **2**(Spring 1971).

B.R. Weingast and M.J. Moran, "Bureaucratic Discretion or Congressional Control? Regulatory Policymaking by the Federal Trade Commission," *Journal of Political Economy*, **91**(October 1983).

J.Q. Wilson. "The Politics of Regulation." in J.Q. Wilson, ed., *The Politics of Regulation*, New York: Basic Books. 1980, pp. 1-31.

7. Optimal Regulation of Natural Monopolies

*W.J. Baumol and D.F. Bradford, "Optimal Departures from Marginal Cost Pricing," *American Economic Review*, **60**(June 1970).

*P. Joskow, "Contributions to the Theory of Marginal Cost Pricing," *Bell Journal of Economics*, **7**(Spring 1976).

*J.C. Panzar and R.D. Willig, "Free Entry and the Sustainability of Natural Monopoly," *Bell Journal of Economics*, **8**(Spring 1977).

*L.W. Weiss, "State Regulation of Public Utilities and Marginal-cost Pricing," in *Case Studies in Regulation: Revolution and Reform*, Boston: Little, Brown, 1981.

*R.D. Willig, "Pareto-Superior Nonlinear Outlay Schedules." *Bell Journal of Economics*, **9**(Spring 1978).

W.J. Baumol. E.E. Bailey and R.D. Willig, "Weak Invisible Hand Theorems on the Sustainability of Prices in a Multi-Product Monopoly," *American Economic Review*, **67**(June 1977).

W.J. Baumol, J.C. Panzar and R.D. Willig, *Contestable Markets and the Theory of Industry Structure*, San Diego: Harcourt. Brace and Jovanovich, ch. 8.

W.A. Brock and J.A. Scheinkman, "Free Entry and the Sustainability of Natural Monopoly: Bertrand Revisited by Cournot," Chapter 9 in D.S. Evans, ed., *Breaking Up Bell*, New York: Elsevier, 1983.

G.R. Faulhaber, "Cross-Subsidization: Pricing in Public Enterprises," *American Economic Review*, **65**(December 1975).

G.R. Faulhaber and S.B. Levison, "Subsidy-Free Prices and Anonymous Equity," *American Economic Review*, **71**(December 1981).

M.S. Feldstein, "Distributional Equity and the Optimal Structure of Public Prices," *American Economic Review*, **62**(March 1972).

A.M. Henderson, "The Pricing of Public Utility Undertakings," *Manchester School of Economics and Social Studies*, **15**(1947), (Reprinted in K.J. Arrow and T. Scitovsky, eds., *Readings in Welfare Economics*, Homewood: Irwin, 1969).

G. Knieps and I. Vogelsang, "The Sustainability Concept under Alternative Behavioral Assumptions," *Bell Journal of Economics*, **13**(Spring 1982).

L.J. Mirman, Y. Tauman, and I. Zang, "Supportability, Sustainability, and Subsidy-Free Pricing," *Rand Journal of Economics*, **16**(Spring 1985).

B.M. Mitchell, "Optimal Pricing of Local Telephone Service," *American Economic Review*, **68** (September 1978).

B.M. Mitchell, W. Manning and J.P. Acton, *Peak Load Pricing: European Lessons for U.S. Energy Policy*, Cambridge: Ballinger, 1978.

J.R. Nelson, ed., *Marginal Cost Pricing in Practice*, Englewood Cliffs: Prentice-Hall, 1964.

J.A. Ordover and J.C. Panzar, "On the Nonexistence of Pareto-Superior Outlay Schedules," *Bell Journal of Economics*, **11**(Spring 1980).

R. Schmalensee, *The Control of Natural Monopolies*, Lexington: D.C. Heath, 1979.

R. Schmalensee, "Monopolistic Two-Part Pricing Arrangements," *Bell Journal of Economics*, **11** (Autumn 1981).

W.W. Sharkey and L.G. Telser, "Supportable Cost Functions for the Multi-product Firm," *Journal of Economic Theory*, **18**(1979).

P. Steiner, "Peak Loads and Efficient Pricing," *Quarterly Journal of Economics*, **71**(November 1957).

R. Turvey, *Optimal Pricing and Investment in Electricity Supply*, Cambridge: MIT Press, 1968.

J. Wenders, "Peak Load Pricing in the Electric Utility Industry," *Bell Journal of Economics*, **7**(Spring 1976).

E.E. Zajac, *Fairness or Efficiency: An Introduction to Public Utility Pricing*, Cambridge: Ballinger, 1978.

8. Actual Regulation of Natural Monopolies

*W.J. Baumol and A.K. Klevorick, "Input Choices and Rate-of-Return Regulation: An Overview of the Discussion," *Bell Journal of Economics and Management Science*, **1**(Autumn 1970).

*R.L. Hagerman and B.T. Ratchford. "Some Determinants of Allowed Rates of Return on Equity to Electric Utilities," *Bell Journal of Economics*, 9(Spring 1978).

*P.L. Joskow, "Inflation and Environmental Concern: Structural Change in the Process of Public Utility Regulation." *Journal of Law and Economics*. 17(October 1974).

*E. Shehinski, "Welfare Aspects of the Regulatory Constraint," *American Economic Review*. 61 (March 1971).

H. Averch and L. Johnson. "Behavior of the Firm Under Regulatory Constraint," *American Economic Review*, 52(December 1962).

E.E. Bailey, *Economic Theory of Regulatory Constraints*, Lexington: Heath, 1973.

R. Braeutigam, "An Analysis of Fully-Distributed Cost Pricing in Regulated Industries," *Bell Journal of Economics*, 11(Spring 1980).

W. Hendricks, "The Effect of Regulation on Collective Bargaining in Electric Utilities," *Bell Journal of Economics*. 6(Autumn 1975).

P.L. Joskow, "The Determination of the Allowed Rate of Return in a Formal Regulatory Hearing," *Bell Journal of Economics and Management Science*. 4(Autumn 1972).

P.L. Joskow, "Pricing Decision of Regulated Firms: A Behavioral Approach," *Bell Journal of Economics*, 4(Spring 1973).

R. Meyer and H.E. Leland. "The Effectiveness of Price Regulation," *Review of Economics and Statistics*, 62(January 1980).

S. Myers, "The Application of Finance Theory to Public Utility Rate Regulation," *Bell Journal of Economics and Management Science*, 3(Spring 1972).

H.C. Peterson. "An Empirical Test of Regulatory Effects," *Bell Journal of Economics*, 6(Spring 1975).

G. Stigler and C. Friedland, "What Can Regulators Regulate? The Case of Electricity," *Journal of Law and Economics*, 5(October 1962).

9. Regulation of Natural Monopolies under Uncertainty

*P.L. Joskow and R. Schmalensee, "Incentive Regulattion For Electric Utilities," *Yale Journal on Regulation*, 4(1986).

*D. Sappington, "Optimal Regualtion of Multiproduct Monopoly with Unknown Technology Capabilities," *Bell Journal of Economics*, 14(Autumn 1983).

D.P. Baron, "Noncooperative Regualtion of a Nonlocalized Externality," *Rand Journal of Economics*, 16(Winter 1985).

D.P. Baron and R. DeBondt. "Fuel Adjustment Mechanisms and Economic Efficiency," *Journal of Industrial Economics*, (March 1979).

D.P. Baron and R. DeBondt. "On the Design of Regulation Price Adjustment Mechanisms." *American Economic Review* 71(February 1981).

D.P. Baron and R.B. Myerson. "Regulating a Monopolist with Unknown Costs." *Econometrica*. 50(July 1982).

D.P. Baron and R.A. Taggart, "A Model of Regulation Under Uncertainty and a Test of Regulatory Bias," *Bell Journal of Economics*, 8(Spring 1977).

M.J. Brennan and E.S. Schwartz. "Consistent Regulatory Policy Under Uncertainty," *Bell Journal of Economics*, 13(Autumn 1982).

R.M. Isaac. "Fuel Adjustment Mechanisms and the Regulated Utility Facing Uncertain Fuel Prices," *Bell Journal of Economics*, 13(Spring 1982).

D. Sappington and D.S. Sibley. "Regulatory Incentive Structures Using Historic Cost Data," (mimeo).

S. Thomadakis. "Price Regulation Under Uncertainty in an Asymmetric Decision Environment," *Quarterly Journal of Economics*, 96(November 1982).

10. Economic Regulation of Non-Monopoly Markets

*K.D. Boyer, "The Costs of Price Regulation: Lessons from Railroad Deregulation." *Rand Journal of Economics*, 18(Autumn 1987).

*R.R. Braeutigam, "Optimal Pricing with Intermodal Competition," *American Economic Review*. 69(March 1979).

*P.L. Joskow, "Cartels, Competition and Regulation in the Property-Liability Insurance Industry," *Bell Journal of Economics*, 4(Autumn 1973).

*R.C. Levin. "Allocation in Surface Freight Transportation: Does Regulation Matter?" *Bell Journal of Economics*. 9(Spring 1978).

*P.W. MacAvoy, *Energy Policy*, New York: W.W. Norton. Ch. 3.

*N.L. Rose, "Labor Rent Sharing and Regulation: Evidence from the Trucking Industry," *Journal of Political Economy*, 95(December 1987).

*R.T. Smith, M. Bradley. and G. Jarrell, "Studying Firm-Specific Effects of Regulation with Stock Market Data: An Application to Oil Price Regulation," *Rand Journal of Economics* 17(Winter 1986).

K.D. Boyer. "Equalizing Discrimination and Cartel Pricing in Transport Rate Regulation," *Journal of Political Economy*, 89(April, 1981).

K.D. Boyer, "Minimum Rate Regulaiton, Modal Split Sensivities and the Railroad Problem," *Journal of Political Economy*, 85(June 1977).

S.G. Breyer and P.W. MacAvoy, *Energy Regulation by the Federal Power Commission*, Washington: Brookings, 1974.

G.W. Douglas and J.C. Miller, *Economic Regulation of Domestic Air Transport: Theory and Policy*, Washington: Brookings, 1975.

R.A. Ippolito, "The Effects of Price Regulation in the Automobile Insurance Industry," *Journal of Law and Economics*, 22(April 1979).

R.A. Ippolito and R.T. Masson, "The Social Cost of Government Regulation of Milk," *Journal of Law and Economics*. 21(April 1978).

T.G. Moore, "Deregulating Surface Frieght Transportation," in A. Phillips, ed., *Promoting Competition in *Regulated Markets*, Washington: Brookings, 1975.

H.D. Jacoby and A.W. Wright, "The Gordian Knot of Natural Gas Pricing," *The Energy Journal*, 3(1982).

T. Keeler, *Railroads, Freight and Public Policy*, Washington: Brookings, 1983.

R.C. Levin, "Railroad Regualtion. Deregulation, and Workable Competition," *American Economic Review*, 71(May 1981).

P.W. MacAvoy, "The Regulation-Induced Shortage of Natural Gas," *Bell Journal of Economics*, 4(Autumn 1973).

N.L. Rose, "The Incidence of Regulatory Rents in the Motor Carrier Industry," *Rand Journal of Economics*, 16(Autumn, 1985).

R. Schmalensee, "Comparative Static Properties of Regulated Airline Oligopolies," *Bell Journal of Economics*, 8(Autumn 1977).

T.S. Ulen, "The Market for Regulation: The ICC from 1887 to 1920," *American Economic Review*, 70(May 1980).

11. Deregulation and Alternatives to Regulation

*E.E. Bailey, D.R. Graham, and D.P. Kaplan, *Deregulating the Airlines*, Cambridge: MIT Press, 1985. Chs. 3,4,5.

*S. Borenstein, "On the Efficiency of Competitive Markets for Operating Licenses," *Quarterly Journal of Economics* 102(1988).

*H. Demsetz. "Why Regulate Utilities?" *Journal of Law and Economics*, 11(April 1968).

*A.E. Kahn. "The Road to More Intelligent Telephone Pricing," *Yale Journal on Regulation*, 1(1984).

*K.E. Train, D.L. McFadden, and M. Ben-Akiva, "The Demand for Local Telephone Service: A Fully Discrete Model of Residential Calling Patterns and Service Choices," *Rand Journal of Economics*, 18(Spring 1987).

*O.E. Williamson, "Franchise Bidding for Natural Monopoly - In General and with Respect to CATV," *Bell Journal of Economics*, 7(Spring 1976).

D.R. Graham, D.P. Kaplan and D.S. Sibley, "Efficiency and Competition in the Airline Industry," *Bell Journal of Economics*, 14(Spring 1983).

L.L. Johnson, "Why Local Rates are Rising," *Regulation*.7(July/Aug, 1983).

P.W. MacAvoy and K. Robinson, "Winning by Losing: The AT&T Settlement and Its Impact on Telecommunications," *Yale Journal on Regulation*, 1(1983).

J.C. Panzar, "Equilibrium and Welfare in Unregulated Airline Markets," *American Economic Review*. 69(May 1979).

M.K. Perry and R.H. Groff, "Trademark Licensing in a Monopolistically Competitive Industry," *Rand Journal of Economics*, 17(Summer 1986).

12. Social Regulation I: Externalities

*R.H. Coase, "The Problem of Social Cost," *Journal of Law and Economics*, **3**(October 1960).

*S. Rose-Ackerman, "Market Models for Water Pollution Control: Their Strengths and Weaknesses," *Public Policy*, **25**(Summer 1977).

*M.L. Weitzman, "Prices vs. Quantities," *Review of Economic Studies*, **41**(1974).

F. Gollop and M. Roberts, "Environmental Regulations and Productivity Growth: The Case of Fossil-fueled Electric Power Production," *Journal of Political Economy*, **91**(August 1983).

A.N. Link, "Productivity Growth, Environmental Regulations and the Composition of R&D," *Bell Journal of Economics*, **13**(Autumn 1982).

L.J. Perl and F.C. Dunbar, "Cost Effectiveness and Cost-Benefit Analysis of Air Quality Regulations," *American Economic Review*, **72**(May 1982).

M. Spence and M. Weitzman, "Regulatory Strategies for Pollution Control," in A.F. Friedlaender, ed., *Approaches to Controlling Air Pollution*, Cambridge: MIT Press, 1977.

L.J. White, *The Regulation of Air Pollutant Emissions from Motor Vehicles*, Washington: American Enterprise Institute, 1982.

13. Social Regulation II: Information and Consumer/Worker Protection

*H. Beales, R. Craswell, and S.C. Salop, "The Efficient Regulation of Consumer Information," *Journal of Law and Economics*, **24**(December 1981).

*S. Borenstein and M.B. Zimmerman, "Market Incentives For Safe Commercial Airline Operation," Institute of Public Policy Studies Discussion Paper #268, University of Michigan, November 1987.

*D. Epple and A. Raviv, "Product Safety: Liability Rules, Market Structure, and Imperfect Information," *American Economic Review*, **68**(March 1978).

*H.A. Grabowski and J.M. Vernon, "Consumer Protection Regulation in Ethical Drugs," *American Economic Review*, **67**(February 1977).

*W.Y. Oi, "The Economics of Product Safety," *Bell Journal of Economics and Management Science*, **4**(Spring 1973).

*C. Shapiro, "Consumer Information, Product Quality, and Seller Reputation," *Bell Journal of Economics*, **13**(Spring 1982).

*S. Peltzman, "An Evaluation of Consumer Protection Legislation: The 1962 Drug Amendments," *Journal of Political Economy*, **81**(September 1973).

*M. Spence, "Monopoly, Quality, and Regulation," *Bell Journal of Economics*, **6**(Autumn 1975).

P. Asch and D.T. Levy, "Does the Minimum Drinking Age Affect Traffic Fatalities?", *Journal of Policy Analysis and Management*, **6**(Winter 1987).

L. Benham, "The Effect of Advertising on the Price of Eyeglasses," *Journal of Law and Economics*, **15**(October 1972).

R. Cooper and T.W. Ross, "Product Warranties and Double Moral Hazard," *Rand Journal of Economics*, **16**(Spring 1985).

N.W. Cornell, R.G. Noll and B. Weingast, "Safety Regulation," in H. Owen and C.L. Schultze, eds., *Setting National Priorities: The Next Ten Years*, Washington: Brookings, 1976.

H.A. Grabowski and J.M. Vernon. *The Regulation of Pharmaceuticals*, Washington: American Enterprise Institute, 1983.

J.E. Harris. "Taxing Tar and Nicotine." *American Economic Review*, 70(June 1980).

P.L. Joskow, "The Effects of Competition and Regulation on Hospital Bed Supply and the Reservation Quality of the Hospital," *Bell Journal of Economics*, 11(Autumn 1980).

P.L. Joskow, *Controlling Hospital Costs: The Role of Government Regulation*, Cambridge: MIT Press, 1981.

L.B. Lave, "Conflicting Objectives in Regulating the Automobile," *Science*, 212(May 22, 1981).

K.B. Leffler, "Physician Licensure: Competition and Monopoly in American Medicine," *Journal of Law and Economics*, 21(April 1978).

S. Peltzman, "The Effects of Automobile Safety Regulation," *Journal of Political Economy*, 83(August 1975).

S. Peltzman, "The Effects of FTC Advertising Regulation," *Journal of Law and Economics*, 24(December 1981).

L. Shepherd, "Licensing Restrictions and the Cost of Dental Care," *Journal of Law and Economics*, 21(April 1978).

M. Spence, "Consumer Misperceptions, Product Failure, and Producer Liability," *Review of Economic Studies*, 44(October 1977).

P. Temin, *Taking Your Medicine: Drug Regulation in the United States*, Cambridge: Harvard University Press, 1980.

W.K. Viscusi, "The Impact of Occupational Safety and Health Regulation, 1973-1983," *Rand Journal of Economics*, 17(Winter 1986).

W.K. Viscusi, "The Impact of Occupational Safety and Health Regulation," *Bell Journal of Economics*, 10(Spring 1979).

W.K. Viscusi, *Risk by Choice*, Cambridge: Harvard University Press, 1983

W.K. Viscusi, W.A. Magat, and J. Huber, "Informational Regulation of Consumer Health Risks: An Empirical Evaluation of Hazard Warnings," *Rand Journal of Economics*, 17(Autumn, 1986).

MIDTERM EXAMINATION – ECON 632
Winter 1988   University of Michigan   Borenstein

- Read the entire exam before beginning.
- Suggested minutes also reflect relative weights in grading.
- Read questions carefully. THINK before you write. Answer concisely, but thoroughly.
- Answer all questions.

1. (20 minutes) Oliver Williamson has suggested a law that would prevent incumbent firms from expanding output in response to new entry into the market. It is claimed that this would prevent predatory pricing and would induce lower prices pre-entry by increasing the importance of limit pricing. Yet, this would be a law about quantities, not prices.

  a) Explain how this law might lessen predatory pricing.

  b) Explain how this law might lower the incumbent's limit price.

2. (30 minutes) For each of the vertical restrictions below, describe what the practice is, explain carefully one reason why an upstream firm might use it, and state whether the use you suggest is likely to be welfare improving or not.

  a) Exclusive dealing contracts.

  b) Quantity Forcing.

  c) Resale Price Maintenance.

3. (30 minutes) Carefully explain three *different* inefficiencies that might result from original cost (also known as historical cost) valuation of capital in a public utility rate making hearing. Examples or graphical/mathematical explanations suggested. (Assume that the rate of return is "correctly" set.)

FINAL EXAMINATION – ECON 632

Winter 1988   University of Michigan   Borenstein

- Read the entire exam before beginning.
- Suggested minutes also reflect relative weights in grading.
- Read questions carefully. THINK before you write. Answer concisely, but thoroughly.
- Answer all questions.

1. (20 minutes) Explain Yardstick Competition as used by public utility regulators to monitor the efficiency of the regulated firm. How is it done? How is it useful to regulators? What are the pitfalls of it?

2. (20 minutes) The Averch-Johnson Effect states that a regulated firm that is allowed a rate of return above the opportunity cost of capital may use a production process that is more capital intensive than is efficient for the quantity that the firm is producing. Prove mathematically or explain intuitively (carefully and precisely) why a slight tightening of the regulatory constraint, that is, a slight lowering of the allowed rate of return from the unregulated monopoly level, is still welfare improving.

3. (40 minutes) Over the last 20 years, regulation of pollution has gradually moved from process standards, such as prescribing smokestack scrubbers for plants that burn high-sulfur coal, to performance standards. Though pollution taxes have been considered, most performance intervention is in the form of quantity setting. Usually, firms are given the right to pollute up to a given amount. Recently, the Environmental Protection Agency has allowed some of these emissions permits to be sold among firms.

    a. Under what conditions will control of pollution through an emissions tax be equivalent to control through transferable emissions permits?

    b. Why must the permits be transferable for this equivalence to hold?

    c. Under what conditions is taxation a better instrument for pollution control than emissions permits?

4. (40 minutes) Regulation of the price of interstate natural gas sales in the 1970's caused shortages in the interstate market. To model this situation, assume that the cost of selling gas interstate and intrastate are the same. Also, assume that when a shortage does occur, allocation in the market that has a shortage is done randomly among customers. Finally, assume that the regulated price is below the unregulated "free-market" equilibrium price, $P*$, but not so low as to completely eliminate supplies in the interstate market.

    a. Explain why price will be the same in the unregulated intrastate and regulated interstate markets, yet the shortage will occur only in the interstate market.

1

b. Explain why the regulation would harm some interstate buyers even if the supply of natural gas were completely inelastic.

c. When a regulated price is announced, a certain consumer in the interstate market who values one unit of gas at R and all further units at zero does not know *ex ante* whether or not she will receive a unit under the random rationing scheme. Are there any values of R above $P*$ for which the consumer would favor regulation? Are there any values of R below $P*$ for which the consumer would favor regulation?

d. (This Question is Harder. Work on it After All Other Questions on the Exam) For a given R above $P*$, describe intuitively and set up the mathematical equation to solve for the (risk-neutral) consumer's optimal P_{reg}, that is, the regulated price that will maximize the consumer's expected consumer surplus.

University of Chicago

Graduate School of Business

BUS 502/ECON 386
Winter 1989

Dennis W. Carlton
Robert H. Gertner

ADVANCED INDUSTRIAL ORGANIZATION I

READING LIST I

Text: Carlton-Perloff (C-P), (in draft form) on Modern Industrial Organization.
   Stigler, G. J., The Organization of Industry, Irwin, 1967.
* Tirole, The Theory of Industrial Organization MIT Press 1988.
Packet of Readings (* indicates article is not in packet).
Recommended: Scherer, F. M., Industrial Market Structure and Economic Performance, 1977.

I. Theory of the Firm

   C-P, Chapter 2.

   Tirole, Introductory Chapter, pp. 15-60.

   Coase, The Nature of the Firm, Economica, 1937, p. 386-405.

   Williamson, Chapter 2 in Markets and Hierarchies: Analysis and Antitrust Implications, Free Press, 1975.

   Klein, Crawford and Alchian, Vertical Integration Appropriable Rents and the Competition Contracting Process, J. of Law and Economics, 1978, p. 297-326.

* Williamson, The Economic Institutions of Capitalism, Free Press, 1985.
* Chandler, The Visible Hand, Harvard University Press, 1977.
* Chandler, Strategy and Structure, MIT Press, 1962.
* Grossman & Hart, The Costs and Benefits of Ownership: A Theory of Lateral and Vertical Integration, Journal of Political Economy 1986, pp. 691-719.

II. Cost Concepts

   C-P, Chapter 3.

   Baumol, Panzar and Willig, Contestable Markets and the Theory of Industry Structure, Chapters 3, 4.

* Stigler, G. J., The Economies of Scale, Chapter 7 in The Organization of Industry.

   Friedlaender, Winston and Wang, Costs, Technology and Productivity on the U.S. Automobile Industry, Bell Journal of Economics, 1983, pp. 1-20.

III. Competition

   C-P, Chapter 4.

* Stigler, G. J., Chapter 2 in The Organization of Industry.

   Baumol, Panzar and Willig, Chapter 2, op. cit.

IV. Monopoly

C-P, Chapter 5.

* Tirole, Chapter 1.

Posner, "The Social Costs of Monopoly and Regulation, <u>J. of Political Economy</u>, 1975.

V. Dominant Firm

C-P, Chapter 8.

Gaskins, "Dynamic Limit Pricing: Optimal Pricing under Threat of Entry", <u>J of Economic Theory</u>, 1971, 3, 306-322.

VI. Oligopoly

C-P, Chapter 9, 10

Bulow, J., Geanakopolos, J. and Klemperer, P., `Multimarket Oliogopoly: Strategic Substitutes and Complements," <u>Journal of Political Economy</u>, 93 (June 1985), 488-511.

* Tirole, Chapters 11, 5, 6.

* Stigler, G. J., "A Theory of Oligopoly," <u>Journal of Political Economy</u> 72 72 (February 1964), 44-61. Chapter 5 in <u>Organization of Industry</u>.

* Stigler, G. J., "Price and NonPrice Competition," Chapter 3 in <u>Organization of Industry</u>, 1968.

Carlton, D. W., "A Reexamination of Delivered Pricing," <u>J. of Law and Economics</u>, 1983.

Green, E. and Porter, R., "Noncooperative Collusion Under Imperfect Price Information," <u>Econometrica</u>, 52 (January 1984), 87-100.

* Maskin, E. and Tirole, J., "A Theory of Dynamic Oligopoly, I-III", mimeo, 1986.

* Gertner, R., "Dynamic Duopoly with Price Inertia," mimeo, 1986.

Rotemberg, J. and Saloner, G., "A Supergame--Theoretic Model of Business Cycles and Price Wars During Booms," <u>American Economic Review</u> 76 (June 1986), 390-407.

* Telser, L., <u>Economic Theory and the Core</u> (especially Chapter 2), 1978.

* Bittlingmayer, G., "Did Antitrust Policy Cause the Great Merger Wave," <u>J. of Law and Economics</u>, April 1985.

VII. Strategic Behavior and Entry Barriers

C-P, Chapters 7, 13.

* Tirole, Chapters 8, 9.

Salop, Strategic Entry Deterrence, <u>American Economics Review</u>, 1979, 335.

Salop and Scheffman, "Raising Rival's Cost", <u>American Economic Review</u>, May 1983, p. 267. Also FTC Working Paper with same title, 1986.

* Gelman and Salop, Judo Economics: Capacity Limitations and Coupon Competition, <u>The Bell Journal of Economics</u>, Autumn 1983, 315-325.

* Spence, "Entry Capacity Investment and Oligopolistic Pricing", <u>The Bell Journal of Economics</u>, Autumn 1977, p. 534.

* Schmalensee, "Economies of Scale and Barriers to Entry," <u>J. of Political Economy</u>, December 1981, p. 241.

Schmalensee, "Product Differentiation Advantage of Pioneering Brands," <u>American Economic Review</u> 1982, 349-365.

Easterbrook, "Predatory Strategies and Counter Strategies," <u>University of Chicago Law Review</u>, 1981.

Milgrom and Roberts, "Predation, Reputation, and Entry Deterrence," <u>J. of Ec. Theory</u>, 1982, 280-312.

Milgrom and Roberts, "Limit Pricing and Entry Under Incomplete Information", <u>Econometrica</u>, 1982, 440-460.

* Bernheim, Strategic Entry Deterrence into an Industry, <u>Rand Journal of Economics</u>, Spring 1984, 1-11.

Baumol, Panzar, Willig, Ch. 10., op. cit.

Bain, <u>Barriers to New Competition</u>, Harvard University Press, 1957, Chapters 1-6 (omit pp. 19-41, 93-113).

* Koller, The Myth of Predatory Pricing: An Empirical Study, <u>Antitrust Law and Economics Review</u>, 105-123, 1970.

Ghemawat and Nalebuff, "Exit", <u>Rand Journal</u>, Summer 1985, 185-194.

* Salop, Strategy, "Strategic Predation and Antitrust Analysis", <u>FTC</u>, 1981.

* Riordan, M., "Imperfect Information and Dynamic Conjectural Variations", <u>Rand Journal</u>, Spring 1985, 41-50.

Burns, M. R., "Predatory Pricing and the Acquisition Costs of Competitors", <u>Journal of Political Economy</u> 1986, 266-296.

Bresnahan, T. and Reiss, P., "Do Entry Conditions Vary Across Markets," <u>Brookings Papers</u>, 1988, special issue.

Dunne, T., N. Roberts and L. Samuelson, "Patterns of Firm Entry and Exit in U.S. Manufacturing Industries," mimeo February 1988.

Jovanovic, B. "Selection and Evolution of Industry," <u>Econometrica</u> 1982, pp. 649-70.

VIII. Monopolistic Competition

   C-P, Chapter 11.

* Tirole, Chapter 7.

   Spence, Product Differentiation and Welfare, <u>American Economic Review</u> May 1976, pp. 407-414.

   Salop, "Monopolistic Competition with Outside Goods," <u>Bell Journal of Economics</u>, Spring 1979, pp. 41-156.

* Dixit and Stiglitz, "Monopolistic Competition and Optimum Product Diversity," <u>American Economic Review</u>, June 1977, pp. 297-308.

   Spence, "Product Selection, Fixed Costs and Monopolistic Competition, <u>Review of Economic Studies</u>, 1976, pp. 217-235.

IX. Concentration and its Relationship to Profits

* C-P, Chapters 7, 12.
* Scherer, Chapters 3 and 9.
* Stigler, "Monopoly and Oligopoly", Chapter 8 in <u>Organization of Industry</u>, 1968.

   Schmalensee, Inter-Industry Studies of Structure and Performance, MIT.

   Ravenscraft, Structure-Profit Relationships at the Line of Business and Industry Level, <u>Review of Economics and Statistics</u>, 1983, p. 22, (included in packet in working paper form).

   Peltzman, The Gains and Losses from Industrial Concentration, <u>J. of Law and Economics</u>, p. 229, 1977.

* Kwoka, "The Effect of Market Share Distribution on Industry Performance", <u>Review of Economics and Statistics</u>, 1979, pp. 101-109.

   Domowitz, et al., "Business Cycles and the Relationship between Concentration and Price Cost Margins", <u>Rand Journal of Economics</u>, pp. 1-17, 1986.

   Kwoka and Ravenscraft, "Cooperation v. Rivalry Price-Cost Margins by Line of Business, <u>Economica</u> 1985, pp. 1-13.

   Fisher, F. M. and McGowan, J., "On the Misuse of Accounting Rates of Return to Infer Monopoly Profits, <u>American Economic Review</u> 73 March 1983, 82-97.

   Bresnahan, "Empirical Studies of Market Power".

   Hall, R., "The Relation Between Price and Marginal Cost in U.S. Industry, <u>JPE</u>, October 1988, pp. 921-947.

G

UNIVERSITY OF CHICAGO
GRADUATE SCHOOL OF BUSINESS

BUSINESS 503/ECONOMICS 387 DENNIS W. CARLTON
Spring 1989 ROBERT H. GERTNER

ADVANCED INDUSTRIAL ORGANIZATION II

Textbooks: Carlton-Perloff (C-P), Modern Industrial Organization
Tirole, Jean, The Theory of Industrial Organization,
MIT Press, 1988.
Packet of Readings

Recommended: Scherer, Industrial Market Structure and Economic Performance

(* Indicates reading is not included in packet.)

I. Price Discrimination Through Two-Part Tariff, Non Linear Pricing, Tie-in Sales

C-P, Chapters 14 and 15.

* Tirole, Chapter 3.

* Scherer, F.M., Chapter 11 through page 324 (in packet).

Singer, E., Chapter 15, An Introduction to Multiple Product Analysis, pp. 185-186 (rest of Chapter 15 optional). Antitrust Economics, Prentice-Hall Incorporated, 1968 Edition.

* Oi, Walter, A Disneyland Dilemma: Two-Part Tariffs for a Mickey Mouse Monopoly, QJE, Vol. (Feb.) 1971, pp. 77-96.

* Schmalensee, Richard, Monopolistic Two-Part Pricing Arrangements, BJE 1981, pp. 445-466.

* Spence, A. Michael, Nonlinear Prices and Welfare, JPE, Vol. 8, 1977, pp. 2-180 (difficult).

Blackstone, E.A., "Restrictive Practices in the Marketing of Electrofax Coping Machines and Supplies: The SCM Corporation Case," J. Ind. Econ., March 1975 23(3): 189-202.

Stigler, George, "United States vs. Leow's Inc.: A Note on Block Booking," The Supreme Court Review, Kurland, University of Chicago Press, 1963 Edition, pp. 152-157.

Singer, Eugene M., Chapter 16, "The Economic Rationale of Typing Arrangements," Antitrust Economics, Prentice-Hall Incorporated, 1968 Edition, pp. 187-195.

* Mussa & Rosen, "Monopoly and Product Quality," JET, 1978, p. 301-317.

Creamer, "On the Economics of Repeat Buying," Rand Journal, Autumn 1984.

II. **Durable Goods**

   C-P, Chapter 19.

   * Tirole, pp. 72-75, 79-87.

   Schmalensee, Richard, Market Structure, Durability, and Quality:
   A Selective Survey, Economic Inquiry, Vol. 17(2) 1979, pp. 177-196.

   Bulow, Jeremy I., Durable-Goods Monopolists, JPE, Vol. 90(2) 1982,
   pp. 314-331.

   Coase, Ronald, "Durability and Monopoly," JLE, Vol. 18 (April) 1972,
   pp. 143-149.

   Carlton, Dennis & Robert Gertner, "Market Power and Mergers in
   Durable Good Industries," Mimeo, 1988.

   * Benjamin, Daniel K. & Roger Kormendi, "The Interrelationship Between
   Markets for New and Used Durable Goods," JLE, Vol. 17(2) 1974,
   pp. 381-401. (Optional)

   * Gul, Sonnenschein and Wilson, "Foundation of Dynamic Monopoly and the
   Coase Conjecture". (Mimeo)

III. **Vertical Relationships Between Firms**

   C-P, Chapter 16.

   * Tirole, Chapter 4.

   Telser, Lester, "Why Should Manufacturers Want Fair Trade?," JLE,
   Vol. 3 (Oct.) 1960, pp. 86-105.

   Easterbrook, Frank H., "Restricted Dealing is a Way to Compete,"
   Regulation, Vol. (Jan.) 1984, pp. 23-27.

   Marvel, Howard and McCafferty, "Resale Price Maintenance and Quality
   Certification, Rand Journal, Autumn 1984.

   Marvel, Howard and McCafferty, "The Economics of Resale Price
   Maintenance, JPE 1986.

   Marvel, Howard P., "Exclusive Dealing," JLE, Vol. 25 (Apr) 1982,
   pp. 1-25.

   * Mathewson, G.F. & R.A. Winter, "An Economic Theory of Vertical
   Restraints," Working Paper, University of Toronto, revised
   December 1982, 36 pages.

   Mathewson, F.G. & R.A. Winter, "Vertical Integration by Contractual
   Restraints in Spatial Markets," JoB, Vol. 56(4) 1983, pp. 497-517.

Caves, Richard E. & William F. Murphy, "Franchising: Firms, Markets, and Intangible Assets," <u>Southern Economic Journal</u>, Vol. 1975, pp. 572-586.

Rubin, Paul, "A Theory of the Firm and the Structure of the Franchise Contract," <u>JLE</u>, Vol. (Apr) 1978, pp. 223-233.

IV. <u>Determination of Price and Availability when Demand is Uncertain</u>

* C-P, Notes on Demand Uncertainty, Chapter 21.

  Carlton, Dennis W., Uncertainty Production Lags and Price, <u>AER</u>, 1977, p. 244.

* Carlton, Dennis W., "Market Behavior with Demand Uncertainty and Price Inflexibility," <u>AER</u>, Sept. 1978 (optional).

* Carlton, Dennis W., "Market Equilibrium When Price and Delivery Lags Clear the Market", <u>BJE</u>, Autumn 1983.

  Carlton, Dennis W., "Contracts, Price Rigidity and Market Equilibrium," <u>JPE</u>, October 1979): 1034-1062.

* Carlton, Dennis W., "The Disruptive Effect of Inflation on the Organization of Markets," in R. Hall, ed., <u>Inflation</u>, 1983.

  Sheshinski and Dreze, Demand Fluctuations, Capacity Utilization, and Costs," <u>AER</u>, 1976, p. 731.

* Carlton, Dennis W., "The General Theory of Allocation and Its Implications for Marketing and Industrial Structure," mimeo, 1987.

V. <u>Antitrust</u>

  C-P, Chapter 22.

VI. <u>Inventories</u>

  Kahn, J., "Inventories and Production," <u>AER</u>, September 1987, pp. 667-679.

  Blinder, A., "Can the Production Smoothing Model of Inventory Behavior Be Saved?," <u>QJE</u>, August 1986, pp. 431-454.

  Blanchard, O., "The Production and Inventory Behavior of the American Automobile Industry, <u>JPE</u>, June 1983, pp. 365-400.

  Miron, J. and Zeldes, S., "Seasonality, Cost Shocks, and the Production Smoothing Models of Inventories," NBER Working Paper #2360, August 1987.

Miron, J. and Zeldes, S., "Production Sales and the Change in Inventories: An Identity that Doesn't Add Up." Mimeo, June 1987.

VII. Advertising and Information

C-P, Chapters 17 and 18.

* Tirole Notes, Chapter 2, pp. 289-295.

Telser, "Advertising and Competition, JPE, 72(6) December 1964, 537-562.

Dixit and Norman, "Advertising and Welfare," BJE, 9, No. 1 (Spring 1978), 1-17.

Benham, "Advertising and the Price of Eyeglasses, JLE, October 1972, 337-52.

Schmalensee, "Advertising and Market Structure," in New Developments in Analysis of Market Structure, MIT Press, 1986, 373-396.

* Scherer, Chapter 14, "Product differentiation, market structure, and competition," in Industrial Structure and Economic Performance (1980), 375-406.

Stigler, "Economics of Information," JPE, 1961. [Chapter 16, The Organization of Industry, University of Chicago Press 1983, 171-190.]

* Diamond, "A Model of Price Adjustment," JET 3(2), June 1971.

Salop and Stiglitz, "Bargains and Ripoffs," R. E. Studies, October 1977.

Nelson, "Advertising as Information," JPE, 82(4) July/August 1974: 729-754.

* Akerlof, "The Market for Lemons: Uncertainty and the Market Mechanism," QJE, 1970, 488-500.

Grossman, "The Informational Role of Warranties and Private Disclosure About Product Quality," JLE, 1981: 461-483.

Klein and Leffler, "The Role of Warranties and Private Disclosure About Product Quality," JPE, 89(4) 1981, pp. 615-641.

* Shapiro, "Consumer Information Product Quality and Seller Reputation," BJE, Spring 1982: 20-35.

IX. R&D and Technological Change

C-P, Chapter 20.

* Tirole, Chapter 10.
* Loury, "Market Structure and Innovation," QJE, August 1979, 395-410.

  Reinganum, "The Timing of Innovation: Research, Development and Diffussion," mimeo, 1985.
* Scherer, Chapter 16, "The Economics of the Patent System," 439-458.
* Griliches, R&D, Patents, and Productivity, University of Chicago Press, 1984.
* Mansfield, Economics of Technological Change, Norton, 1960.

  Pakes, "Patents as Options: Some Estimates of the Value of Holding European Patent Stocks," mimeo, 1984.

  Spence, "Cost Reduction, Competition and Industry Performance," Econometrica, 52 Vol. 1, (January 1984): 101-121.
* Kamien and Schwartz, Market Structure and Innovation, Cambridge University Press, 1982.
* Nordhaus, Invention, Growth and Welfare, MIT Press, 1969.

  Spence, "The Learning Curve and Competition," BJE, Spring 1981, 49-70.

  Farrell and Saloner, "Standardization, Compatibility and Innovation," Rand J of Econ, Spring 1985, 16(1) pp. 70-83.

  Carlton, "The Need for Coordination Among Firms, With Special Reference to Network Industries," University of Chicago Law Review 50(2), Spring 1983, 446-465.

  Wright, B., "The Economics of Invention Incentives: Patents and Prizes, and Research Contracts," AER, 83(4), September, 1983, 691-707.

G

University of California at Santa Barbara

Econ 216 A-B   Industrial Organization
Mr. Frech   Revised March 1990

READING LIST AND COURSE OUTLINE

REQUIRED TEXTS: Stigler, The Organization of Industry (S)
                  Scherer, Industrial Market Structure and Economic
                     Performance, 2nd ed. (Sh)
                  Xeroxes, at Kinko's

   There are also numerous readings from National Bureau of Economic
Research, Business Concentration and Price Policy (NBER) and American
Economic Association, Readings in Industrial Organization and Public
Policy (AEA), Weston and Ornstein The Impact of Large Firms on the
U.S. Economy (WO) and McGee, In Defense of Industrial Concentration
(M), Sherman, Oligopoly: An Empirical Approach, and Tirole, The
Theory of Industrial Organization (T).

   You may find it helpful to consult the following to review some
of the material covered in the course: Needham, Economic Analysis and
Industrial Structure, and Singer, Antitrust Economics.

   Antitrust law and case precedent is not covered extensively in
the course. For a review see Neale, The Antitrust Laws of the U.S.A.;
cases are covered in Stelzer, Selected Antitrust Cases and in Warren,
Antitrust in Theory and Practice.

   For case studies of specific industries, which will not be
covered extensively in class are Adams, The Structure of American
Industry and Weiss, Case Studies in American Industry.

   Recommended for the analysis of regulation are Kahn, The
Economics of Regulation, 2 vols.; Olson, The Logic of Collective
Action; Kolko, The Triumph of Conservatism; Buchanan and Tullock, The
Calculus of Consent; Bailey, Economic Theory of Regulatory Constraint.

   The following journal abbreviations are used:

   AER -   American Economic Review
   QJE -   Quarterly Journal of Economics
   JPE -   Journal of Political Economy
   JLE -   Journal of Law and Economics
   RES -   Review of Economics and Statistics
   BJ   -   Bell Journal of Economics
   JOB -   Journal of Business

Especially recommended are readings marked (*).

I.   Oligopoly

       A.   Traditional Models

            *Intriligator, Mathematical Optimization and Economic
                Theory, pp. 205-219
            *SH, Chs. 5-8
            *S, Ch. 5

*Schwartzman, David, <u>Innovation in the Pharmaceutical Industry</u>, Ch. 12
Cournot, <u>Researches in the Mathematical Principles of the Theory of Wealth</u>, Chs. 7,8
Fellner, <u>Competition Among the Few</u>
R.G.D. Allen, <u>Mathematical Analysis for Economists</u>, pp. 200-204, 345-347
Chamberlin, <u>The Theory of Monopolistic Competition</u>, Ch. 3
Baumol, <u>Business Behavior, Value and Growth</u>, Part I
Machlup, <u>The Economics of Sellers Competition</u>, Ch. 13
Henderson & Quandt, <u>Microeconomic Theory</u>, pp. 222-234
Posner, Ch. 6

B. Game Theoretic Approaches

*SH, pp. 160-165
*Thompson & Faith, "A Pure Theory of Strategic Behavior and Social Institutions", <u>AER</u>, Vol. 71, No. 3 (June 1981), pp. 366-380
T, Chs. 11,5,6
Axelrod, Robert, <u>The Evolution of Cooperation</u>, New York: Basic Books (1984)
Faith & Thompson, "Social Interaction under Truly Perfect Information", <u>J. Math. Sociology</u>
Borch, <u>The Economics of Uncertainty</u>, Ch. 9-11
Luce & Raiffa, <u>Games and Decisions</u>
Faith Thompson, "A Model of Rational Non-Competitive Interdependence"
Sherman, Chs. 1-5, 9

C. Market Sharing

Nicholls, <u>Imperfect Competition within Agricultural Industries</u>, pp. 120-130

D. Price Leadership

Markham, "The Nature and Significance of Price Leadership", in AEA

E. Predation

*McGee, "Predatory Price Cutting: The Standard Oil (N.J.) Case", <u>JLE</u>, 1958
*Comanor & Frech, "Strategic Behavior in Antitrust", <u>AER</u>, 1984
T, Ch. 9

F. Cartels

Patinkin, "Multiple Plant Firms, Cartels and Imperfect Competition", QJE, Feb. 1947

II. **Monopolistic Competition and the Economics of Selling Expenditures**

   A. The Theory of Monopolistic Competition

   *SH, Ch. 14
   *Chamberlin, The Theory of Monopolistic Competition, Chs. 4-7

   1. Welfare Implications

      *Chamberlin, "Product Heterogeneity and Public Policy", in AEA
      Chamberlin, Theory of Monopolistic Competition, Appendix E & F

   B. The Critique of the Theory

   *S, Appendix
   *Barzel, "Excess Capacity in Monopolistic Competition", JPE, Sept/Oct 1970
   Archibald, "Chamberlin versus Chicago", Review of Economic Studies, October 1961
   Damsetz, "The Nature of Equilibrium in Monopolistic Competition", JPE, Feb 1959
   _____, "The Welfare and Empirical Implications of Monopolistic Competition", Economic Journal, Sept 1964
   _____, "Do Competition and Monopolistic Competition Differ?", JPE, Feb 1968
   _____, "The Inconsistencies in Monopolistic Competition: A Reply", JPE, May/June 1972

   C. Selling Expenditures and the Economics of Information

   *S, Chs. 16, 17
   *Benham, "The Effect of Advertising on the Price of Eyeglasses", JLE, Oct 1972
   *Nelson, "Economic Consequences of Advertising", JOB, April 1975
   *Klein & Leffler, "The Role of Market Forces in Assuring Contractual Performance", JPE, 89, 4, Aug 1981, pp. 615-641
   *Pauly & Satterthwaite, BJ, 12, 2, Autumn 1981, pp. 488-506
   *_____, "Advertising as Information", JPE, July/Aug 1974
   *Frech & Rochlin, "... Advertising as a ... Public Good", Econ. Inquiry, 7/1979
   T, Ch. 2
   Buchanan, "Advertising Expenditures: A Suggested Treatment", JPE, August 1942
   Telser, Advertising and Competition, JPE, 1964
   _____, The Supply and Demand for Advertising Messages, AER, May 1966
   Schmalensee, The Economics of Advertising, Ch. 1
   Kaldor, "Economic Aspects of Advertising", Review of Economic Studies, 50-51, Vol. 18

Churbak, "Mail-Order Giants Lure Buyers by Employing Multiple Identities", PC Week, Vol. 4, No. 23, pp. 1, 167
Frech & Rochlin, "A New View of Advertising", J. of Advertising, 1982
Comanor & Wilson, Advertising and Market Power, Chs. 2,3
Akerlof, "The Market for 'Lemons' Quality Uncertainty and the Market Mechanism", QJE, Aug 1970
Heal, "Do Bad Products Drive Out Good", QJE, Aug 1976
Stigler & Becker, "De Gustibus Non Est Disputandum", AER, March 1977
Schwartzman, David, Innovation in the Pharmaceutical Industry, Ch. 11

D. Newer Theories

*Archibald & Rosenbluth, "The 'New Theory' of Consumer Demand and Monopolistic Competition", QJE, November 1975
*Hotelling, "Stability in Competition", Economic Journal, March 1929
*_____, "Monopoly, Quality and Regulation", BJ, Autumn 1975
*Krugman, "Intraindustry Specialization and the gains from Trade"
*Spence, "Nonprice Competition", AER, Feb 1977
T, Ch. 7
Lancaster, "Socially Optimal Product Differentiation", AER, September 1975
Leland, "Quality Choice and Competition", AER, March 1977
Rosen, "Hedonic Prices and Implicit Markets: Product Differentiation in Pure Competition", JPE, Jan/Feb 1974
Spence, "Product Selection, Fixed Costs, and Monopolistic Competition", RES, June 1976
_____, "Monopoly Quality and Regulation", BJ, Fall 1975
Dixit and Stiglitz, "Monopolistic Competition and Optimum Product Diversity", AER, June 1977
Hirshleifer, Price Theory and Applications, Ch. 9

III. Some Determinants of Market Structure

*SH, Ch. 4

A. Mergers

*Butters & Lintner, "Effects of Taxes on Concentration", in NBER
*S, Ch. 8
*Coase, "The Nature of the Firm", in RPT
*Markham, "Survey of the Evidence on Mergers", in NBER
Nelson, Merger Movements in American Industry
Weston, The Role of Mergers in the Growth of Large Firms
Butters & Lintner, "Effects of Mergers on Industrial Concentration", RES, 1950
Gort, "An Economic Disturbance Theory of Mergers", QJE, Nob 1969

B. Firm Growth

   Peltzman, "The Gain and Losses from Industrial
      Concentration", JLE, 20, 2, Oct 1977, pp. 229-265
   Nelson & Winter, "The Schumpeterian Trade-offs Revisited",
      AER, 72, 1, Mar 1982, pp. 114-132
   Hymer & Pasigian, "Firm Size and Rate of Growth", JPE, Dec
      1962
   Mansfield, "Entry, Gibrat's Law ..." AER, Dec 1962
   Sion & Bonini, "The Size Distribution of Business Firms",
      AER, Sept 1958
   Whalen, Gary, "Concentration and Profitability in non-SMSA
      Banking Markets", Economic Review, Federal Reserve Bank
      of Cleveland, Quant. 1, 1987, pp. 1-89

C. Economies of Scale and Barriers to Entry

   *S, Chs. 7,6
   *Frech & Ginsburg, "Optimal Scale in Medical Practice: A
      Survivor Analysis", JOB, Jan 1974
   Baumol, "On the Proper Cost Tests for Natural Monopoly in a
      Multi-product Industry",AER, Dec 1977
   Panzer & Willig, "Free Entry and the Sustainability of
      Natural Monopoly", BJ, Spring 1977
   Smith, "Survey of Empirical Evidence on Economies of Scale",
      & Reply by Friedman in NBER, pp. 213-38
   Bain, Barriers to New Competition
   EAG Robinson, The Structure of Competitive Industry, Ch. 207
   Williamson, "Selling Costs as a Barrier to Entry", QJE, Feb
      1963
   Nerlov, Estimation and Identification of Cobb-Douglas
      Production Functions, 1965
   Peltzman, "Entry in Commercial Banking", JLE, Oct 1965
   Baumol, "Contestable Markets: On Uprising in the Theory of
      Industrial Structure", AER, 72, 1, Mar 1982, pp. 1-15
   Demsetz, "Barriers to Entry", AER, 72, 1, Mar 1982, pp. 47-
      57

D. Limit Entry Pricing

   *Bain, "A Note on Pricing in Monopoly and Oligopoly", in AEA
   T, Ch. 8
   Osborne, "The Role of Entry in Oligopoly Theory", June 1961
   Kemien & Schwartz, "Limit Pricing and Uncertain Entry",
      Econometrica, May 1971
   Bain, "Economies of Scale ...", in AEA
   Modigliani, "New Developments on the Oligopoly Front", JPE,
      1958
   Pashigian, "Limit Price and the Market Share of the Leading
      Firm", Journal of Industrial Economics, July 1968
   Wenders, "Collusion and Entry", JPE, Nov 1971

E. Patents, Copyrights and Innovation

   *SH, Ch. 16

*Kitch, "The Nature and Function of the Patent System", JLE, Oct 1977
T, Ch. 10
Plant, "Economic Theory Concerning Patents for Invention", Economica, 1945
_____, "Economic Aspects of Copyright in Books", Economics, 1934
Young, "Increasing Returns and Economic Progress", Economic Journal, 1928
Bowman, Ward S., Patent and Antitrust Law: A Legal and Economic Appraisal, Chicago: U of Chicago Press, 1973

IV. Pricing

   A. Price Discrimination

   *SH, Ch. 11
   T, Ch. 3
   J. Robinson, Economics of Imperfect Competition, Bk., V
   Pigou, Economics of Welfare, Ch. 17
   Oi, "A Disneyland Dilemma: Two Part Tariffs for a Mickey Mouse Monopoly", QJE, Feb 1971

   B. Uniform Delivered Prices -- Basing Point Methods

   *S, Ch. 14
   Machlup, The Basing Point System
   Kaysen, "Basing Point Pricing and Public Policy", in AEA
   J.M. Clark, "Basing Point Methods", Canadian Journal of Economics and Political Science, 1938
   DeCanio, "Delivered Pricing and Multiple Basing Point Equilibria, a Re-evaluation", QJE, Vol. 99, No. 3, May 1984, pp. 329-347

   C. Price Rigidity

   *SH, Ch. 13
   *Stigler & Kindahl, The Behavior of Industrial Prices, Basic Methods and Conclusions
   Carlton, Dennis W., "The Rigidity of Prices", AER 76(4) (Sept. 1986), pp. 637-658
   Mason, "Price Inflexibility", Rev. of Econ. and Stat., 1938
   National Bureau of Econ. Research, The Price Statistics of the Federal Government, pp. 393-412, 419-31
   S., Ch. 19
   U.S. Senate, Antitrust Subcommittee, Administered Prices: A Compendium, 1963
   Means, "Industrial Prices and Their Relative Inflexibility", Journal of the American Statistical Association, 1935
   _____, "The Administered Price Thesis Reconfirmed", AER, June 1972
   Blair, Economic Concentration, Pt. 4
   Sweezy, "Demand Under Conditions of Oligopoly", and companion article by Stigler in AEA Readings in Price Theory (latter also in S., Ch. 18)

53

V. **Vertical Relations**

   *Oliver Williamson, "Reflections on the New Institutionalist Economics", Zeitschrift für die Gesampte Staatswissenschaft, 141, 1, Mar 1985, pp. 187-195
   *Steiner, "Basic Relationship in Consumer Goods Industries", Research in Marketing, 7, 1984, pp. 165-208
   Blair, Roger D. & David L. Kogerman, Law and Economics of Vertical Integration and Control

   A. Vertical Integration

   *S, Ch. 12
   *Alchian, Crawford & Klein, "Vertical Integration Appropriable Rents and the Competitive Contracting Process", JLE, Oct 1978
   T, Ch. 4
   Allen "Vertical Integration and Foreclosure", JLE, April 1971
   Warren-Boulton, Vertical Control of Market, 1978
   _____, "Vertical Control with Variable Proportions", JPE, July/Aug 1974
   _____, "Vertical Control with Variable Proportions", JPE, July/Aug 1975
   Machlup & Taber, "Bilateral Monopoly ...", Economica, May 1960
   Bork, "Vertical Integration and the Sherman Act", University of Chicago Law Review, Autumn 1954
   Liebeler, "Toward a Consumer's Antitrust Law: The FTC and Vertical Mergers in Cement", UCLA Law Review, June 1968
   McGee & Bassett, "Vertical Integration Revisited", JLE, April 1976

   B. Resale Price Maintenance

   *Telser, "Why Should Manufacturers Want Fair Trade?", JLE, 1958
   *SH, pp. 591-4
   Bowman, "The Pre-requisites of Resale Price Maintenance", University of Chicago Law Review, 1955
   Bork, "The Rule of Reason ..." Yale Law Journal, 1965, 1966
   Andrews, Fair Trade, 1960
   Springer, R.F. & H.E. Frech III, "Deterring Fraud: The Role of Resale Price Maintenance", November 1985

   C. Tie-in Selling and Full Line Forcing

   *Burstein, "A Theory of Full Line Forcing", Northwestern University Law Review, Feb 1969
   *_____, "The Economics of Tie-in Sales", RES, Feb 1960
   *S., Ch. 15
   Bowman, "Trying Arrangements and the Leverage Problem", Yale Law Journal, Nov 1957
   R.G.D. Allen, Math. Analysis for Economists, pp. 359-62
   Markovits, "Tie-in, Leverage and the American Antitrust Laws", Yale Law Journal, 1967, 1970

Pashigian, *The Distribution of Automobiles*

D. Exclusive Dealing

Frech, H.E. III & W.S. Comanor, "The Competitive Effects of Vertical Agreements", AER, 75, 3, June 1985, pp. 539-546

Mathweson, G. Frank and Ralph A. Winter, "The Competitive Effects of Vertical Agreements: Comment." AER 77 (5) (Dec. 1987): 1057-62

Schwartz, Marius. "The Competitive Effects of Vertical Agreements: Comments." AER 77 (5) (Dec. 1978): 1063-68

Comanor, William S. and H.E. Frech III. "The Competitive Effects of Vertical Agreements: Reply." AER 77 (5) (Dec. 1987): 1069-72

Marvel, Howard P., "Exclusive Dealing", JLE, Vol. 25, No. 1, April 1982, pp.1-25

VI. Welfare Aspects

*SH, Ch. 2, including Appendix
*Harberger, "Monopoly and Resource Allocation", AER, May 1954
*Tullock, "The Welfare Costs of Tariffs, Monopolies and Theft", WEJ, 5, 3, June 1967
Stigler, "The Statistics of Monopoly and Merger", JPE, Feb 1965
Schwartzman, "The Burden of Monopoly", JPE, Dec 1960
Bergson, "On Monopoly Welfare Loss", AER, Dec 1976
McGee, *In Defense of Industrial Concentration*
Tullock, "The Cost of Transfers", WEJ, July 2, 1970
Posner, "The Social Cost of Monopoly and Regulation", JPE, 83, 4, Aug 1975
Adams & Yellen, "Commodity Bundling and the Burden of Monopoly", QJE, Aug 1976

VII. Empirical Studies of Market Structure and its Consequences

A. Measurement of Market Structure

*S, Ch. 4
*Rosenbluth, "Measurement of Concentration", in NBER
*Adelman, "Concept and Measurement of Vertical Integration", in NBER
*Saving, "Concentration Ratios and the Degree of Monopoly", *International Economic Review*, Feb 1970
Scitovsky, "Economic Theory and the Measurement of Concentration", in NBER

B. Market Structure in the United States

*SH, Ch. 3
*Nutter and Einhorm, *The Extent of Enterprise Monopoly in the United States: 1899-1958*
Adelman, "Measurement of Industrial Concentration", in AEA
Stigler, *Five Lectures on Economic Problems*, Ch. 5

Nelson, *Concentration in the Manufacturing Industries of the U.S.*
Pashigian, "Market Concentration in the U.S. and Great Britain", JLE, Oct 1968
Stigler, "The Economic Effect of the Antitrust Laws", JLE, 1966
Kemerschen, "An Empirical Test of Oligopoly Theories", JPE, July 1968

C. Market Structure and Profits

*WO, Chs. 3-6, 11, 14-16
*SH. 17-21
*Bain, "The Relation of the Profit Rate to Industry Concentration", QJE, 1951
*Collins & Preston, *Price-Cost Margins in Manufacturing* (contains summary of results of other studies)
*Brozen, "Bain's Concentration and Rates of Return Revisited", JLE, Oct 1971
S., Ch. 13
McConnell, "Corporate Earnings by Size of Firm", *Survey of Current Business*, May 1945
Stigler, *Capital and Rates of Return in Manufacturing*
Hall & Weiss, "Firm Size and Profitability", RES, Aug 1967
Kilpatrick, "Stigler on the Relationship Between Profits and Concentration", JPE, May 1963
Weiss, "Econometric Studies of Industrial Organization", unpublished
Posner, Chs. 7,8
Demsetz, "Industry Structure, Market Rivalry, and Public Policy", JLE, April 1973

1. Advertising and Profits

Telser, "Advertising and Cigarettes", JPE, Oct 1962
Comanor & Wilson, "Advertising, Market Structure and Performance", RES, Nov 1967
Weiss, "Advertising, Profits and Corporate Taxes", RES, Nov 1960
Peles, "Rate of Amortization of Advertising", JPE, Oct 1971
Schmalensee, Chs. 4, 7
Ayanian, "Advertising and the Rate of Return", unpublished
Block, "Advertising and Profitability: A Reappraisal", JPE, March/April 1974
Comanor & Wilson, *Advertising and Market Power*

IX. Technological Change and Market Structure

*SH, Ch. 15
*Schumpeter, *Capitalism, Socialism and Democracy*, Chs. 7-8
Boulding, "In Defense of Monopoly", QJE, 1945
Villard, "Competition, Oligopoly, and Research", JPE, 1958
Stigler, "Industrial Organization and Economic Progress", in *State of the Social Sciences*
Abramovitz, "Monopolistic Selling", QJE, 1938

Mansfield, *Industrial Research and Technological Innovation*, Ch. 5
Nutter, "Monopoly, Bigness and Progress", JPE, 1956
Scherer, "Firm Size, Market Structure and the Output of Patented Invention", AER, Dec 1965
Schmookler, *Invention and Economic Growth*
Williamson, "Innovation and Market Structure", JPE, Feb 1965
Mansfield, "Industrial Research and Development", JPE, 1964
_____, "Rate of Return from Industrial Research and Development", AER, May 1965

X. **Government Regulated and Government Owned Industries**

*Coase, "The Federal Communications Commission", JLE, Oct 1969
*Stigler & Friedland, "What Can Regulators Regulate? The Case for Electricity", JLE, Oct 1962
*SH, Chs. 18, 22
*George J. Stigler, "The Theory of Economic Regulation", BJ, II (1971), 3-21
*William A. Jordan, "Producer Protection, Prior Market Structure and the Effects of Government Regulation", *Journal of Law and Economics*, XV (1972), 151-176
*Ruben Kessel, "Price Discrimination in Medicine", JLE, I (1958), 20-53 (also in Breit & Hochman)
*Peltzman, "An Evaluation of Consumer Protection Legislation: The 1962 Drug Amendments", JPE, 81, 5 (Sept/Oct 1973)
* _____, "Pricing in Public and Private Enterprise ...", JLE, Apr 1971
W.S. Comanor & B.M. Mitchell, "Cable Television and the Impact of Regulation", BJ, II (1971), 154-212
_____, The Costs of Planning: The FCC and Cable Television", JLE, April 1972
Averch & Johnson, "Behavior of the Firm Under Regulatory Constraint", AER, Dec 1962
Hilton, "The Consistency of the Interstate Commerce Act", JLE, 1966
Demeetz, "Why Regulate Utilities?", JLE, 1968
Baumol & Klevorick, "Input Choices and Rate-of-Return Regulation", BJ, Autumn 1970
MacAvoy, "The Effectiveness of the Federal Power Commission", BJ, Autumn 1970
Peltzman, "Capital Investment in Commercial Banking", JPE, Jan 1970
Sloss, "Regulation of Motor Freight Transportation", BJ, Autumn 1970
Friedlaender, *The Dilemma of Freight Transportation Regulation*
Meyer et al., *The Economics of Competition in the Transportation Industries*
Kolke, *The Triumph of Conservatism*, Chs. 1,2,6,9,10
Olson, *The Logic of Collective Action*
Alfred E. Kahn, *The Economics of Regulation* (New York: John Wiley & Sons, Inc., 1970), 2 vols.
Ed Renshaw, "Utility Regulation", *Journal of Business*, XXI (1958), 335-343

George W. Hilton, "The Basic Behavior of Regulatory
   Commissions", AER LXII (May 1972), 47-54
Richard Posner, "Natural Monopoly and Its Regulation",
   Stanford Law Review, XXI (1969), 548-643
Horace M. Gray, "The Passing of the Public Utility Concept",
   American Economic Association, Readings in the Social
   Control of Industry, 280-303
Bailey, Economic Theory of Regulatory Constraint
Posner, Chs. 9-14
George W. Hilton, "The Costs to the Economy of the
   Interstate Commerce Commission", The Economics of
   Federal Subsidy Programs (Joint Economic Committee,
   Congress of the United States, 1973), Part 6, pp. 707-
   733
William A. Jordan, Airline Regulation in America
E. Kitch, "Regulation of the Federal Power Commission", JLE,
   XI (1968), 243-280
Paul MacAvoy, "The Regulation-Induced Shortage of Natural
   Gas", JLE, XIV (1971), 167-199
Robert W. Gerwig, "Natural Gas Production: A Study of the
   Costs of Regulation", JLE, V (1962), 69-92
E. Erickson & R. Spann, "Supply Response in a Regulated
   Industry: The Case of Natural Gas", BJ, II (1971), 94-
   121
Thomas G. Moore, "The Petroleum Industry", The Structure of
   American Industry, Walter Adams, ed., 4th ed., 1971,
   pp. 117-155
Kenneth Dam, "Implementation of Import Quotas: The Case of
   Oil", JLE, XIV (1971), 1-60
Thomas G. Moore, "Electric Utility Prices", Southern
   Economic Journal, XXXVI (1970), 365-375
Ross D. Eckert & George W. Hilton, "The Jitneys", JLE, XV
   (1972), 293-325
R. West & S. Tinic, "Minimum Commission Rates on New York
   Stock Exchange Transactions", BJ, II (1971), 57-605
William F. Baxter, "NYSE Fixed Commission Rates: A Private
   Cartel Public", Stanford Law Review, XXII (1970), 675-
   712
J. Fred Barron, "Business and Professional Licensing --
   California, A Representative Example", Stanford Law
   Review, XVIII (1966), 64-0665
Simon Rottenberg, "The Economics of Occupational Licensing",
   National Bureau of Economic Research, Aspects of Labor
   Economics, pp. 3-20
Caves, Air Transport and its Regulators
Posner, "Taxation by Regulation", BJ, Spring 1971
Jordan, "Producer Protection, ...", JLE, Apr 1972
Moore, "The Effectiveness of Regulation of Electric Utility
   Prices", Southern Econ. Journal, 1970
Davies, "The Efficiency of Public v. Private Firms", JLE,
   Apr 1971
Keeler, "Airline Regulation and Market Performance", BJ,
   Autumn 1972
Peltzman, "An Evaluation of Consumer Protection Legislation:
   The 1962 Drug Amendments", JPE, Sept/Oct 1973
Kessel, "Transfused Blood, Serum Hepatitis, and the Coase
   Theorem", JLE, Oct 1974

University of California at Santa Barbara

Final Examination   Economics 216A   Mr. Frech
TIME: 3 hours   (100 points possible)   1985

GENERAL INSTRUCTIONS: Read each question carefully. Plan your answers; excessive wordiness and poor organization will be penalized. Explain all answers. Note carefully the point value of all questions.

1. **The U.S. Auto Industry (20 points)**
In recent years, it has been obseved that the U.S. auto firms have been disintegrating. For example, GM is purchasing engineering services from Getrag in Germany. Ford is purchasing both engineering and parts from Mazda. Chrysler is purchasing complete V8 engines from Mitsubishi. Explain this behavior.

2. **Oligopoly Models (14 points)**
   a. In what sense is the Bertrand model more stable than the Cournot?
   b. How would you choose between the two models to represent behavior in an actual industry? What empirical facts would you observe to help you choose?

3. **Scale Economies in Advertising (15 points)**
Some economists argue that there are scale economies in advertising. Is this correct? What empirical evidence bears on your answer?

4. **Oligopoly and Game Theory (18 points)**
Consider the following bimatrix of payoffs to two competing firms:

	firm b's price		
firm a's price	$5	$4	$3
$5	(6,3)	(5,4)	(2,3)
$4	(7,2)	(6,3)	(3,2)
$3	(10,0)	(7,0)	(4,1)

   a. What are the Nash-Bertrand equilibrium price pair(s), if any?
   b. What are the preferred price pair(s) for each firm.
   c. Are the preferred price pairs attainable as Faith-Thompson equilibria?
   d. Write down the committments that would achieve all of the Faith-Thompson equilibria.

5. **Predatory Behavior (15 points)**
Carefully define predatory behavior. Does predatory behavior on the part of sellers help or harm consumers?.

6. **Information (15 points)**
Does better market information help or harm consumers?

7. **The Course (5 points)**
What is the most striking idea you have come across in your reading or lectures in this course? How has it affected your thinking?

Final Examination Economics 216A Mr. Frech
TIME: 3 hours Winter, 1986

GENERAL INSTRUCTIONS: Read each question carefully. Plan your answers; excessive wordiness and poor organization will be penalized. Write in ink or dark pencil. Be sure that your writing is readable. Explain all answers. Note carefully the point value of all questions.

1. **Advertising (24 points)**
Some economists analyze advertising as information.
   a. What is (are) the alternative views?
   b. What empirical evidence would you use to distinguish among these various theories of advertising?

2. **Oligopoly and Game Theory (24 points)**
An oligopoly is modelled with the following bimatrix.

		firm b	
	1. high price	2. medium price	3. low price
firm a 1. high price	(10, 9)	(8, 10)	(-5, 13)
2. medium price	(11, 6)	(10, 7)	(-3, 6)
3. low price	(10, -4)	(8, -2)	(-2, 0)

   a. Identify the Nash-Bertrand equilibrium price pair(s) if, any.
   b. Identify the preferred price pair for each firm.
   c. Are these preferred pairs attainable as Faith-Thompson equilibria?
   c. Write down committments that would achieve these preferred pairs.

3. **The Course (5 points)**
What is the most striking idea that you have come across in the reading or the lecture of this course? How has it affected your thinking?

4. Omitted for copyright reasons.

5. Omitted for copyright reasons.

University of California at Santa Barbara

Final Examination   Economics 216A   Mr. Frech
TIME: 3 hours   Winter 1985

GENERAL INSTRUCTIONS: Read each question carefully. Plan your answers; excessive wordiness and poor organization will be penalized. Be sure that your writing is readable. Explain all answers. Note carefully the point value of all questions.

1. **The Computer Market--Announcements (18 points)**
It has been observed that computer hardware and software makers sometimes announce products, in detail, substantially (perhaps many months) before they are ready to be sold.
    a. Can you explain this behavior using economic analysis?
    b. What does this behavior tell you about the degree of competitiveness of the industry?
    c. What, if any, are the implications of this behavior for public policy?

2. **Cost Savings (20 points)**
A supermarket has argued that if its customers help reduce theft, the supermarket will save costs and these costs will be passed along to the shoppers there.
    a. In the short run, is this argument by the supermarket correct?
    b. In the long run, allowing for exit and entry, how is your answer different?

3. **Symmetry (18 points)**
Several times in class the issue of symmetry in monopolistic competition models has come up.
    a. What does the assumption of symmetry mean in these models?
    b. What difference does this assumption make for the analysis?
    c. What difference does it make for the results of the models?

4. **Oligopoly and Game Theory (18 points)**
An oligopoly is modelled with the following bimatrix.

	firm b high price	low price
firm a high price	(5,4)	(-6,4)
medium price	(8,1)	(-5,0)
low price	(9,-3)	(-4,-2)

    a. Identify the Nash-Bertrand equilibrium pair(s) if any.
    b. Identify the Faith-Thompson equilibrium pair(s), if any.
    c. Write down the Faith-Thompson committment made by firm a if it is maker.

5. Omitted for copy reasons.

6. **The Course (6 points)**
What is the most striking idea that you have come across in the reading or the lectures of this course? How has it affected your thinking?

University of California at Santa Barbara

Winter 1984   Economics 216A   Mr. Frech
                        Final Examination

General Instructions: Answer all questions. Carefully note the point values of the questions. Answer each one as clearly and briefly as possible. Excessive wordiness is not in your best interest. Be sure that your writing and your penmanship is clear. You will be penalized if it is not. Explain <u>all</u> answers.

Time: 3 hours.

1. **Advertising for Eyeglasses** (15 points)

    The Benham article on advertising has implications for the effect of advertising on the elasticity of demand for goods.
    a.   What are these implications?
    b.   What does this, in turn, imply about whether advertising would be oversupplied or undersupplied in this market? (Hint: Among other arguments, Spence's is relevant here.)

2. **The Computer Market** (21 points)

    It has been observed that some computer manufacturers make computers that have less performance than would be possible at that cost. These are the junior models of higher performance computers.
    a.   Can you explain this behavior using economic analysis?
    b.   What does this behavior tell you about the degree of competitiveness of this industry?
    c.   What, if any, are the policy implications of your analysis?

3. **Vertical Integration** (9 points)

    How would you predict which markets would be bridged by vertical integration?

4. **Oligopoly and Game Theory** (30 points)

An oligopoly is modelled with the following bimatrix.

	firm b high price	firm b low price
firm a high price	(9,5)	(-6,4)
firm a low price	(12,-2)	(-4,-1)

a. Does a Nash-Bertrand equilibrium exist? Identify it (them).
b. Identify the collusive solution(s).
c. Suppose that we are at a collusive solution. Starting from it (them), what is the gain to firm a from cheating on the agreement? What is the gain to firm b for such cheating?
d. Does a Faith-Thompson solution exist? Identify it (them).
e. Now suppose that punishment prices are allowed. Answer question d. again.

5. **The Course** (5 points)

What is the most striking idea you have come across in the reading or the lectures for this course? How has it affected your thinking?

6. **Chrysler v. General Motors and Toyota** (20 points)

Chrysler is currently suing General Motors and Toyota on the grounds that their joint venture to produce small cars in San Francisco is anticompetitive. Chrysler states further that this joint venture will hurt Chrysler. How would you argue for and against Chrysler?

University of California at Santa Barbara

Winter 1982   Economics 216A   Mr. Frech
Final Examination

General Instructions: Answer all questions Carefully note the point values of the questions. Answer each one as clearly and briefly as possible. Excessive wordiness is not in your interest. Explain all answers.

Time: 3 hours.

1. **Oligopoly Models** (20 points)

   For each of the following oligopoly models, briefly explain the assumptions and results, then state the characteristics of an actual oligopoly where you think the model would be useful for analysis.
   a. Cournot.
   b. Bertrand.
   c. Faith/Thompson.
   d. Limit entry pricing.
   e. Stigler (cheating on collusion).

2. **The Theory of Advertising** (20 points)

   There are many arguments in the literature that firms that supply relatively good buys for consumer will advertise more heavily than other firms. State the arguments. Do you agree? Explain.

3. **The Lectures** (5 points)

   What argument of the professor do you most disagree with? Explain.

4. **Resale Price Maintenance** (25 points)

   Resale price maintenance is now illegal in most cases. Present the arguments for and against prohibiting it.

5. Ommitted for Copyright Reasons

Fall 1980

University of California at Santa Barbara
Economics 216A
Final Examination

Mr. Frech

General Instructions: Answer all questions. Carefully note the point values of the questions. Answer each question as clearly and briefly as possible. Excessive wordiness is not in your interest. Explain all answers.

Time: 3 Hours

1. Limit Entry Pricing - (30 points)

   How would a firm that is originally practicing limit entry pricing react to:

   a. Technical change so that the minimum efficient scale of firm declines from 50,000 units per year to 25,000 units per year.
   b. For a handsome fee, the firm's consulting economist tells the management that the demand elasticity has changed from -2.0 to -5.0.
   c. The appropriate discount rate falls from 15% to 5%.

2. Game Theory and Oligopoly - (20 points)

   An oligopoly is modeled with the following bimatrix.

	firm b high price	firm b low price
firm a high price	(8,4)	(-6,3)
firm a low price	(10,-2)	(-5,-1)

   a. Does a Faith-Thompson Equilibrium exist? If so, identify it (them).
   b. If the firms are initially colluding, what is the gain to firm b in cheating on the collusion?

3. The Lectures - (10 points)

   What argument made by the professor do you most disagree with? Explain your disagreement.

4. The Oligopoly Problem - (20 points)

   Is the assumption of complete information and maximizing behavior sufficient to find the equilibrium of an ologopoly market? Explain.

5. Product Choice - (20 points)

   It is traditionally argued that firms choose products to produce which have less elastic demands so that they can more profitably exercise whatever monopoly power they may have. Do you agree? Explain whichever position you take.

University of California at Santa Barbara

Fall 1979   FINAL EXAMINATION   Mr. Frech
Economics 216A

GENERAL INSTRUCTIONS: Answer all questions. Carefully note the point values. Answer each question as clearly and briefly as possible. Poor organization and excessive wordiness are not in your interest.

Time: 2 1/2 hours. Students whose native language is not English will be allowed an extra one half hour.

1. Oligopoly Models - (15 points)

    Some argue that the study of oligopoly models is a waste of time because there are so many of them -- the general theory of oligopoly has not been invented yet. Do you agree? Explain.

2. Advertising - (20 points)

    Recently the Supreme Court struck down state laws prohibiting advertising of perscription drug prices. Who, among the following groups, do you expect to gain and who to lose? Explain your answers.

    a. Retail druggists.
    b. Consumers of lifetime drugs (those with chronic illnesses).
    c. Consumers of drugs for only a short period (those with brief acute illnesses).
    d. Pharmaceutical manufacturers.

3. First Entrant Advantage - (20 points)

    It is often argued that the first firm in an industry has a long-lasting advantage over later entrants.

    a. Why would this be?
    b. Is this (supposed) fact a cause for policy concern? Does it leat to inefficiency? Explain.

4. Product Differentiation - (15 points)

    Chamberlain and his legacy leads to the idea that there is too much differentiation in both monopolistically competitive and oligopolistic markets. Do you agree? Explain.

5. The Readings - (5 points)

    What is the most striking idea you have come across in your readings for the course? How has it affected the way you think?

6. Market Share Stability - (20 points)

    Suppose that the plaintiff in an antitrust case argued that the top eight oil firms collude because the market shares of the leading 8 firms were almost constant over the last 10 years. If you were the expert hired by the defendants, how would you argue against the proposition? Specifically:

Mr. Frech
Econ 216A
Fall 1979

6. (continued)

   a. What alternative arguments are there for market share stability?
   b. What other empirical implications are there of the existence of collusion by the largest 8 oil firms?

7. **The Reading List** - (5 points)

   What is your new title for the section of the reading list on new monopolistic competition and old location-based oligopoly models?

Duke University

Economics 206S

Regulation and Industrial Economics

Fall 1989   Professor Grabowski

This is a seminar course. There will be no lectures or exams. There will be weekly readings and class presentations with an emphasis on discussion and debate.

For each topic, two or three student presenters will be selected. They will research the topic in greater depth than the rest of the class, organize the material and prepare an outline or "road map" for handout. The rest of the class will read a few background articles on the topic so as to be generally familiar with the key questions and issues. They will also be required to hand in one page prior to class outlining key points on the discussion questions (based on the background readings).

Each student will have two class presentations on different topics. In addition, a short paper (10 to 15 pages) will be required. This can be an analysis of a public policy issue discussed in class. Grades in the class will be based on the two class presentations, the term paper, and overall class participation.

You will have an opportunity to purchase a course packet with the required readings in xerox form. Many of these readings will also be available in the library on reserve.

My office is 314 Social Sciences Building. My office hours are by appointment. My telephone number is 684-6484.

Background Reading Assignments (First two weeks)

Week 1

Readings:

    Henry Grabowski and John Vernon, Chapter 1 "Introduction" and Chapter 2 "Market Failure; The Normative Basis for Government in a Market Economy" xerox.

Discussion Questions:

1. What is the Pareto efficiency criterion? How does it relate to the benefit-cost principle? Why is the benefit-cost principle a useful benchmark for judging public policy actions?

2. What is meant by the term "natural monopoly?" What economic efficiency problems does it result in?

3. What is meant by the term "externality" or "spillover effects?" What economic efficiency problem does it give rise to? What are the options for government policy in the case of externality type market failure?

4. What is the basis for the contention that the private market tends to produce too little information--especially in the case of product characteristics like health and safety hazards? What are the government options for remedying these kinds of market failures?

5. Why are the concepts of "destructive competition" and "government paternalism" more suspect rationales for government regulatory intervention? Are these rationales consistent with the economists concept of Pareto efficiency?

Background Reading Assignments

Week 2

Readings:

1. Henry Grabowski and John Vernon, Chapter 3 "Sources of Non-Market Failure" xerox.

2. Alfred Kahn, "The Political Feasibility of Regulatory Reform: How Did We Do It" in L. Graymer and F. Thompson, Reforming Social Regulation, pp. 247-263.

3. Mark Levinson, "The Verdict on Deregulation," Dun's Business Month, Nov. 1986, pp. 30-34.

Discussion Questions:

1. What is Stigler's economic theory of regulation? What are its key assumptions?

2. What kind of benefits can regulation provide to an industry? What limitations or constraints arise in capturing these benefits?

3. Can Stigler's model explain the deregulation movement in various industries such as airlines, trucking and telecommunications? What factors outside his model might explain these reforms?

4. What kind of "non-market" failures tend to occur in the case of health and safety regulation?

5. What kind of regulatory reforms are useful to consider in the health and safety area?

Airlines

Readings:
1. Daniel Kaplan "The Changing Airline Industry" in Leonard Weiss and Michael Klass, Regulatory Reform What Really Happened. Little Brown (1986) Pp. 40-77.

2. "Airline Deregulation: Turbulent Skies Ahead" and "Airline Deregulation: Is Flying the Cheaper Skies Safe," The Margin, Dec. 1987 and Sept. 1988 issue.

3. S.A. Mornson and C. Winston "Air Safety, Deregulation and Public Policy" The Brookings Review Winter, 1988.

4. Congressional Budget Office, Policies for the deregulated Airline Industry, Ch. IV, p 57-70. Alfred Kahn, "Raise the Cost of Landing at Peak Hours", NY Times, Sept. 9, 1984.

Discussion Questions:

1. Was regulation of the airline industry prior to the mid 1970s a good example of Stigler's capture theroy?

2. Who are the main winners and losers from airline deregulation? Can one persuasively argue that the benefits of deregulation have exceeded the costs in airlines?

3. What is the best approach for solving the congestion problem that now exists at several major airports in the United States?

4. Should the major airlines be prohibited from further merger activity? Should constraints be placed on airlines owning computer reservation systems? on Frequent Flier Programs?

Health Care

Readings:
1. Alain Enthoven, "The Health Care Economy in the USA," in G.S. Smith, Health Economics: Prospects for the Future. pp. 57-70.

2. Burton Weisbrod, "America's Health Care Dilemma," Challenge, Sept./Oct., 1985, pp. 30-34.

3. Wall Street Journal, recent articles on health care costs.

4. Vicente Navarro, "A National Health Program is Necessary" Challenge, May/June 1989.

5. Louise B. Russell, Proposed a Comprehensive Health Care System for the Poor, Brookings Review, Summer, 1989.

Discussion Questions:

1. What are the major factors behind the rapid use in health care costs over the last few decades in the U.S.?

2. Are prospective payment schemes likely to be an effective means of controlling health care costs? What adverse effects are they likely to produce?

3. Should the government encourage the spread of health maintenance organizations?

4. Should Congress enact a program to provide long-term care for the elderly? a comprehensive health care system for the poor?

5. Should the U.S. adopt a national health program like that in Canada or other developed countries.

Telephones

Readings:

1. Roger Noll and Bruce Owen "The Anticompetitive Uses of Regulation: US vs. AT&T" in J.E. Kwoka and L.J. White, eds. The Antitrust Revolution, p 290-330.

2. Alfred Kahn, "The Road to More Intelligent Pricing" Yale Journal of Regulation, Vol I, No. I, 1983 pp. 31-42

3. Robert Crandall "Has the AT&T Break-up Raised Telephone Rates" Brookings Review, Winter 1987, p. 37-44, and "Surprises from Telephone Deregulation and the AT & T Divesture". American Economic Review, May 1988, P 323-27.

4. Roger Noll, "The Twisted Pair: Regulation and Competiton in Telecommunications", Regulation, p 15 - 22.

Discussion Questions:

1. What have been the main short run effects of the AT&T breakups? What are the likely long-term consequences?

2. Should cross-subsidization in telephone rates be eliminated? If not, how should these subsidies be structured in the face of the new competition in long distance services?

3. Should local calls be subject to usage sensitive fees as is currently the case for long distance calls?

4. Should all regulation of AT&T Long Lines Division in the intercity telecommunications market be ended?

5. Should the local operating companies be allowed to compete in other businesses including long distance services?

Readings:

1. Henry Grabowski and John Vernon, The Regulation of Pharmaceuticals: Balancing the Benefits and Risks, Washington, D.C.: American Enterprise Institute (1982), pp. 1-13.

2. William Wardell, "Rx: More Regulation or Better Therapies," Regulation, Sept./Oct. 1979, pp. 25-33.

3. Carolyn Asbury, Orphan Drugs Medical vs. Market Value, pp. 1-5, 38-42, 265.

4. Henry Grabowski "Impact of Patent and Regulatory Policies on Drug Innovation" paper presented to Shearson Lehman Hutton Conference, New York, Oct. 13, 1988

5. Wall Street Journal, editorial and article excerpts.

Discussion Questions:

1. Is it desirable for the FDA to err on the side of caution in approving new drugs? What are the adverse consequences of doing so?

2. Is the Orphan Drug Act sound public policy? Is it likely to be effective in stimulating the development of new drugs for rare diseases?

3. Should drug prices be restrained by government policy? How can one explain the fact that "brand name" prices frequently increase after patent expiration?

4. Should patent policies for pharmaceuticals be modified in light of current regulatory and economic trends in the industry?

Cigarettes and the Tobacco Industry

Readings:

1. John Calfee, "The Ghost of Cigarette Advertising Past," Regulation, Nov. - Dec. 1986 and Kenneth Warner, Testimony on Proposed Cigarette Advertising Ban Before House Committee, 1986.

2. Willard Manning et al. "The Taxes of Sin: Do Smokers and Drinkers Pay their Way" Journal American Medical Association March 17, 1989, Vol. 261, no. 11, p 1604 - 9.

3. Jasper Womach, "Summary: Tobacco Programs of U.S. Dept. of Agriculture" and "The Tobacco Price Support Program: Policy Issues", Congressional Research Service, July 12, 1985.

Discussion Questions:

1. Should all tobacco advertising be prohibited?

2. Should excise taxes be increased on tobacco?

3. Should cigarette smoking be totally banned in airplanes and other public places?

4. Should the tobacco price support program be modified or ended?

Product Liability

Readings

1. Robert Litan and Clifford Winston, *Liability: Perspectives and Policy*, Bookings Institution, 1988, Ch. 1 and Ch. 8.

2. Edmund Kitch "Vaccines and Product Liability" *Regulation* May/June 1985 pp 11-18.

3. William 'Bennett "Pluses of Malpractice Suits" *New York Times Magazine*, July 24, 1988.

4. "Tobacco Goes Back on Trial" *NY Times* Aug. 16, 1987 "Business Lobby Softens Push for Liability Limits in a Tacital Change Aimed at Wooing Congress *Wall Street Journal* August. 22, 1989.

Discussions Questions:

1. Should there be a national system of tort law? If so, what should be its main characteristics?

2. Should vaccine manufactures be strictly liable for all injuries resulting from their usage? What adverse consequences would this produce?

3. Should health warnings on cigarettee packages permit firms to be excused from legal liability for deaths and illnesses from smoking?

4. Should the liability system for medical malpractice be altered?

Banking

Readings:

1. William Haraf, "Bank and Thrift Regulation" *Regulation*, 1988, no. 3 p 50-56.

2. E. Dan Brumbaugh and Robert Litan "The S&L Crisis: How to Get out and Stay out" *Brookings Review* Spring, 1989

3. Financial Restructuring: Articles by Robert Guttman, James Tobin and Robert Litan in *Challenge*, Nov./Dec. 1987.

4. Thomas Cargill "Glass Steagall Is Still Needed" *Challenge*, Nov./Dec. 1988.

Discussion Questions:

1. Should the FDIC system of deposit insurance be modified?

2. Should banks be allowed to compete freely in other businesses?

3. Should there be a separate thrift industry? If so how should it be regulated?

4. Should geographical restrictions on banks be ended?

SEC and Financial Regulation

Readings:

1. Douglas Ginsburg and John Robinson, "The Case Against Federal Intervention in the Market for Corporate Control" and F. M. Scherer, "Takeovers Present and Future Dangers", The Brookings Review, Winter Spring 1986, pp. 9-21.

2. "Senate Showdown Expected Over Shareholder Rights," Congressional Quarterly, June 4, 1988, pp. 1506-1509.

3. "Corporate Takeovers; Who Wins: Who Loses: Who Should Regulate?" Regulation 1988, number 1.

4. "After the Crash: Linkages Between Stocks and Futures" Regulation 1988, number 2.

Discussion Questions:

1. Do current SEC rules favor either party in a hostile takeover attempt? Should they be modified?

2. Should information disclosure rules be changed? Can insider trading rules be made more effective?

3. Should programming trading and other practices be restricted?

4. Should SEC enforcement powers and budgets be increased?

Automobiles

Emissions Standards, Safety, and Fuel Economy

Readings:

1. Robert Crandall et al. Regulating the Automobile, Ch. 1 Overview, pp. 1-8; Ch. 8 conclusions, pp. 155-161.

2. Lawrence J. White, The Regulation of Air Pollutant Emissions from Motor Vehicles pp. 3-10 and pp. 78-110.

3. John Graham, "Secretary Dole and the Future of Automobile Airbags," The Brookings Review, Summer 1985, pp. 10-15.

4. Robert Crandall "Why Should We Regulate Fuel Economy at All" Brookings Review, Spring 1985, p 3-7.

Discussion Questions:

1. What are the main policy alternatives to mandatory belt usage or regulations on passive restraints systems?

2. Should the fuel economy standards be phased out?

3. What are unintended side effects of instituting standards with very amibtious decreases in auto emission levels over a short time span?

4. Should the auto emissions standards be changed.

Duke University

Economics 389

Industrial Organization II

Henry Grabowski   Spring 1989

For Journals the following abbreviations are used:

AER	American Economic Review
BJE	Bell Journal of Economics
JEL	Journal of Economic Literature
JIE	Journal of Industrial Organization
JLE	Journal of Law and Economics
JPE	Journal of Political Economy
QJE	Quarterly Journal of Economics
RJE	Rand Journal of Economics
RE Stat	Review of Economics and Statistics
IJIO	International Journal of Industrial Organization

Readings marked with an (*) are highly recommended. We will not attempt to cover all the items under each topic. Several items are included to provide a bibliography for further study.

Students will be asked to discuss at least one article in class. The schedule of potential articles to be discussed is given at the end of the reading list.

There will be a final at the end of the semester. Each student will also be required to turn in a short paper (note length) by the end of the semester critiquing or extending an article covered in the course or one within the general field of industrial organization.

I. Technological Change and Industrial Innovation

1. R and D Inventive Activity - Basic Characteristics

   *F.M. Scherer Industrial Market Structure and Economic Performance, 2nd edition, Rand-McNally, 1980, ch. 15.

   *Jean Tirole, The Theory of Industrial Organization, MIT Press, 1988, 389-94.

   *Kenneth Arrow, "Economic Welfare and the Allocation of Resources for Invention" in NBER volume Rate and Direction of Inventive Activity.

   *William Wardell, "The History of Drug Discovery, Development and Regulation" in Robert Chien, Issues in Pharmaceutical Economics, D.C. Health and Co., 1979, 3-12.

   Morton Kamien and Nancy Schwartz, Market Structure and Innovation, Cambridge University Press, 1982.

   Richard Nelson and Sidney Winter, An Evolutionary Theory of Economic Change, Harvard University Press, 1982.

   F.M. Scherer, Innovation and Growth, MIT Press, 1984.

2. Optimal Patent Policy

   *William Nordhaus, Invention Growth and Welfare, MIT Press, 1969, Ch. 5, pp 70-90.

   *F.M. Scherer, "Nordhaus' Theory of Optimal Patent Life," AER (June 1972) and Reply by Nordhaus, 422-31.

   *F.M. Scherer, Industrial Market Structure and Economic Performance, Ch. 16.

   *Henry Grabowski and John Vernon, "Longer Patents for Lower Imitation Barriers: the 1984 Drug Act, AER, 76 (May 1986), 195-8.

   Pankaj Tandon, "Optimal Patents with Compulsory Licensing, JPE (June 1982) 470-86.

   Larry De Brock, "Market Structure, Innovation and Optimal Patent Life," JLE (April 1985) 223-244.

   Zvi Grilliches, ed. R & D Patents and Productivity, NBER, 1985.

3. R and D Rivalry and Patent Races

   *Jean Tirole, The Theory of Industrial Organization, Ch. 10, 394-401.

   *Partha Dasgupta and Joseph Stiglitz, "Uncertainty Industrial Structure and the Speed of R & D" BJE (Spring 1980), 1-20.

*R.K. Sah and Joseph Stiglitz, "The Invariance of Market Innovation to the Number of Firms" RJE (Spring 1987) vol 18; no 1.

J. Vickers, "The Evolution of Market Structure When There is a Sequence of Innovations," JIE, 35, September 1986, 1-12.

*Jennifer Reinganum, "Practical Implications of Game Theoretic Models of R & D," AER (May 1984) 61-67.

4. Spillovers and Appropriability

*A. Michael Spence, "Cost Reduction, Competition and Industry Performance," Econometrica (Jan. 1984) 101-21.

Adam Jaffe, "Technological Opportunity and Spillovers of R & D: Evidence from Firms' Patents, Profits and Market Value," AER (Dec. 1986) 984-1001.

*Richard Levin, "Appropriability, R & D Spending and Technological Performance, AER (May 1988), 424-428.

Richard Levin and Peter Reiss, "Cost Reducing and Demand Increasing R & D," Stanford University, Nov. 1986.

Edwin Mansfield, "How Rapidly Does New Industrial Technology Leak Out," JIE, 91 (Dec. 1985), 217-24.

*R. Mark Issac and Stanley Reynolds, "Appropriability and Market Structure In a Stochastic Invention Model," forthcoming in QJE, 1989; (also "Schumpeterian Competition in Experimental Markets," University of Arizona, 1988).

*Richard Levin, Wesley Cohen and David Mowery, "R & D Appropriability, Opportunity and Market Structure: New Evidence on the Schumpeterian Hypothesis" AER (May 1985) 20-24.

5. Private and Social Returns to R & D

*Edwin Mansfield, et al, "Social and Private Rates of Return from Industrial Innovation," QJE, (May 1977) pp 221-240.

*Henry Grabowski and Dennis Mueller, "Industrial R & D and Profit Rates," BJE (Autumn 1978) pp 328-42.

*Ariel Pakes and Mark Schankerman, "The Rate of Obsolescence of Patents, Research Gestation Lags and the Private Rate of Return to Research Resources" in Grilliches, ed. R & D, Patents and Productivity, 1984.

Henry Grabowski and John Vernon, "A New Look at the Returns and Risks to Pharmaceutical R & D," Duke University, 1988.

Manuel Trajtenberg, "The Welfare Analysis of Product Innovations with an Application to CT Scanners," NBER Working Paper no. 1724, Oct. 1985.

6. **Public Policy Issues - International Competitiveness Joint Ventures, Government Support of Research**

   *Edwin Mansfield, "Industrial R & D in Japan and U.S.: A Comparative Study," <u>AER</u> (May 1988) 223-228.

   *Zvi Grilliches, "Productivity R & D and Basic Research at the Firm Level in the 1970s," <u>AER</u> (March 1986).

   Henry Grabowski, "Innovation and International Competitiveness in Pharmaceuticals" forthcoming 1989.

   *Edwin Mansfield, "R & D and Innovation: Some Empirical Findings" in Zvi Grilliches, <u>R & D Patents and Productivity</u>, 127-154.

   J.A. Ordover and R.D. Willig, "Antitrust for High-Technology Industries: Assessing Research Joint Ventures and Mergers," <u>Journal of Law and Economics</u>, 28 (May 1985), 311-334.

   F.R. Lichtenberg, "The Effect of Government Funding on Private Research and Development: A Re-assessment," <u>Journal of Industrial Economics</u>, 36 (September 1987) 97-104.

II. Government Regulation of Industry

1. **Political Economy of Regulation and Deregulation**

   *Charles Wolf, <u>Markets or Governments</u>, Cambridge: MIT Press, 1988.

   *George Stigler, "The Economic Theory of Economic Regulation," <u>BJE</u>, 2 (Spring 1971) 3-21.

   Sam Peltzman, "Toward a More General Theory of Regulation," <u>JLE</u>, 19 (August 1976) 211-240.

   Gay Becker, "A Theory of Competition Among Pressure Groups for Political Influence," <u>QJE</u> 98 (August 1983) 371-400.

   *T. Romer and H. Rosenthal, "Modern Political Economy and the Study of Regulation," in E.E. Bailey, ed., <u>Public Regulation: Perspectives on Institutions and Policies</u>, Cambridge: MIT Press, 1987.

   Roger Noll, "Economic Perspectives on the Politics of Regulation," in R. Schmalensee and R.D. Willig, <u>Handbook of Industrial Organization</u>, Amsterdam: North-Holland, forthcoming.

   Joe Kalt and Mark Zupan, "Capture and Ideology in the Economic Theory of Politics," <u>AER</u> 74 (June 1984) 279-300.

   *Barry Weingast and M.J. Moran, "Bureaucratic Discretion or Congressional Control? Regulatory Policymaking by the Federal Trade Commission, <u>JPE</u> 91 (October 1983) 765-800.

2. Measuring the Impact of Regulation & Deregulation

   *G.W. Schwert, "Using Financial Data to Measure the Effects of Regulation," JLE 24 (April 1981) 121-158.

   J.J. Binder, "Measuring the Effects of Regulation with Stock Price Data," RJE 16 (Summer 1985) 167-183.

   *G. Jarrell and S. Peltzman, "The Impact of Product Recalls on the Wealth of Sellers, JPE 93 (June 1985) 512-536.

   R.T. Smith, M. Bradley and G. Jarrell, "Studying Firm Specific Effects of Regulation with Stock Market Data: An Application to Oil Price Regulation" RJE 17 (Winter 1986) 467-489.

3. Deregulation of Multi-Firm Industries - Airlines

   *Daniel Kaplan, "The Changing Airline Industry" in Leonard Weiss and Michael Klass, ed. Regulatory Reform What Actually Happened, pp 40-77.

   *Alfred Kahn, "Surprises of Airline Deregulation," AER 78 (May 1988) 316-322.

   *Steven Morrison and Clifford Winston, The Economic Effects of Airline Deregulation, Washington, D.C., Brookings Institution, 1986.

   *Gregory Call and Ted Keeler, "Airline Deregulation, Fares and Market Behavior: some Empirical Evidence" in Andrew Daugety Analytical Studies In Transport Economics, Cambridge University Press, 1986.

   *Steven Morrison and Andrew Winston, "Empirical Implications and Tests of the Contestability Hypothesis," vol 33, April 1987, pp 53-66.

   Michael Levine, "Airline Competition in Deregulated Markets: Theory Firm Strategy and Public Policy," Yale Journal of Regulation, vol 4, no 2, Spring 1987, pp 393-494.

   Elizabeth Baily, David Graham and Daniel Kaplan, Deregulating the Airlines, the MIT Press, 1985.

   S. Borenstein, "Hubs and High Fares: Increasing Market Power and Efficiency in the Deregulated U.S. Airline Industry, Michigan, Nov. 1987.

4. Information, Product Differentiation and Advertising

   *F.M. Scherer, Industrial Market Structure and Economic Performance, Ch. 15, 407-438.

   William Comanor and Tom Wilson, "Advertising and Competition: A Survey," Journal of Economic Literature (June 1979), 453-456.

Lynn Schmeider, Benjamin Klein and Kevin Murphy, "Government Regulation of Cigarette Health Information," JLE (Dec. 1981) 575-610.

*Lee Benham, "The Effects of Advertising on the Price of Eyeglasses," JLE (Oct. 1972) 357-72.

*Richard Schmalensee, "Entry Deterrence in the Ready to Eat Breakfast Cereal Industry," BJE (Autumn 1978) 303-327.

F.M. Scherer, "The Welfare Economics of Product Variety: An Application to the Ready to Eat Cereals Industry," JIE (Dec. 1979) 113-134.

5. **Regulation of Product Safety Standards - Automobiles**

   *Richard Arnould and Henry Grabowski, "Automobile Safety Regulation: A Review of the Evidence," Review in Law and Economics, vol 5, 233-267.

   *Robert Crandall, Howard Grunspecht, Theodore Keeler and Lester Lave, Regulating the Automobile, chapters 1 & 4, pp 1-8; 45-84.

   *Sam Peltzman, "The Effects of Automobile Safety," JPE (August 1975) 677-725.

   Clifford Winston and Fred Mannering, "Consumer Demand For Automobile Safety," AER (May 1984) 316-319.

6. **New Product Screening - Pharmaceuticals**

   *Henry Grabowski and John Vernon, The Regulation of Pharmaceuticals: Balancing the Benefits and Risks, American Enterprise Institute, 1983, 1-48.

   Martin Baily, "Research and Development Costs and Returns: The U.S. Pharmaceutical Industry," JPE (Jan/Feb, 1972).

   Henry Grabowski, John Vernon and Lacy Thomas, "Estimating the Effects of Regulation on Innovation: An International Comparative Analysis of the Pharmaceutical Industry," JLE April 1978.

   Steven Wiggins, "The Impact of Regulation on Pharmaceutical Research Expenditures: A Dynamic Approach," Economic Inquiry, Jan. 1983.

   *Elizabeth Jensen, "Research Expenditures and the Discovery of New Drugs," JIE (Sept. 1987), 83-95.

   Lacy Thomas, "Regulation and Firm Size: FDA Impacts on Innovation," Columbia University Working Paper, September 1987.

   *Sam Peltzman, "The Health Effects of Mandatory Prescriptions," JLE (Oct. 1987), 207-238.

Economics 389

Spring 1989

Articles For Class Discussion

Week of

Jan. 22   Scherer "Nordhaus' Theory of Optimal Patent Life" and "Reply" by Nordhaus

Jan. 29   Sah and Stiglitz "The Invariance of Market Innovation to the Number of Firms"

Feb. 5   Issac and Reynolds "Appropriability and Market Structure In a Stochastic Invention Model"

Feb. 12   Mansfield et. al. "Social and Private Rates of Return from Industrial Innovation"

Feb. 19   Grilliches "Productivity, R & D and Basic Research at the Firm Level in the 1970s"

Feb. 26   Weingast and Moran "Bureaucratic Discretion or Congressional Control? Regulatory Policymaking by the Federal Trade Commission"

March 5   Jarrell and Peltzman "The Impact of Product Recalls on the Wealth of Sellers"

March 19 Call and Keeller "Airline Deregulation, Fares and Market Behavior" and Morrison and Winston "Empirical Implications and Tests of the Contestability Hypothesis"

March 26 Benham "The Effects of Advertising on the Price of Eyeglasses"

Massachusetts Institute of Technology

U

14.23   <u>Government Regulation of Industry</u>   Spring 1989

Professor Paul L. Joskow
E52-280B
253-6664

The readings for this course come from several different sources. Copies of all of the readings will be on reserve in Dewey Library, but I think that you will find it convenient to purchase the following:

1. L.W. Weiss and M.W. Klass, editors, <u>Regulatory Reform: What Really Happened?</u> Little, Brown and Company, 1986 (at the Coop).

2. **Class Notes for 14.23.** A set of these notes can be purchased at the graphic arts department in the basement of E52. It includes copies of most of the readings listed below.

There will be **two exams**--a mid-term and a final-- and (by popular demand) three of four problem sets (of sorts) that will determine your grade in the course. Both exams will be given in class.

I. Introduction

P. Joskow and R. Noll, "Regulation in Theory and Practice: An Overview," <u>Studies in Public Regulation</u>, A. Fromm, editor, MIT Press, 1981.

Weiss and Klass, Chapter 1.

P. Joskow and N. Rose, "The Effects of Economic Regulation," in <u>Handbook of Industrial Organization</u> (In Press).

R.A. Posner, "Theories of Economic Regulation," <u>Bell Journal of Economics</u>, Autumn 1974, pp. 335-58.

J.Q. Wilson, "The Politics of Regulation," in J.Q. Wilson, editor, <u>The Politics of Regulation</u>, Basic Books, 1980.

R. Noll, "Regulation After Reagan," <u>Regulation</u>, 1988(3), pp. 13-20.

II. Natural Monopoly and Its Regulation

R. Schmalensee, The Control of Natural Monopolies, D.C. Heath, 1979, Chapters 1 and 2.

S. Brown & O. Sibley, The Theory of Public Utility Pricing, Cambridge University Press, 1986, Chapter 3.

W. Baumol and D. Bradford, "Optimal Departures from Marginal Cost Pricing," American Economic Review June 1970, pp. 265-82.

W. Baumol and A. Klevorick, "Input Choices and Rate of Return Regulation: An Overview of the Discussion," Bell Journal of Economics, Autumn 1970, pp. 162-190.

P. Joskow, "Inflation and Environmental Concern: Structural Change In the Process of Public Utility Price Regulation," Journal of Law and Economics, October 1974, pp. 291-327.

G. Stigler and C. Friedland, "What Can Regulators Regulate?" Journal of Law and Economics, October 1962, pp. 1-16.

P. Joskow and R. Schmalensee, "Incentive Regulation in the Electric Utility Industry," Yale Journal of Regulation, December 1986, pp. 1-49.

V.L. Smith, "Currents of Competition in Electricity Markets," Regulation No. 2, 1987, pp. 23-29.

III. Regulation and Deregulation in Telecommunications

D. Evans, Ed., Breaking Up Bell, North-Holland, 983, Chapters 1 and 2.

Weiss and Klass, Chapter 7.

G. Faulhaber, "Cross-Subsidization: Pricing in Public Enterprises," American Economic Review, December 1975, pp. 966-77.

A.E. Kahn and W.B. Shew, "Current Issues in Telecommunications Regulation: Pricing," Yale Journal on Regulation, Spring 1987, pp. 191-256.

R. Noll and B. Owen, "United States vs. AT&T: An Interim Assessment," (mimeo) June 1987.

U.S. Federal Communications Commission, "Notice of Proposed Rulemaking: In the Matter of Policy and Rules Concerning Rates for Dominant Carriers," August 1987.

R. Crandall, "Telecommunications Policy in the Reagan Era," Regulation, 1988(3), pp. 28-32.

IV. Municipal Franchise Regulation and Cable TV

H. Demsetz, "Why Regulate Utilities?", *Journal of Law and Economics*, April 1980, pp. 55-65.

O. Williamson, "Franchise Bidding for Natural Monopoly--In General and with Respect to Cable TV," *Bell Journal of Economics*, Spring 1976, pp. 73-104.

Weiss and Klass, Chapter 3.

W. Shew, "Costs of Cable Television Franchise Requirements," 1984 (mimeo).

E. Lindenberg and S. Ross, "Tobin's q Ratio and Industrial Organization," *Journal of Business*, January 1981, pp. 1-32

NTIA, *Video Program Distribution: Current Policy Issues and Recommendations*, June 1988; Introduction and Chapters 1-3.

V. Regulation and Deregulation in the Airline Industry

S. Breyer, *Regulation and its Reform*, Harvard University Press, 1982, Chapter 11.

Douglas and Miller, "Efficiency in the Price Constrained Airline Market," *American Economic Review*, September 1974.

Weiss and Klass, Chapter 2.

E. Bailey, D.R. Graham, and D.P. Kaplan, *Deregulating the Airlines*, Cambridge, MIT Press, 1985, ch. 9 (rest of book is recommended).

S. Borenstein, "Hubs and High Fares: Increasing Market Power and Efficiency in the Deregulated U.S. Airline Industry, (mimeo) March 1988.

S. Borenstein and M. Zimmerman "Market Incentives for Safe Commercial Airline Operation," *American Economic Review*, December 1988.

VI. Regulation and Deregulation in Surface Freight Transportation

S. Breyer, *Regulation and Its Reform*, Harvard University Press, 1982, Chapter 12.

Weiss and Klass, Chapter 1.

N. Rose, "An Economic Assessment of Surface Freight Transportation Deregulation," (mimeo) 1987.

N. Rose, "The Incidence of Regulatory Rents in the Motor Carrier Industry," *Rand Journal of Economics*, Autumn 1985, pp. 299-318.

C. Barnekov, "Railroad Deregulation: The Track Record," *Regulation*, No. 1., 1987, pp 19-27.

R. Willig and W. Baumol, "Railroad Deregulation! Using Competition as a Guide," *Regulation*, No. 1., 1987, pp. 28-35.

T. Moore, "Transportation Policy," *Regulation*, 1988(3), pp. 57-62.

VII. Federal Bank Regulatory Policies

W.S. Haraf, "Bank and Thrift Regulation," *Regulation*, 1988(3), pp. 50-56.

J. Kareken, "Federal Bank Regulatory Policy: A Description and Some Observations," *Journal of Business*, 1986, pp. 3-48.

D. Diamond and P. Dybvig, "Banking Theory, Deposit Insurance, and Bank Regulation," *Journal of Business*, 1986 (1), pp. 55-68.

R. Litan, "Evaluating and Controlling the Risks of Financial Product Deregulation," *Yale Journal On Regulation*, 1985, pp. 1-52.

VIII. The Liability Insurance Crisis: Regulatory And Antitrust Responses

R. Litan and C. Winston, *Liability: Perspectives and Policy*, Brookings, 1988, pp. 1-41

S. Harrington, "The Impact of Rate Regulation on Prices and Underwriting Results in the Property-Liability Insurance Industry: A Survey," *Journal of Risk and Insurance*, 1984, pp. 577-623.

R. Clark, et. al., "Sources of the Crisis," in *Yale Journal On Regulation*, Summer 1988, pp. 367-396.

N. Lacey, "The Competitiveness of the Property-Casualty Insurance Industry," in *Yale Journal on Regulation*, Summer 1988, pp. 501-516

MIT Department of Economics	Paul L. Joskow
Spring 1990	Andrea Shepard

INDUSTRIAL ORGANIZATION II: 14.272

This course is a continuation of 14.271. Four books will be used in several sections of the course:

R. Posner and F. Easterbrook, <u>Antitrust: Cases, Economic Notes, and Other Materials</u>, 2nd Ed., St. Paul: West Publishing, 1981. (Hereafter <u>P&E</u>)

L. Weiss and M. Klass, <u>Regulatory Reform: What Actually Happened</u>, Boston: Little-Brown, 1986. (Hereafter <u>W&K</u>)

J. Tirole, <u>The Theory of Industrial Organization</u>, Cambridge: MIT Press, 1988. (Hereafter <u>Tirole</u>)

S. Brown and D. Sibley, <u>The Theory of Public Utility Pricing</u>, Cambridge: Cambridge University Press, 1986. (Hereafter <u>Brown and Sibley</u>)

(W&K and Brown and Sibley will be available in the Coop, but you are not required to purchase them; P&E and Tirole should have been purchased for 14.271.) The following texts also provide useful background information:

A. Kahn, <u>The Economics of Regulation</u>, 2 volumes, New York: John Wiley, 1970, 1971 (republished by MIT Press, 1988).

S. Breyer, <u>Regulation and its Reform</u>, Cambridge: Harvard University Press, 1982.

In the list that follows, starred items are especially recommended, and copies of them will be on reserve. We will not attempt to cover all of the subtopics listed under each major section of the list. The list's length reflects an attempt to provide a useful bibliography for further study and research.

Grading in this course will be based on in-class midsemester and final examinations. Several problem sets (which will not affect the grade directly) will be distributed during the term.

1. MERGERS AND MARKET POWER

A. Market Definition and Market Power

*P&E, ch. III.

W.M. Landes and R.A. Posner, "Market Power in Antitrust Cases," *Harvard Law Review*, 94 (March 1981), 937-996.

R. Schmalensee, "Another Look at Market Power," *Harvard Law Review*, 95 (June 1982), 1789-1816.

G.J. Stigler and R.A. Sherwin, "The Extent of the Market," *Journal of Law and Economics*, 28 (October 1985), 555-586.

*P.T. Spiller and C.J. Huang, "On the Extent of the Market: Wholesale Gasoline in the Northeastern United States," *Journal of Industrial Economics*, 35 (December 1986), 131-146.

D.T. Scheffman and P.T. Spiller, "Geographic Market Definition under the DOJ Guidelines," *Journal of Law and Economics*, 30 (April 1987), 123-147.

M.E. Slade, "Exogeneity Tests of Market Boundaries Applied to Petroleum Products," *Journal of Industrial Economics*, 34 (March 1986), 291-304.

*V.Y. Suslow, "Estimating Monopoly Behavior with Competitive Recycling: An Application to Alcoa," *Rand Journal of Economics*, 17 (Autumn 1986), 389-403.

B. Horizontal Mergers

*P&E, ch. IV.

*U.S. Department of Justice, *Merger Guidelines*, revised June 1984.

*S.C. Salop, L.J. White, F.M. Fisher, and R. Schmalensee, "Symposium: Horizontal Mergers and Antitrust," *Journal of Economic Perspectives*, 1 (Fall 1987), 3-54.

*H.R. Varian et al., "Symposium on Takeovers," *Journal of Economic Perspectives*, 2 (Winter 1988), 3-68.

B.E. Eckbo, "Mergers and the Market Concentration Doctrine: Evidence from the Capital Market," *Journal of Business*, 58 (July, 1985), 325-349.

*S. Bhagat, A. Shleifer, R.W. Vishny, "The Aftermath of Hostile Takeovers," mimeo, 1989.

R. McAffee and M. Williams, "Can Event Studies Detect Anticompetitive Mergers," *Economic Letters*, 1988, 199-203.

F. Lichtenberg and D. Siegel, "The Effect of Takeovers on the Employment and Wages of Central-Office and other Personnel," mimeo, June 1989.

2. VERTICAL RELATIONS AND VERTICAL RESTRAINTS

*Tirole, ch. 4.

*P&E, ch. II.C.2.

*P. Rey and J. Tirole, "The Logic of Vertical Restraints," _American Economic Review_, 76 (December 1986), 921-939.

*S.I. Ornstein and D.M. Hanssens, "Resale Price Maintenance: Output Increasing or Restricting? The Case of Distilled Spirits in the United States," _Journal of Industrial Economics_, 36 (September 1987), 1-18.

*G.F. Mathewson and R.A. Winter, "An Economic Theory of Vertical Restraints," _Rand Journal of Economics_, (1984), 27-38.

*J.A. Ordover, G. Saloner, and S.C. Salop, "Equilibrium Vertical Foreclosure," mimeo, (1989).

U.S. Department of Justice, _Vertical Restraints Guidelines_, January 1985.

T.G. Krattenmaker and S.C. Salop, "Anticompetitive Exclusion: Raising Rivals' Cost to Achieve Power Over Price," _Yale Law Journal_, 96 (November 1986), 209-295.

R.F. Springer and H.E. Frech, III, "Deterring Fraud: The Role of Resale Price Maintenance," _Journal of Business_, 59 (July 1986), 433-450.

O. Hart and J. Tirole, "Vertical Integration and Market Foreclosure," mimeo, 1989.

3. ADMINISTRATIVE REGULATION: INTRODUCTION AND OVERVIEW

*P.L. Joskow and R. Noll, "Regulation in Theory and Practice: An Overview," in G. Fromm, ed., _Studies in Public Regulation_, Cambridge: MIT Press, 1981.

*P.L. Joskow and N.L. Rose, "Economic Regulation and its Effects," in R. Schmalensee and R.D. Willig, eds., _Handbook of Industrial Organization_, Amsterdam: North-Holland, forthcoming.

*A.E. Kahn, Vol. I, ch. 1.

4. OPTIMAL PRICING POLICIES FOR NATURAL MONOPOLIES (FULL INFORMATION)

*R. Schmalensee, The Control of Natural Monopolies, Lexington: D.C. Heath, 1979, chs. 1 and 2.

Kahn, Vol. I, chs. 3-7.

S.J. Brown and D.S. Sibley, The Theory of Public Utility Pricing, Cambridge: Cambridge University Press, 1986.

A. Peak Load Pricing

*Brown and Sibley, Chapter 3, pages 26-34.

*Kahn, Vol. I, ch. 2.

P.L. Joskow, "Contributions to the Theory of Marginal Cost Pricing," Bell Journal of Economics, 7 (Spring 1976), 197-206.

B.M. Mitchell, W. Manning, and J.P. Acton, Peak Load Pricing: European Lessons for U.S. Energy Policy, Cambridge: Ballinger, 1978.
M.A. Crew and P.R. Kleindorfer, The Economics of Public Utility Regulation, Cambridge: MIT Press, 1986, chs. 3 and 4.

R. Park and B. Mitchell, Optimal Peak Load Pricing For Local Telephone Calls, Rand Corporation (R-3404-1-RC), March 1987

B. Optimal Pricing with Scale and Scope Economies

*W.J. Baumol, J.C. Panzar, and R.D. Willig, Contestable Markets and the Theory of Industry Structure, San Diego: Harcourt, Brace, Jovanovich, 1982, ch. 8. [Chs. 3, 4, and 7 recommended for review.]

*R. Braeutigam, "Optimal Policies for Natural Monopolies," forthcoming in R. Schmalensee and R.D. Willig, eds., Handbook of Industrial Organization.

*Brown and Sibley, ch. 3, pp. 34 - 60; chs. 4, 5, and 7.

W.W. Sharkey, The Theory of Natural Monopoly, Cambridge: Cambridge University Press, 1982.

W.J. Baumol and D.F. Bradford, "Optimal Departures from Marginal Cost Pricing," American Economic Review, 60 (June 1970), 265-282.

A.B. Atkinson and J.E. Stiglitz, Lectures on Public Economics, New York: McGraw-Hill, 1980, lectures 12 and 15.

R.R. Braeutigam, "Socially Optimal Pricing with Rivalry and Economies of Scale," Rand Journal of Economics, 15 (Spring 1984), 127-134.

G.R. Faulhaber, "Cross-Subsidization: Pricing in Public Enterprises," American Economic Review, 65 (December 1975), 966-977.

G. Knieps and I. Vogelsang, "The Sustainability Concept Under Alternative Behavioral Assumptions," Bell Journal of Economics, 13 (Spring 1982), 234-241.

R.D. Willig, "Pareto-Superior Nonlinear Outlay Schedules," Bell Journal of Economics, 9 (Spring 1978), 56-69.

5. OPTIMAL REGULATORY INSTITUTIONS AND MECHANISMS (ASYMMETRIC INFORMATION)

*D. Baron, "Design of Regulatory Institutions and Mechanisms," in R. Schmalensee and R.D. Willig, eds., Handbook of Industrial Organization, Amsterdam: North-Holland.

*J.J. Laffont and J. Tirole, "Using Cost Observations to Regulate Firms," Journal of Political Economy, 94 (June 1986), 614-641.

*A. Shleifer, "A Theory of Yardstick Competition," Rand Journal of Economics, 16 (Autumn 1985), 319-327.

*P.L. Joskow and R. Schmalensee, "Incentive Regulation for Electric Utilities," Yale Journal on Regulation, 4 (December 1986), 1-49.

*J.J. Laffont and J. Tirole, "A Theory of Incentives in Procurement and Regulation," mimeo, 1989.

B. Caillaud, R. Guesnerie, P. Rey, and J. Tirole, "Government Intervention in Production and Incentives Theory: A Review of Recent Contributions," Rand Journal of Economics, 19 (Spring 1988).

H. Demsetz, "Why Regulate Utilities?" Journal of Law and Economics, 11 (April 1968), 55-65.

O.E. Williamson, "Franchise Bidding for Natural Monopoly -- In General and With Respect to CATV," Bell Journal of Economics, 7 (Spring 1976), 73-104.

M.H. Riordan and D.E.M. Sappington, "Awarding Monopoly Franchises," American Economic Review, 77 (June 1987), 375-387.

T.R. Lewis and D.E.M. Sappington, "Regulating a Monopolist with Unknown Demand and Cost Functions," Rand Journal of Economics, 19 (Autumn 1988), 438-457.

J.P. Acton and I. Vogelsang, et al. "Symposium on Price-Cap Regulation," Rand Journal of Economics, 20 (Autumn 1989), 369-472.

J.J. Laffont and J. Tirole, "Provision of Quality and Power of Incentive Schemes in Regulated Industries," MIT Working Paper No. 528, August 1989.

X. Freixas, R. Guesnerie, and J. Tirole, "Planning Under Incomplete Information and the Ratchet Effect," <u>Review of Economic Studies</u>, 52 (April 1985), 173-192.

J.J. Laffont and J. Tirole, "Repeated Auctions of Incentive Contracts, Investment, and Bidding Parity with an Application to Takeovers," <u>Rand Journal of Economics</u>, 19 (Winter 1988), 516-537.

6. PUBLIC UTILITY REGULATION OF LEGAL MONOPOLIES IN PRACTICE

*Kahn, Vol. II, ch. 2

S. Myers, "The Application of Finance Theory to Public Utility Rate Regulation," <u>Bell Journal of Economics and Management Science</u>, 3 (Spring 1972), 58-97.

B.C. Greenwald, "Rate Base Selection and the Structure of Regulation," <u>Rand Journal of Economics</u>, 15 (Spring 1984), 85-95.

*G. Stigler and C. Friedland, "What Can Regulators Regulate ?" <u>Journal of Law and Economics</u>, 5 (October 1962), 1-16.

A. The A-J Debate and the Electric Power Industry

*W.J. Baumol and A.K. Klevorick, "Input Choices and Rate-of-Return Regulation: An Overview of the Discussion," <u>Bell Journal of Economics and Management Science</u>, 1 (Autumn 1970), 162-190.

E.E. Bailey, <u>Economic Theory of Regulatory Constraint</u>, Lexington: D.C. Heath, 1973.

*P.L. Joskow, "Inflation and Environmental Concern: Structural Change in the Process of Public Utility Price Regulation," <u>Journal of Law and Economics</u>, 17 October 1974), 291-327.

*W. Hendricks, "The Effects of Regulation on Collective Bargaining in Electric Utilities," <u>Bell Journal of Economics</u>, 6 (Autumn 1975), 451-465.

H.C. Petersen, "An Empirical Test of Regulatory Effects," <u>Bell Journal of Economics</u>, 6 (Spring 1975), 111-126.

R.M. Isaac, "Fuel Adjustment Mechanisms and the Regulated Utility Facing Uncertain Fuel Prices," <u>Bell Journal of Economics</u>, 13 (Spring 1982), 158-169.

P.L. Joskow, "Regulatory Failure, Regulatory Reform, and Structural Chankge in the Electric Power Industry," <u>Brookings Papers on Economic Activity</u>, 1989, 125-208.

3. Multiproduct Problems: Telecommunications

*W&K, case 7.

*R. Noll and B. Owen, "United States vs. AT&T: An Interim Assessment," in Bradley and Hausman, eds. Future Competition in Telecommunications, 141-192.

*A.E. Kahn and W. Shew,"Current Issues in Telecommunications Regulation: Pricing," Yale Journal On Regulation, Spring 1987, 191-256.

  P. Temin, The Fall of the Bell System, Cambridge: Cambridge University Press, 1987.

  R. Braeutigam, "An Analysis of Fully-Distributed Cost Pricing in Regulated Industries," Bell Journal of Economics, 11 (Spring 1980), 182-196.

7. REGULATION & DEREGULATION OF MULTI-FIRM INDUSTRIES

*G.W. Schwert, "Using Financial Data to Measure the Effects of Regulation," Journal of Law and Economics, 24 (April 1981), 121-158.

  J.J. Binder, "Measuring the Effects of Regulation with Stock Price Data," Rand Journal of Economics, 16 (Summer 1985), 167-183.

  Kahn, Vol. II, ch. 5.A. Air Transportation

*W&K, case 2.

  R. Schmalensee, "Comparative Static Properties of Regulated Airline Oligopolies," Bell Journal of Economics, 8 (Autumn 1977), 565-576.

*E.E. Bailey, D.R. Graham, and D.P. Kaplan, Deregulating the Airlines, Cambridge: MIT Press, 1985, ch. 9. (rest is recommended, esp. chs. 1 & 2.)

*S. Morrison and C. Winston, "Enhancing the Performance of the Deregulated Air Transport System," Brookings Papers on Economic Activity, 1989, 61-124.

*G. Hurdle et al., "Concentration, Potential Entry, and Performance in the Airline Industry," Journal of Industrial Economics, forthcoming.

*S. Borenstein, "Hubs and High Fares: Airport Dominance and Market Power in the U.S. Airline Industry," Rand Journal of Economics, 20 (Autumn 1989), 344-368.

  M.E. Levine, "Airline Competition in Deregulated Markets: Theory, Firm Strategy, and Public Policy," Yale Journal on Regulation, 4 (Spring 1987), 393-494.

  S. Borenstein, "On the Efficiency of Competitive Markets for Operating Licenses," Quarterly Journal of Economics, 103 (May 1988), 357-385.

*S. Borenstein and M.B. Zimmerman, "Market Incentives for Safe Commercial Airline Operation," *American Economic Review*, 78 (December 1988), 913-935.

N.L. Rose, "Profitability and Product Quality: Economic Determinants of Airline Safety Performance," Sloan Working Paper #2032-88, June 1988.

B. Surface Freight Transportation

*W&K, case 1.

T.S. Ulen, "The Market for Regulation: The ICC from 1887 to 1920," *American Economic Review*, 70 (May 1980), 306-310.

*T. Keeler, *Railroads, Freight, and Public Policy*, Washington: Brookings, 1983, chs. 2, 3, 5, and 7.

K.D. Boyer, "The Costs of Price Regulation: Lessons from Railroad Deregulation," *Rand Journal of Economics*, 18 (Autumn 1987), 408-416.

P.V. Garrod and W. Miklius, "'Captive Shippers' and the Success of Railroads in Capturing Monopoly Rent," *Journal of Law and Economics*, 30 (October 1987), 423-442.

*N.L. Rose, "The Incidence of Regulatory Rents in the Motor Carrier Industry," *Rand Journal of Economics*, 16 (Autumn 1985), 299-318.

*N.L. Rose, "Labor Rent Sharing and Regulation: Evidence from the Trucking Industry," *Journal of Political Economy*, 95 (December 1987), 1146-1178.

C. Other Markets

W&K, cases 3-6.

R.T. Smith, M. Bradley, and G. Jarrell, "Studying Firm-Specific Effects of Regulation with Stock Market Data: An Application to Oil Price Regulation," *Rand Journal of Economics*, 17 (Winter 1986), 467-489.

J.P. Kalt and R.A. Leone, "Regional Effects of Energy Price Decontrol: The Roles of Interregional Trade, Stockholding, and Microeconomic Incidence," *Rand Journal of Economics*, 17 (Summer 1986), 201-213.

R.E. Litan, "Evaluating and Controlling the Risks of Financial Product Deregulation," *Yale Journal on Regulation*, 3 (Fall 1985), 1-52.

S. Harrington, "The Impact of Rate Regulation on Prices and Underwriting Results in the Property-Liability Insurance Industry: A Survey," *Journal of Risk and Insurance*, 51 (1984), 577-623.

8. PUBLIC vs. PRIVATE OWNERSHIP

*J. Vickers and G. Yarrow, *Privatization: An Economic Analysis*, Cambridge: MIT Press, 1988, chs. 1, 2, 5, and 6.

D.E.M. Sappington and J.E. Stiglitz, "Privatization, Information and Incentives," *Journal of Policy Analysis and Management*, 6 (1987), 567-582.

D.G. Davies, "The Efficiency of Public Vs. Private Firms: The Case of Australia's Two Airlines," *Journal of Law and Economics*, 14 (April 1971), 149-165.

*R. Teeples and D. Glyer, "Cost of Water Delivery Systems: Specification and Ownership Effects," *Review of Economics and Statistics*, 69 (August 1987), 399-408.

*A. Boardman and A. Vining, "Ownership and Performance in Competitive Environment," *Journal of Law and Economics*, April 1989, 1-34.

9. RESEARCH, INNOVATION AND PUBLIC POLICY

A. Theory

*Tirole, Ch. 10.

*C. Shapiro, "Patent Licensing and R&D Rivalry," *American Economic Review*, 75 (May 1985), 25-30.

A.M. Spence, "Cost Reduction, Competition, and Industry Performance," *Econometrica*, 52 (January 1984), 101-122.

*R.K. Sah and J.E. Stiglitz, "The Invariance of Market Innovation to the Number of Firms," *Rand Journal of Economics*, 18 (Spring 1987), 98-108.

J. Vickers, "The Evolution of Market Structure When There is a Sequence of Innovations," *Journal of Industrial Economics*, 35 (September 1986), 1-12.

N.T. Gallini, "Deterence by Market Sharing," *American Economic Review*, 74 (December 1984), 931-941.

*J.F. Reinganum, "The Timing of Innovation: Research, Development and Diffusion," in R. Schmalensee and R.D. Willig, ed., *Handbook of Industrial Organization*, North-Holland.

*D. Fudenberg and J. Tirole, "Understanding Rent Dissipation: On the Use of Game Theory in Industrial Organization," *American Economic Review*, 77 (May 1987), 176-183.

B. Empirical Work

*W.M. Cohen and R.C. Levin, "Empirical Studies of Innovation and Market Structure;" in R. Schmalensee and R.D. Willig, ed., Handbook of Industrial Organization, North-Holland, forthcoming.

R.C. Levin, et al., "Appropriating the Returns from Industrial Research and Development," Brookings Papers on Economic Activity, 3:1987, 783-831.

E. Mansfield, et al., "Social and Private Returns from Industrial Innovations," Quarterly Journal of Economics, 91 (May 1977), 221-240.

*S. Oster, "The Diffusion of Innovation Among Steel Firms: The Basic Oxygen Furnace," Bell Journal of Economics, 13 (Spring 1982), 45-56.

*A. Pakes, "Patents as Options: Some Estimates of the Value of Holding Patent Stocks," Econometrica, 54 (1986), 390-409.

N.L. Rose and P.L. Joskow, "The Diffusion of New Technologies: Evidence From the Electric Utility Industry," Rand Journal of Economics, forthcoming.

*Z. Griliches, "Productivity, R&D and Basic Research at the Firm Level in the 1970's," American Economic Review, 76 (March 1986), 141-154.

F.M. Scherer, "Inter-Industry Technology Flows and Productivity Growth," Review of Economics and Statistics, 64 (November 1982), 627-634.

M.B. Lieberman, "Patents, Learning by Doing, and Market Structure in the Chemical Processing Industries," International Journal of Industrial Organization, 5 (September 1987), 257-276.

S. Fischer, ed. "Symposium: The Slowdown in Productivity Growth," Journal of Economic Perspectives, 2 (Fall 1988), 3-98.

R.C. Levin, and P.C. Reiss, "Cost-Reducing and Demand-Creating R and D with Spillovers," Rand Journal of Economics, 19 (Winter 1988), 538-556.

Z.J. Acs and D.B. Audretsch, "Innovation in Large and Small Firms: An Empirical Analysis," American Economic Review, 78 (September 1988), 678-690.

C. Policy

P&E, chs. II.C.3 and VI.D, and pp. 663-668.

J.A. Ordover and R.D. Willig, "Antitrust for High-Technology Industries: Assessing Research Joint Ventures and Mergers," Journal of Law and Economics, 28 (May 1985), 311-334.

F.R. Lichtenberg, "The Effect of Government Funding on Private Research and Development: A Re-assessment," Journal of Industrial Economics, 36 (September 1987), 97-104.

R.R. Nelson, ed., Government and Technical Progress: A Cross Industry Analysis, New York: Pergamon Press, 1982.

R.P. Taylor, "Licensing in Theory and Practice: Licensor-Licensee Relationships," Antitrust Law Journal, 53 91984), 561-609.

G.M. Grossman and C. Shapiro, "Research Joint Ventures: An Antitrust Analysis," Journal of Law, Economics, and Organization, 2 (Fall 1986), 315-337.

10. THE POLITICAL ECONOMY OF REGULATION AND DEREGULATION

*G.J. Stigler, "The Theory of Economic Regulation," Bell Journal of Economics, 2 (Spring 1971), 3-21.

*T. Romer and H. Rosenthal, "Modern Political Economy and the Study of Regulation," in E.E. Bailey, ed., Public Regulation: Perspectives on Institutions and Policies, Cambridge: MIT Press, forthcoming.

*R. Noll, "Economic Perspectives on the Politics of Regulation," in R. Schmalensee and R.D. Willig, Handbook of Industrial Organization, Amsterdam: North-Holland, forthcoming.

S. Peltzman, "Toward a More General Theory of Regulation," Journal of Law and Economics, 19 (August 1976), 211-240.

G. Becker, "A Theory of Competition among Pressure Groups for Political Influence," Quarterly Journal of Economics, 98 (August 1983), 371-400.

J.Q. Wilson, "The Politics of Regulation," in J.Q. Wilson, ed., The Politics of Regulation, Cambridge: Harvard University Press, 1980.

M. Derthick and P.J. Quirk, The Politics of Deregulation, Washington: Brookings, 1985.

*J.P. Kalt and M.A. Zupan, "Capture and Ideology in the Economic Theory of Politics," American Economic Review, 74 (June 1984), 279-300.

*R. Calvert, M. McCubbins, and B. Weingast, "A Theory of Political Control and Agency Discretion," American Journal of Political Science, 1989, 670-699.

*B.R. Weingast and M.J. Moran, "Bureaucratic Discretion or Congressional Control? Regulatory Policymaking by the Federal Trade Commission," Journal of Political Economy, 91 (October 1983), 765-800.

W.A. Magat, A.J. Krupnick, and W. Harrington, Rules in the Making, Washington: Resources for the Future, 1986.

Economics 432 - Government Regulation of Industry

The University of Michigan
Fall 1988

Prof. Avery Katz
210 Lorch Hall (4-2447) or 941 Legal Research (7-4039)
Office hours: T 4:00-5:00 and W 3:00-4:00 (at Lorch) and by appointment

Class location: 2225 Angell Hall, 9:30 - 11:00, Tuesday and Thursday.

Purposes: This course studies the causes and effects of economic regulation, focusing both on the substance of regulations and on the procedures and institutions used to implement them. There are four main parts to the course. First, we consider normative and positive explanations of economic regulation. Second, we examine the effects of traditional price, output, and entry regulation. We will also consider a set of regulatory issues which arise from imperfect or costly information: regulation of fraud, product quality, and health and safety. Third and more briefly, we consider the regulatory aspects of the civil liability system, in which compliance with policy rules depends upon their enforcement by private individuals. Fourth and finally, we take up the federal antitrust laws. Topics to be covered include monopolization, collusion, and other restrictive practices.

Requirements: All students registering for this class are expected to have taken Economics 401 or its equivalent. Grades for the course will be based 25% on each of two hour exams, 40% on a final exam, and 10% on class participation.

Policy on rescheduled or makeup exams: There will be no makeups for missed hour exams. If you must miss an exam and have a valid, documented excuse, you have the option of (1) writing a short (6-8 page) paper on a topic approved by me, or (2) increasing proportionately the weight of the other exams and having the final grade determined accordingly. Illness documented by a physician's note or similar documented incapacity is a valid excuse; another exam or a job interview on the same day is not. I will attempt to schedule the hour exams to minimize your conflicts with other obligations.

Neither of these options is available for the final exam, which you must take in order to pass the course. It will be given Friday, December 16, at 1:30 P.M. Please arrange your schedule now to avoid a conflict.

Readings: Two books are required: Gujarati, Government and Business (McGraw-Hill, 1984), and Breyer, Regulation and its Reform (Harvard, 1982). There is also a coursepack of readings that may be purchased at Dollar Bill Copying on Church Street.

A course outline and reading list is found below. Some assignments may be modified later. The assignments have been carefully selected and you should assume that all readings are required unless you are told otherwise in class. I have tried to keep the quantity to a minimum in order to make this a reasonable requirement. A few of the readings may presume a legal background on the reader's part. I will try to fill in such gaps, but be sure to ask me if you have any questions in this regard.

Economics 432 syllabus — Page 2

I. Introduction: Theories of regulation

   A. Background: The setting of the debate

       Gujarati, chapters 1, 4
       Friedman, *Capitalism and Freedom*, chapters 1,2
       Galbraith, *Economics and the Public Purpose*, chapters 2,3,25
       Sweezy, *The Theory of Capitalist Development*, chapter 13

   B. Public interest theories

       Gujarati, chapter 2
       Breyer, chapter 1
       Stokey and Zeckhauser, *A Primer for Policy Analysis*, chapter 13
       Posner, "The Social Costs of Monopoly and Regulation," *Journal of Political Economy*, 1975.

   C. The political economy approach

       Posner, "Theories of Economic Regulation," *Bell Journal of Economics*, Autumn 1974.
       Kalt & Zupan, "Capture and Ideology in the Economic Theory of Politics," *American Economic Review*, June 1984, 279-300.

II. Direct public regulation

   A. Price and output regulation

       1. Theory and legal background

           Weiss, "State Regulation of Public Utilities and Marginal-Cost Pricing"
           Breyer, chapters 2,3
           Smyth v. *Ames*
           FPC v. *Hope Natural Gas Co.*

       2. Airlines: a case study

           Gujarati, chapters 12
           Breyer, chapter 10, 11

       3. Trucking: a case study

           Gujarati, chapter 11
           Breyer, chapter 12

Economics 432 syllabus — Page 3

B. Licensing and franchise bidding

>   Demsetz, "Why Regulate Utilities?" *Journal of Law and Economics*, 1968.
>   Breyer, chapter 4

C. Information, quality, and safety regulation

>   Beales, Craswell, & Salop, "The Efficient Regulation of Consumer Information," *Journal of Law and Economics*, December 1981.
>   Breyer, chapter 7
>   Breyer and Stewart, *Administrative Law and Regulatory Policy*, 1979, pp. 804-815
>   Gujarati, chapter 14 (OSHA)
>   "Value of One Life? From $8.37 to $10 Million," *New York Times*, 6/26/85.
>   Akerlof, "The Market for Lemons: Qualitative Uncertainty and the Market Mechanism," *Quarterly Journal of Economics*, 1971.

III. Private regulation — the liability system

>   Breyer, chapter 8
>   Coase, R., "The Problem of Social Cost," *Journal of Law and Economics*, 1960, sections I-VI
>   Shavell, S., *Economic Analysis of Accident Law*, 1987, chapters 2,11.
>   Shavell, S., "Liability for Harm Versus Regulation for Safety," *Journal of Legal Studies*, 1984.
>   Henningsen v. Bloomfield Motors

IV. Antitrust policy

  A. Monopolization

   1. Substantive issues and legal background

>   Gujarati, chapters 6,7
>   U.S. v. Alcoa

   2. Procedural issues and legal background

>   Blair & Kaserman, *Antitrust Economics*, chapter 4, "Private Enforcement" (1985).
>   Breit & Elzinga, "Antitrust Enforcement and Economic Efficiency: The Uneasy Case for Treble Damages," *Journal of Law and Economics*, 1974.

Economics 432 syllabus -- Page 4

   3. Case study -- the IBM case

   Fisher, McGowan & Greenwood, *Folded, Spindled, and Mutilated:
      Economic Analysis and US v. IBM*, 1983, chapters 1,8.
   Thomas, "Antitrust and the Issue of Competitive Advantage," *American
      Bar Foundation Journal*, 1985.

B. Collusion

   Gujarati, chapter 8
   Stigler, "A Theory of Oligopoly," in *Economic Analysis and Antitrust
      Law*, ed. Calvani & Siegfried
   Theater Enterprises v. *Paramount Film Distributing Corp.*

C. Vertical restraints

   Gujarati, pp. 206-218
   Kaserman, "A Survey of the Literature on Vertical Integration," in
      Economic Analysis and Antitrust Law, ed. Calvani & Siegfried
   "Round and Round on RPM," *Regulation*, Jan. 1984 [symposium with
      Areeda, Easterbrook, Pitofsky, and Miller]

D. Mergers

   Gujarati, chapter 10
   "US Issues Guidelines on Vertical Accords," *New York Times*, 1/24/85.

V. Regulatory reform

   Breyer, chapter 17

Name:_____

Economics 432
Government Regulation of Industry
University of Michigan
Prof. Avery Katz

First Hour Examination

October 18, 1988

Instructions: Write your name at the top of the page. This is a closed book examination. You have 80 minutes to complete it. Answer all questions in the space provided; if you need more room, use the back of the page. If you need to make any assumptions in your answers, state them explicitly. Use diagrams where appropriate. Please write legibly and in ink. Good luck.

Part I: Short answer (35 minutes) Explain in a brief paragraph or two.

A. In a few sentences, define and explain the significance of the following concepts. Where two concepts are listed, explain the difference between them, and the significance of the difference.

   1. Kaldor-Hicks improvement (5)

   2. Positive economics and normative economics (5)

   3. Inverse elasticity rule (5)

   4. Economic rent (5)

B. State whether the following statements are true, false, or uncertain, and briefly explain. Credit depends upon the explanation.

   1. Most systems of price regulation involve some amount of cross-subsidization. (5)

   2. Empirical measurements show that the deadweight loss from monopoly is at most a small fraction of GNP. (5)

   3. The economic theory of regulation holds that the demand for and supply of regulation combine to produce the optimal level and type of regulation. (5)

Economics 432
Fall 1988

1st hour exam
Page 2

Part II: (25 minutes) Explain, using diagrams where appropriate. Both graphical and verbal explanation is required for full credit.

Consider a regulated firm that has constant short-run marginal cost and a fixed level of capacity in the short-run. Suppose that capacity is sufficiently small that the firm cannot serve the quantity that would be demanded if price were set equal to short-run MC.

- A. What price is first-best efficient if the firm does not have to worry about covering its fixed cost? Show graphically and explain. (7)

- B. Suppose the price indicated by part A. does not allow the firm a normal rate of return. Also suppose there is only one identifiable group of consumers purchasing the firm's product. What pricing policy could you recommend for the firm's regulators? Explain. (6)

- C. Now suppose the firm's consumers can be separated into two groups consuming at different times: peak and off-peak. Assume both peak and off-peak demands would exhaust capacity if they were charged short-run MC. What prices are efficient? Show graphically and explain. (6)

- D. In the situation described in C., would it be desirable to increase the level of capacity in the long run? Explain. (6)

Part III: Essay (20 minutes) Space is limited, so for full credit, plan and organize your answer before you write.

As we have discussed, government transfer payments are commonly made in kind rather than in cash, despite the fact that standard consumer theory suggests it is inefficient to restrict the recipient to the purchase of particular goods. Which theories of regulation can account for this apparent inefficiency? Be sure to relate your answer to specific theories of regulation that we have studied, and not just to general arguments of social desirability.

END OF EXAM

Name:_____

Economics 432
Government Regulation of Industry
University of Michigan
Prof. Avery Katz

Second Hour Examination

November 17, 1988

Instructions: Write your name at the top of the page. This is a closed book examination. You have 80 minutes to complete it. Answer all questions in the space provided; if you need more room, use the back of the page. If you need to make any assumptions in your answers, state them explicitly. Use diagrams where appropriate. Please write legibly and in ink. Good luck.

Part I: Short answer (40 minutes) Choose 5 of 6. Explain in a paragraph or two.

A. Describe the objections that might be raised to the procedure of inferring the value of health and safety from market price differentials (as for example, in land and labor markets.) (8)

B. Describe the effects of price regulation on nonprice competition. (8)

C. Could it ever be efficient to restrict entry into a regulated industry? (8)

D. Explain how rate-of-return regulation in general can result in an inefficient mix of factors of production. (8)

E. Explain how litigation costs can affect the ability of the civil liability system to encourage the optimal level of precaution.

F. Explain in words the case against interfering with product quality in a competitive market. (8)

Part II: (22 minutes) Explain, using diagrams where appropriate.

A. Explain how bounded rationality can cause markets with imperfect information to fail. (6)

B. Explain and show graphically why adverse selection can cause markets with imperfect information to fail. Also explain the difference between the problems of adverse selection and bounded rationality. (8)

Economics 432
Fall 1988

2d hour exam
Page 2

C. Give two reasons why adverse selection does not cause all private markets for insurance to collapse in practice. (8)

Part III: Essay (18 minutes) Choose either A or B. Space is limited, so for full credit, plan and organize your answer before you write. Write your answer in the space provided.

A. Under what circumstances is the case strongest for choosing monopoly franchise bidding over traditional direct regulation? Could franchise bidding be used to control market power in any of the industries we have discussed?

B. What are the normative justifications for the regulation of workplace safety? Can the performance of OSHA be explained in terms of these justifications?

Economics 432
Government Regulation of Industry
Prof. Avery Katz

Final Examination — Written section
December 16, 1988

Instructions: Write your name at the top of the page. This is a closed book examination. Please write this section of the exam in ink.

Part II: Short answer (40 minutes) Choose only five of six. The points possible for each question are in parentheses.

1. What were the primary difficulties with the government's economic arguments in the IBM case? (8)

2. Explain the inefficiency that occurs when people reduce their purchases of aspirin because they overestimate the risk that someone has tampered with the package. (8)

3. Briefly outline the arguments for and against the pass-through rule in antitrust, as established by the Hanover Shoe case. (8)

4. In the capture theory of regulation, why are the captors more likely to be the regulated firms than to be consumer interest groups? (8)

5. Explain the difference between per se rules and rules of reason, and the principal advantage of each. (8)

6. Identify one possible competitive and one possible anticompetitive motivation for product tying. (8)

Part III: True/False/Uncertain (20 minutes) **Choose four of five.** Answer in the space provided; credit depends upon the explanation.

1. In a civil antitrust case, the government will typically argue for a broader market definition, and the accused firm will typically argue for a narrower market definition. (5)

2. Underinvestment in a public utility is more likely when the firm's regulators use the historical cost method to value the firm's rate base than when the regulators use the replacement cost method. (5)

3. Resale price maintenance is more likely to be anticompetitive in the market for videocassette recorders than in the market for beer. (5)

4. If off-peak demand for electricity falls, the optimal capacity for the electric company's power plant will fall as well. (5)

5. Increasing the number of taxicabs licensed to operate in New York City would be a Pareto improvment. (5)

U

Economics 224
Antitrust Economics
M. W. F. 9:00-9:50 a.m.

R. Miller
Spring 1990
Wesleyan University

SYLLABUS

The preservation of competitive rivalry in the U.S. economy. Examples of governmental intervention through the antitrust statutes (Sherman, Clayton, F.T.C., Robinson-Patman, and Cellar-Kefauver acts) on cartels, price-fixing conspiracies, predation, mergers, monopolizing, unfair acts and practices, and tie-in sales. Readings: selected court opinions since 1890. Procedure: class dicussion and final exam.

* * * * * * * *

This course deals with an important aspect of microeconomic public policy: the preservation of competitive markets. The antitrust laws are the major statutory embodiment of that policy; they touch on, affect, prohibit and/or influence the decisions of businessmen, and they may even have some influence, for good or ill, on resource allocation and hence on consumers' welfare. Occasionally someone invokes antitrust enforcement as an anti-inflation tool.

The case law--the opinions of various courts as cases are brought before them under the antitrust laws--provides the detailed applications of those statutes to business decisions. The area of business activities includes price and output decisions, agreements among firms, resale price maintenance, exclusive dealing arrangements, tying contracts, boycotts, division of markets and mergers. Most of these areas will be mentioned during the course.

The procedure will be class discussion of assigned articles and cases, supplemented with occasional lectures. Please bring with you to class your copy of the case(s) assigned for that class session.

Required Texts:

(a) Kwoka, John E., Jr. and Lawrence J. White (eds.), The Antitrust Revolution, Scott Foresman (paperback) 1989 (KW)

(b) A set of reproduced materials, available at the Economics Department Office (123 PAC). The set of materials will cost you $10.00--to be returned at the end of the semester (prior to submission of a final grade; i.e., your final grade will not be submitted until the materials are returned). If you choose to keep the materials, you may do so for an additional payment of $5.00, or a total of $15.00.

Prerequisites: One of the following:

(a) Econ 111 and 112
(b) Econ 105
(c) Econ 108

Economics 224
Antitrust Economics
Syllabus (continued)

R. Miller
Spring 1990

Class Procedure:

Since most of the class sessions will be discussions, you should be prepared for each class; reading the case(s) assigned is usually (by itself) insufficient. In addition, you should think about the facts, the law, and the economics. The following questions will provide a start:

1. Who are the parties? (The plaintiff, the defendant.)

2. What act(s) was (were) involved? What was the charge?

3. What practices are involved?

4. Who won; who lost? Why? (i.e., what argument prevailed?)

5. How do those practices affect competition? If the practices were actually employed, why were they employed (i.e., why did the practitioner use them and how did they affect profits)?

6. What was (or what could be expected as) the effect on price and on output?

7. Do you agree with the verdict? Why? (i.e., what is _your_ argument and what would be, thus, the decision in this case?)

8. What was the remedy if any imposed by the court? What was the court's reasoning for this remedy?

9. Do you agree with the remedy? Why or why not?

Grading:

Your grade will be based on one paper, class discussion, and the final examination as scheduled by the registrar during the final exam period in May. "Incomplete" is not an available grade in this course.

The paper will be a _compilation_ of short economic essays, one each on five of the cases which we discuss in class. The _entire_ paper (not pieces thereof) is due two days after the last class; i.e., 9:00 A.M., Friday, May 11, 1990. Your choice of cases should reflect at least four of the five sections of the course as the reading list indicates.

I aim for fairness in grading. Please remember that grading is a subjective process whose end is not always satisfactory to everyone, and that "grades" measure at most only a few of the dimensions of intelligence. Also please remember that your grade in this course is not a prediction of your success after graduation, nor is it an evaluation of your worth as a person.

Economics 224
Antitrust Economics
Syllabus (continued)

R. Miller
Spring 1990

Honor System:

You are urged to familiarize yourself with the Honor System. Quizzes and tests are not proctored or monitored by the instructor. The Honor System is based on "universal acceptance of certain enduring and quite specific standards of academic conduct." Those standards are "set forth as the Honor Code and are enforced by the Honor Board." Each individual at Wesleyan, student and faculty member, has an obligation to uphold those standards of academic conduct by adherence to the Honor Code. The Code includes three parts, covering:

"(A) Acts constituting a violation of the Honor Code;"
"(B) Constructive action," which obligates individuals in the Wesleyan Community "to take constructive action" under certain circumstances; and
"(C) The Pledge," which reads in its entirety: "A Student must sign a pledge on any formal academic exercise, if so requested by the instructor concerned. The pledge reads, 'Pledge, no aid, no violations.'"

By now each of you should have memorized this pledge.

The Honor Code is applied in this course to tests, quizzes, papers, and the final exam, in which no communication is permitted.

Promptness:

The curtain rises promptly at 9:00 a.m. for each performance; late comers will be seated at the discretion of the management.

Readings:

I. Single Firm Monopolizing

 1. Standard Oil Co. of N.J. v. U.S., 221 U.S.1 (1911)
 2. U.S. v. U.S. Steel Corporation, 251 U.S. 417 (1920)
 3. U.S. v. Aluminum Company of America, et al., 148 F.2d 416 (1945)
 4. U.S. v. E.I. duPont de Nemours & Company, 351 U.S. 378 (1956)
 5. U.S. v. Grinnell, 384 U.S. 563 (1966)
 6. Berkey Photo, Inc. v. Eastman Kodak Company, 603 F.2d 263 (1979)
 7. Aspen Skiing Co. v. Aspen Highlands Skiing, 105 S.Ct. 2847 (1985)

II. Agreement Among Firms

 A. Collusion

 1. U.S. v. Addyston Pipe & Steel Company, 85 F.271 (1898)
 2. U.S. v. Trenton Potteries Company, 273 U.S. 392 (1927)
 3. U.S. v. Container Corporation of America, 393 U.S. 333 (1969)
 4. U.S. v. U.S. Gypsum, 438 U.S. 422 (1978)
 5. F.T.C. v. Superior Trial Court Lawyers Assoc., 1990-1 Trade Cases (CCH) §68,895 (U.S. Supreme Court January 22, 1990)

Economics 224
Antitrust Economics
Syllabus (continued)

R. Miller
Spring 1990

Readings (continued)

B. Trade Associations

1. American Column & Lumber Company v. U.S., 257 U.S. 377 (1921)
2. U.S. v. American Linseed Oil Company, 262, U.S. 372 (1923)
3. Maple Flooring v. U.S., 268 U.S. 563 (1925)

C. Shared Monopolies

1. American Tobacco Company v. U.S., 328 U.S. 781 (1946)
2. E.I. duPont de Nemours v. F.T.C., 729 F.2d 128 (1984); KW ch 7

D. Professionals (and other issues)

1. Parker v. Brown, 317 U.S. 341 (1943)
2. Goldfarb v. Virginia State Bar, 421 U.S. 773 (1975)
3. U.S. v. National Society of Professional Engineers, 435 U.S. 679 (1978)
4. Bates v. State Bar of Arizona, 433 U.S. 350 (1977); KW ch 5

III. Business Practice

A. Tying

1. International Business Machine Corporation v. U.S., 298 U.S. 131 (1936)
2. Northern Pacific Railway Company v. U.S., 356 U.S. 1 (1958)
3. U.S. v. Loew's, Inc., 371 U.S. 38 (1962)
4. Fortner Enterprises v. U.S. Steel Corporation, 394 U.S. 495 (1969)

B. Exclusive Dealing

1. Standard Oil Co. v. U.S., 337 U.S. 293 (1949)

C. Predatory Pricing and Discrimination

1. Utah Pie Company v. Continental Baking Company, et al., 386 U.S. 865 (1967)
2. Northeastern Telephone Co. v. AT&T, 651 F.2nd 76 (1981)
3. Matsushita Elect. Ind. Co. v. Zenith, 106 S.Ct. 1348 (1986); KW ch 9
4. Cargill of Colorado v. Monfort of Colorado, 107 S.Ct. 484 (1986)
5. A.A. Poultry Farms, Inc. v. Rose Acre Farms, Inc. 881 F.2d 1396 (1989)
6. Trans America Corp. v. IBM, 698 F.2d 1377 (1983); KW ch 6
7. Western Concrete Structures v. Mitsui & Co., 760 F.2d 1013 (1985)

Economics 224 　　　　　　　　　　-5-　　　　　　　　　　R. Miller
Antitrust Economics　　　　　　　　　　　　　　　　　　　Spring 1990
Syllabus (continued)

Readings (continued)

D. Vertical Restraints

1. Continental T.V. v. GTE Sylvania, 433 U.S. 36 (1977); KW ch 10
2. United Airlines, Inc. v. CAB, 766 F.2d 1107 (1985); KW ch 12
3. Monsanto v. Spray-Rite 104 S.Ct. 1764 (1984); KW ch 13
4. Business Electronics v. Sharp Electronics, 108 S.Ct. 1515 (1988)

E. Joint Ventures

1. Broadcast Music, Inc. v. Columbia Broadcasting System, Inc. 441 U.S.1 (1978)
2. NCAA v. Board of Regents, 468 U.S. 85 (1984)
3. Northwest Wholesale Stationers, Inc. v. Pacific Stationery & Printing 472 U.S. 284 (1985)

IV. Mergers

1. Waugh Equipment Company, Arthur Meeker, Frederick W. Ellis, J.B. Scott, 15 F.T.C. 232 (1931)
2. Brown Shoe Company v. U.S., 370 U.S. 294 (1962)
3. U.S. v. Von's Grocery Company, 384 U.S. 270 (1966)
4. Mobil v. Marathon, 669 F.2d 366 and 669 F.2d 378 (1981); KW ch 1
5. F.T.C. v. Coca-Cola 641 F. Supp 1128 (1986); KW ch 3

V. Remedies and Relief

1. International Shoe Co. v. F.T.C., 280 U.S. 291 (1930)
2. Wall Products Co. v. National Gypsum Co., et al., 326 F. Supp. 295 (1971) and 357 F. Supp. 832 (1973)
3. Brunswick Corp. v. Pueblo Bowl-O-Mat, 429 U.S. 477 (1977)

224-SYL
rev030690m

112

Economics 221
Industrial Organization
P.A.C. 002
Office P.A.C. 306

Richard A. Miller
Fall 1989
M W F, 9:00-9:50am
Wesleyan University

SYLLABUS

Industrial Organization: The Role and significance of large corporations in the U.S. economy; the analysis of concentration and superconcentration, advertising, predation, integration, mergers and technical change as they affect market performance; limits to and the uses of power.

Prerequisites: Economics 111 & 112 [212], or 105 by itself.

Text: Steven Martin, <u>Industrial Economics</u>, New York: Macmillan Publishing Co., 1988

Tests: One examination on Friday, October 20.
Final examination (scheduled by the Registrar) during exam week, 18-22 December.

Papers: A number of short papers (about 2 pages, maximum) are required throughout the term, selected from specific topics to be announced.

Grading: Grading will be based on written work (tests, papers) and on class participation (discussion, reports). "Incomplete" is not an available grade in this course. I aim for fairness in grading. Please remember that grading is a subjective process whose end is not always satisfactory to everyone. Also please remember that your grade in this course is not a prediction of your success after graduation, nor is it an evaluation of your worth as a person.

Honor System: You are urged to familiarize yourselves with the Honor System. Quizzes and tests are not proctored or monitored by the instructor. The Honor System is based on "universal acceptance of certain enduring and quite specific standards of academic conduct. These standards are "set forth as the Honor Code and are enforced by the Honor Board." Each individual at Wesleyan, student and faculty member, has an obligation to uphold those standards of academic conduct by adherence to the Honor Code. The Code includes three parts, covering:

"(A) Acts constituting a violation of the Honor Code,"
"(B) Constructive action," which obligates individuals in the Wesleyan Academic Community "to take constructive action" under certain circumstances, and
"(C) The Pledge," which reads in its entirety: "A student must sign a pledge on any formal academic exercise, if so requested by the instructor concerned. The pledge reads, 'Pledge, no aid, no violations'."

In this course, the Honor Code applies to tests, the final examination, and papers. You should acquaint yourselves with the discussion section of the Honor Code in the Student Handbook. As a rule of thumb, ideas taken from another's work require citation (footnotes), and three or more words (and individual words or phrases which are unusual or peculiar) require both quotation marks and citation (footnote).

Economics 221
Industrial Organization
Syllabus (continued)

R.A. Miller
Fall 1989

Reading Assignments:

Not everything on this syllabus will be assigned to be read. I expect that you will read the selections assigned (and on time) and that the readings will be useful for more intensive study in preparation for writing your short papers.

I. Introduction: Monopoly, Competition, and the Competitive Process

    1. Martin, Chs. 1, 2, & 3

R 2. F.M. Scherer, Appendix to Ch. 2, Industrial Market Structure and Economic Performance, (2nd ed., 1980) pp. 595-600

R 3. Fisher et al, Folded, Spindled, and Mutilated, Economic Analysis and U.S. vs. I.B.M., Chapter 2

R 4. Schumpeter, Capitalism, Socialism and Democracy, Chap. 7

    5. W. Ducan Reekie, Industry, Prices and Markets, Chaps. 1 & 6

    6. Israel M. Kirzner, Competition and Entrepreneurship, Ch. 1 & 2

    7. R.R. Nelson & S.G. Winter, An Evolutionary Theory of Economic Change (Cambridge: Belknap Press of Harvard U. Press, 1982) Chaps. 2, 3 & 13.

    8. Cowling and Meuller, "The Social Cost of Monopoly Power," Economica, 1978

    9. Joseph Shaanan, "Welfare and Barriers to Entry: An Empirical Study," 54 Southern Economic Journal, 1988, pp. 746-762

R 10. M.L. Dertouzos, R.R. Lester, & R.M. Solow, Made in America, (MIT Press, 1989), Appendices A (Automobile), C (Commercial Aircraft) & G (Steel)

II. Oligopoly: The Dominant Firm Shares

    1. Martin, Ch. 4

R 2. Gaskins, "Dynamic Limit Pricing: Optimal Pricing Under Threat of Entry," J. of Economic Theory, September 1971, pp. 306-322

R 3. J.S. Bain, "Theory Concerning the Condition of Entry" Chap. 7 in Essays on Price Theory and Industrial Organization, Little Brown, 1972, 2nd ed., pp. 252-269

Economics 221
Industrial Organization
Syllabus (continued)

R.A. Miller
Fall 1989

III. Oligopoly: "Mutual Interdependence Recognized"

    1. Martin, Ch. 5

R 2. Hannah and Kay, Concentration in Modern Industry, Ch. 2 "Concentration and Market Power"; Ch. 4 "The Measurement of Concentration"

R 3. Stigler, "A Note on Profitability, Competition and Concentration" The Organization of Industry, Ch. 13, pp. 142-146

    4. R.A. Miller, "The Herfindahl-Hirschman Index as a Market Structure Variable: An Exposition for Antitrust Practitioners," 27 Antitrust Bulletin (Fall 1982), 593-618.

IV. Oligopoly: Collusion, Conspiracies, Agreements, and Understandings

    1. Martin, Ch. 6

    2. Chamberlin, The Theory of Monopolistic Competition, Chap. 3 (esp. Paragraphs 4 & 5); Chap. 4

    3. Yarrow, "Executive Competition and the Objectives of the Firm" in K. Cowling (ed.), Market Structure and Corporate Behavior, pp. 149-173

R 4. Mund, "Identical Bid Prices," J. of Political Economy, April 1960, pp. 150-169

R 5. Phillips, Market Structure, Organization, and Performance, Ch. 8 "The Trenton Potteries Case"

R 6. Hay & Kelley, "An Empirical Survey of Price Fixing Conspiracies," JLE, April 1974

    7. Fraas and Greer, "Market Structure and Price Collusion: An Empirical Analysis," JIE, September 1977, pp. 29-33

    8. Asch and Seneca, "Characteristics of Collusive Firms," JIE, March 1975

R 9. Markham, "The Nature and Significance of Price Leadership," American Economic Review, December 1951, pp. 891-905

    10. Erichson, "Price Fixing Conspiracies: The Long Term Impact," JIE, March 1976.

R 11. Brief for Appellee United States of America, U.S. vs. American Radiator and Standard Sanitary Corp., et al. (The Plumbing Fixtures Case), Appeal from Final Judgement W.D. Penna.: Criminal No. 66-295 to 3rd Circuit (1969) pp. 57-73; 224-225; 242; 251-256

Economics 221 -4- R.A. Miller
Industrial Organization Fall 1989
Syllabus (continued)

IV. **Oligopoly: Collusion, Conspiracies, Agreements, and Understandings** (continued)

R 12. M.A. Demaree, "How Judgement Came for the Plumbing Conspirators," Fortune (December 1969)

R 13. Plaintiff's memorandum in support of a proposed Modification to the Final Judgment entered on October 1, 1962 against each defendant, U.S. vs. GE and Westinghouse, Civil No. 28228, filed with Stipulations Modifications by Consent of Final Judgment entered October 1962, filed December 10, 1976, Federal Register, vol. 42, No. 61 - Wednesday, March 30, 1977

V. **Some Empirical Evidence**

1. Martin, Ch. 7

2. Liebowitz, "What Do Price-Cost Margins Measure?" 25 JLE, (2) October 92, 231-246

3. Fisher and McGowan, "On the Misuse of Accounting Rates of Return to Infer Monopoly Profits," 73 American Economic Review (1983) pp. 82-97

4. "Comments" by Ira Horowitz, W.F. Long and D.J. Ravenscraft, Stephen Martin and M. F. van Breda, 74 (3) American Economic Review (June 1984) pp.492-509 and "Reply," by Fisher, pp. 509-517

5. F.M. Fisher "On the Misuses of the Profits-Sales Ratio to Infer Monopoly Power," 18 Rand Journal of Economics (1987) pp. 384-396

6. Kwoka, "Does the Choice of A Concentration Ratio Really Matter?" JIE

R 7. Kwoka, "The Effect of Market Share Distribution on Industry Performance," REStat, February 1979, pp. 101-109

R 8. Willard F. Mueller and Douglas F. Greer, "The Effect of Market Share Distribution on Industry Performance Reexamined," 66 (2) Review of Economics and Statistics (May 1984) pp. 353-358

R 9. J.E. Kwoka, "Reply," pp. 358-361

10. Miller, "Numbers Equivalents, Relative Entropy, and Concentration Ratios," Southern Economic Journal, July 1972

11. Meehan and Duchesneau, "The Critical Level of Concentration: An Empirical Analysis," JIE. September 1973

12. Dalton & Penn, "The Concentration-Profitability Relationship: Is there a Critical Concentration Ratio?" 25 JIE, December 1976

Economics 221   -5-   R.A. Miller
Industrial Organization   Fall 1989
Syllabus (continued)

V. Some Empirical Evidence (continued)

13. D. Mueller, Profits in the Long Run (Cambridge University Press, 1986)

14. W.J. Baumol, "Contestable Markets: An Uprising in the Theory of Industry Structure," 72(1) American Economic Review (March 1982) 1-15

15. Michael Spence, "Contestable Markets and the Theory of Industry Structure: A Review Article," 21 (3) J. of Economic Literature September 1983, pp. 981-90

16. William G. Shepherd, "'Contestability' vs. Competition," 74 (4) American Economic Review September 1984, pp. 572-585

17. Elizabeth E. Bailey and William J. Baumol, "Deregulation and the Theory of Contestable Markets," 1 (2) Yale Journal on Regulation (1984) pp. 111-137

R 18. Bain, "Relation of Profit Rate to Industry Concentration: American Manufacturing 1936-40," QJE, August 1951, pp. 293-324

R 19. Yale Brozen, "Bain's Concentration and Rates of Return Revisited," 14(2) J. of Law and Economics, October 1971, pp. 351-369

20. Yale Brozen, "The Antitrust Task Force Deconcentration Recommendations," 13(2) J. of Law and Economics, October 1970, pp. 279-92

21. Harold Demsetz, "Industry Structure, Market Rivalry, and Public Policy," (16) J. of Law and Economics, 1973, pp. 1-9

22. Weiss, "The Concentration-Profit Relationship" in Goldschmid, et al., Industrial Concentration The New Learning, 1974

23. Demsetz, "Two Systems of Belief About Monopoly" in Goldschmid, et al., Industrial Concentration The New Learning, 1974

24. Cowling and Waterson, "Price-Cost Margins and Market Structure," Economica, May 1976, pp. 267-274

25. Almarin Phillips, "Market Concentration and Performance," 61 Notre Dame Law Review, 1986, pp. 1099-1108

26. R.F. Allen, "Efficiency, Market Power, and Profitability in American Manufacturing," 49 SEJ, April 1983, pp. 993-940

27. Malcolm B. Coate, "Comment"

28. Robert F. Allen, "Reply," 51(1) Southern Economic Journal, July 1984, pp. 274-281

Economics 221   R.A. Miller
Industrial Organization   Fall 1989
Syllabus (continued)

V. **Some Empirical Evidence** (continued)

29. Amato and Wilder, "The Effects of Firm Size on Profit Rates in U.S. Manufacturing," 52 *Southern Economic Journal*, 1985, pp. 181-190

30. Chappell and Cottle, "Sources of Concentration-Related Profits," 51 *Southern Economic Journal*, 1985, pp. 1031-1037

31. Lean, Ogur, and Rogers, "Does Collusion Pay...Does Antitrust Work?" 51 *Southern Economic Journal*, 1985, pp. 828-841

32. M. Smirlock, T. Gilligan, and W. Marshall, "Tobin's q and the Structure-Performance Relationship," 74(5) *American Economic Review*, December 1984, pp. 1051-1060

33. M.A. Salinger, "Tobin's q, Unionization, and the Concentration-Profits Relationship," 15(2) *The Rand Journal of Economics*, Summer 1984, pp. 159-170

34. F.H. Harris, "Market Structure and Price-Cost Performance Under Endogenous Profit Risk," 35 *J. of Industrial Economics*, 1986, pp. 35-60

35. F.H. Harris, "Testable Competing Hypotheses from Structure-Performance Theory: Efficient Structure versus Market Power," 36 (3) *J. of Industrial Economics* (March 1988), 267-280.

36. F.M. Scherer, Appendix to Chapter 3, *Industrial Market Structure and Economic Performance*, 2nd edition, 1980, pp. 601-606

37. Fischer Black, "The Trouble with Econometric Models," 38(2) *Financial Analysts Journal*, March/April 1982, pp. 29-37

VI. **Barriers to Entry and Scale Economies**

1. Martin, Ch. 8

2. Bain, *Barriers to New Competition*, Ch. 1, "Importance of the Condition of Entry"

3. Michael Porter, *Competitive Strategy*, pp. 3-33, "The Structural Analysis of Industries"

4. Bain, "Economies of Scale, Concentration, and The Condition of Entry in the Twenty Manufacturing Industries," 44 *AER* (March 1954)

R 5. Demsetz, "Barriers to Entry," 72 *AER* (March 1982) pp. 47-57

R 6. Stigler, *The Organization of Industry*, Ch. 6 "Barriers to Entry, Economics of Scale and Firm Size," pp. 67-70

R 7. Dixit, "Recent Developments in Oligopoly Theory," 72 *AER* (1982) pp. 12-17

Economics 221
Industrial Organization
Syllabus (continued)

R.A. Miller
Fall 1989

VI. **Barriers to Entry and Scale Economies** (continued)

8. C.F. Pratten, *Economies of Scale in Manufacturing Industry*, Ch. 1 & 2 plus selections from Chs. 3-28

9. Stigler, "The Economies of Scale, *J. of Law & Economics*, October 1958

10. Shepherd, "What Does the Survivor Technique Show about Economies of Scale?" *SEJ*, June 1967

11. Cookenboo, "Production and Cost Functions for Oil Pipelines," in D.S. Watson, *Price Theory in Action* (any edition)

12. Spence, "Entry, Capacity, Investment and Oligopolistic Pricing" 8(2) *Bell Journal*, Autumn 1977

13. Schmalensee, "Economies of Scale and Barriers to Entry," 89 *JPE*, December 1981

14. M.E. Porter, "Interbrand Choice, Media Mix and Market Performance," 66(2) *American Economic Review*, May 1983, pp. 398-406

15. S.C. Salop and D.T. Scheffman, "Raising Rivals' Costs," 73(2) *American Economic Review*, May 1983, pp. 267-271

VII. **Sizes of Firms: Horizontal Size and Vertical Integration**

1. Martin, Chs. 9 & 10

2. R. Coase, "The Nature of the Firm," 4 *Economica*, November 1937, pp. 386-405, reprinted in Stigler and Boulding (eds.), *AEA Readings in Price Theory*, pp. 331-351

3. J. Hirshleifer, "On the Economics of Transfer Pricing," 29 *J. of Business*, July 1956, pp. 172-184

4. O.E. Williamson, *Markets and Hierarchies*, Ch. 2, "The Organizational Framework," Ch. 5, "Intermediate Product Markets and Vertical Integration"

R 5. Vernon & Graham, "Profitability of Monopolization by Vertical Integration." 79(4) *JPE*, July/August 1971

R 6. Perry, "Forward Vertical Integration by Alcoa: 1888-1930," *JIE*, September 1980

7. Bolch & Damon, "The Depletion Allowance and Vertical Integration in the Petroleum Industry," *SEJ*, July 1978

Economics 221
Industrial Organization
Syllabus (continued)

R.A. Miller
Fall 1989

VII. **Sizes of Firms** (continued)

8. Mancke, "Iron Ore and Steel--Vertical Integration," *JIE*, 1972

R 9. Stigler, The Theory of Price, 3rd ed., 81-83; 209-214.

10. Alan J. Auerbach (ed.), *Corporate Takeover: Causes and Consequences* (1988)

11. Alan J. Auerbach (ed.), *Mergers and Acquisitions* (1988)

12. Browne & Rosengren (eds.), *The Merger Boom* (F.R. Bank of Boston, 1987)

13. Ravenscraft & Scherer, *Mergers, Sell-offs, & Economic Efficiency* (1987)

VIII. **Advertising**

1. Martin, Ch. 11

2. Comanor and Wilson, "Advertising, Market Structure and Performance," *REStat*, November 1967

R 3. Brozen, "Entry Barriers: Advertising and Product Differentiation" and Mann, "Advertising, Concentration, and Profitability: The State of Knowledge and Directions for Public Policy" both in Goldschmid et al. eds., *Industrial Concentration: The New Learning*

R 4. Benham, "The Effect of Advertising on the Price of Eyeglasses," *JLE*, October 1972

5. Comanor and Wilson, "The Effect of Advertising on Competition: A Survey" 7(2) *JEL*, June 1979, 453-76

6. Bolch, "The Effect of Advertising on Competition: Comments on a Survey"

7. Simon, "On Firm Size and Advertising Efficiency: A Comment"

8. Comanor and Wilson, "On the Economics of Advertising: A Reply to Bolch and Simon," all in 10(5) JEL, (September 1980) 1063-1078

9. G.R. Butters, "A Survey of Advertising and Market Structure" 66(2) *American Economic Review*, 1976, pp. 392-397

10. Strickland and Weiss, "Advertising, Concentration and Price-Cost Margins," 84 *J. of Political Economics*, 1976, pp. 1109-1121

11. Schroeter, Smith, & Cox, "Advertising and Competition in Routine Legal Service Markets, An Empirical Investigation," 36 *J. of Industrial Economics*, 1987, pp. 35-48

Economics 221　　　Industrial Organization　　　Syllabus (continued)　　　R.A. Miller　　　Fall 1989

IX. Technical Change

1. Martin, Ch. 12

2. Sumrall, "Diffusion of the Basic Oxygen Furnace in the U.S. Steel Industry," JIE, June 1982, pp. 421-438

3. Lynn, "New Data on the Diffusion of the Basic Oxygen Furnace in the U.S. and Japan," 30(2) JIE, December 1981, pp. 123-136

4. Oster, "The Diffusion of Innovation Among Steel Firms: The Basic Oxygen Furnace," 13(1) Bell Journal, Spring 1982, pp. 45-56

5. Scherer, "Demand-Pull and Technological Invention: Schmookler Revisited," 30(3) JIE, March 1982, pp. 225-235

6. Mukhopadhyay, "Technical Progress and Change in Market Concentration in the U.S., 1963-77," 52 Southern Economic Journal, 1985, pp. 141-150

X. International

1. Martin, Ch. 13

XI. Strategy

1. Martin, Chs. 15 & 16

XII. Some Policy Matters

1. Martin, Chs. 17 & 18

2. Gerald W. Brock, "The Regulatory Change in Telecommunications: The Dissolution of AT&T" in Weiss and Klass, eds., Regulatory Reform, What Actually Happened, Little, Brown & Co., 1986, pp. 210-233

3. Manley R. Irwin, "The Telecommunications Industry" in Walter Adams, The Structure of American Industry, 7th ed., MacMillan, 1986, pp. 261-289

R 4. Daniel P. Kaplan, "The Changing Airline Industry," in Weiss and Klass, pp. 40-77

5. P. Asch and R. Seneca, Ch. 13, "Regulation: Rationale and Basic Principles," and Ch. 14, "Regulatory Responses to the Basic Problem," in Government and the Market Place, Dryden, 1986, pp. 257-291

6. Levine, Michael S., "Airline Competition in Deregulated Markets: Theory, Firm Strategy, and Public Policy," Yale Journal on Regulation 4(2) Spring 1987, pp. 393-494

G

UNIVERSITY OF CHICAGO
Graduate School of Business

Business 305/Economics 380　　　　　　　　　　　　Mr. Peltzman
Industrial Organization

READING LIST AND COURSE OUTLINE

Text: Stigler, The The Organization of Industry(S)
Packet of Readings (P).

There are also numerous readings from Universities-National Bureau of Economic Research, Business Concentration and Price Policy (NBER) and American Economic Association, Readings in Industrial Organization and Public Policy (AEA) and Readings in Price Theory (RPT).

You may find it helpful to consult the following to review some of the material covered in the course: Scherer, Industrial Market Structure and Economic Performance, and Hay and Morris, Industrial Economics: Theory and Evidence.

Antitrust law and cases are not covered extensively in the course. For a review, see Neale, The Antitrust Laws of the U.S.A.; cases are covered in Stelzer, Selected Antitrust Cases.

The following journal abbreviations are used:

AER	-- American Economic Review
QJE	-- Quarterly Journal of Economics
JPE	-- Journal of Political Economy
JLE	-- Journal of Law and Economics
RES	-- Review of Economics and Statistics
BJ or RJ	-- Bell Journal of Economics and Management Science (now Rand Journal of Economics)
EJ	-- Economic Journal
JB	-- Journal of Business
JEL	-- Journal of Economic Literature
AEI	-- American Enterprise Institute (monograph series)
JIE	-- Journal of Industrial Economics

Especially recommended readings are marked (*) and should be on reserve in the library.

I. The Structure of Markets: Effects on Price and Output

   A. Monopoly and Competition--review on your own.

   B. Oligopoly: When is non-competitive pricing likely?
      (1) Classic Oligopoly Models: Bertrand, Cournot and their descendants.

      "Cournot, Research in the Mathematical Principles of the Theory of Wealth, Ch. 7 (P), Ch. 8.
      *S, Ch. 5.
      Fellner, Competition Among the Few.
      R. G. D. Allen, Mathematical Analysis for Economists, pp. 200-204, 345-347.
      Chamberlin, The Theory of Monopolistic Competition Ch. 3.
      Perry, "Oligopoly and Consistent Conjectural Variation," BJ, Sp. 82.

      Baumol, "Contestable Markets," AER, 3/82.
      _____, Panzar and Willig, Contestable Markets and the Theory of Industry.
      Hotelling, "Stability in Competition," in RPT.

      (2) Market Sharing.
          *Nicholls, Imperfect Competition Within Agricultural Industries, pp. 120-130.

      (3) Price Leadership.
          Markham, "The Nature and Significance of Price Leadership," in AEA.
      (4) Uniform Delivered Prices -- Basing Point Methods.
          *S, Ch. 14.
          Machlup, The Basing Point System.
          Haddock, "Basing Point Pricing," AER June 1982.

   C. The Problem of Entry: When can it be deterred and how?

      1. Limit Entry Pricing
         *Bain, "A Note on Pricing in Monopoly and Oligopoly, " in AEA.
         Bain, "Economies of Scale...," AEA.
         Modigliani, "New Developments on the Oligopoly Front, " JPE, 1958.
         Gaskins, "Dynamic Limit Pricing," Journal of Econ. Theory, 1971.
         Schmalensee, "Economies of Scale and Barriers to Entry," JPE, December 1981.
         Von Weizsacker, Barriers to Entry.

      2. Other Entry-Deterring Strategies.
         Bain, Barriers to New Competition.
         Williamson, "Selling Costs as a Barrier to Entry," QJE, February 1963.
         Von Weizsacker, "Welfare Analysis of Barriers to Entry, " BJ, Fall 1980.
         *Spence, "Entry, Capacity, Investment and Oligopolistic Pricing," BJ, Fall 1977.

_____, "Investment Strategy and Growth in a New Market,"
   BJ, Spring 1979.
Salop, "Strategic Entry Deterrence," AER, May 1979.
Krattenmaker and Salop, "Anticompetitive Exclusion: Raising
   Rivals' Costs," Yale Law Journal, December 1986.
Williamson, Markets and Hierarchies, Ch. 5.
Schmalensee, "Product Differentiation Advantages of Pioneering
   Brands," AER, June 1982.
_____, "Advertising and Entry Detterrence," JPE, August 1983.
West, "Testing for Market Preemption..." BJ, Sp. 1981.
Lieberman, "Excess Capacity as a Barrier to Entry: An Empirical
   Appraisal," JIE, 1987.

D. Cartels
   *Patinkin, "Multiple Plant Firms, Cartels and Imperfect
      Competition," QJE, Feb. 1947.
   Griffin, "OPEC Behavior", AER, December 1985.

E. Predatory Pricing: Does it Pay to Price Below Cost?
   *McGee, "The Standard Oil Case, " JLE, October 1958 (P).
   _____, "Predatory Pricing Revisited," JLE, October 1980.
   Elzinga, "Predatory Pricing: The Case of the Gunpowder Trust,"
      JLE, April 1970.
   Williamson, "Predatory Pricing," Yale Law Journal, 12/77.

II. The Role of Advertising, Product Differentiation and Information

   A. The Theory of Monopolistic Competition.
      *Chamberlin, The Theory of Monopolistic Competition, Chs. 4-7

      1. Welfare Implications.
         Kaldor, "Economic Aspects of Advertising," Review of Economic
            Studies, 1949-50.
         Chamberlin, Theory of Monopolistic Competition, Appendix E and F.
         *Chamberlin, "Product Heterogeneity and Public Policy," in AEA.

      2. The Critique of the Theory
         *S, Appendix.
         Archibald, "Chamberlin versus Chicago," Review of Economic
            Studies, October, 1961.
         *Demsetz, "The Nature of Equilibrium in Monopolistic
            Competition, " JPE, February 1959 (P).
         Demsetz, "Do Competition and Monopolistic Competition Differ?"
            JPE, February 1968.
         Margolis, "Monopolistic Competition and Multiproduct Brand
            Names," Journal of Business, April 1989.

      3. Recent Developments
         Dixit and Stiglitz, "Monopolistic Competition and Product
            Diversity," AER, June 1977.
         Salop, "Monopolistic Competition with Outside Goods," BJ Sp. 79.
         Grabowski, "Effects of Advertising on the Interindustry
            Distribution of Demand," NBER, Exploration in Econ. Research,
            Winter 1976.

Roberts and Samuelson, "An Empirical Analysis of Dynamic
Non Price Competition and Oligopolistic Industry," RJ, Sum. 88.
B. The Economics of Information: Another Approach to Advertising.
*S, Chs. 16, 17.
Nelson, "Information and Consumer Behavior," JPE, March 1970.
Nelson, "Advertising as Information," JPE, July 1974 (P).
Klein and Leffler, "The Role of Market Forces in Assuring
Contractual Performance", JPE, August 1981.
Schmalensee, "A Model of Advertising and Product Quality," JPE,
June 1978.
Kotowitz and Mathewson, "Advertising, Information and Product
Quality," BJ, Fall 1979.
*Ehrlich and Fisher, "The Derived Demand for Advertising," AER,
June 1982.
Pratt, Wise & Zeckhauser, "Price Differences in Almost Competitive
Markets," QJE, May 1979.

C. Other Models of Advertising
Dorfman and Steiner, "Optimal Advertising and Optimal Quality,"
AER, Dec. 1954, also in F. M. Bass (ed.) *Mathematical Models
and Methods in Marketing.*
Schmalensee, *Economics of Advertising.*
*Telser, "Advertising and Competition," JPE, 1964.
Telser, "The Supply and Demand for Advertising Messages," AER,
May, 1966.

III. Some Determinants of the Structure of Firms and Markets

A. Vertical Integration: The firm's "make" or "buy" decision.

1. The Theory of Vertical Integration
   *S, ch. 12.
   *Coase, "The Nature of the Firm, " in RPT. (P)
   *Klein, Alchian and Crawford, "Vertical Integration,
   Appropriable Rents..., " JLE, October 1978 (P).
   Monteverde and Teece, "Appropriable Rents... ," JLE,
   October 1982.
   Caves, "Corporate Strategy and Structure," JEL, March 1980.
   Williamson, "The Vertical Integration of Production", AER 5/71.
   _____, *Markets and Hierarchies.*
2. The Measurement of Vertical Integration
   *Adelman, "Concept and Measurement of Vertical Integration," in
   NBER. (P)
   Laffer, "Vertical Integration by Corporations, " RES,
   February 1969.

3. The Effects of Vertical Integration on Competition and Welfare
   Machlup and Taber, "Bilateral Monopoly... ,"*Economica*, May 1960.
   *Bork, "Vertical Integration and the Sherman Act," University of Chicago Law Review, Autumn 1954.
   Liebeler, "Toward a Consumer's Antitrust Law: The FTC and Vertical Mergers in Cement," UCLA Law Review, June 1968.
   McBride, "Spatial Competition and Vertical Integration: Cement Revisited", AER 12/83.
   Vernon and Graham, "Profitability of Monopolization by Vertical Merger," JPE, July 1971.
   McGee, "Vertical Integration Revisited," JLE, April 1975.
   Peterman, "The Brown Shoe Case," JLE, April 1975.
   Warren-Boulton, "Vertical Control with Variable Proportions," JPE; August 1974.
   Walters, "Reciprocity Reexamined: The Consolidated Foods Case," JLE 10/86.
   Kaserman, "Theories of Vertical Integration," Antitrust Bulletin, Fall 1978.
   Westfield, "Vertical Integration: Does Product Price Rise or Fall?" AER, June 1981.
   Masten, "The Organization of Production: Evidence from the Aerospace Industry" JLE, October 1984.

B. Economies of Scale and the size of firms.
   *S, Chs. 7, 6.
   Saving, "Estimation of Optimum Plant Size by the Survivor Technique, " QJE, November 1961.
   Weiss, "The Survival Technique and the Extent of Suboptimal Capacity," JPE, June 1964.
   Scherer et al. , The Economics of Multi-Plant Operations.
   *Scherer, "Economies of Scale and Industrial Concentration" in Goldschmid Industrial Concentration: The New Learning.

C. Mergers
   *S. Ch. 8.

IV. Vertical Relationships between Firms

A. Resale Price Maintenance, Exclusive Dealing and Franchising.
   *Telser, "Why Should Manufacturers Want Fair Trade?" JLE, 1958 (P).
   Bork, "The Rule of Reason..., " Yale Law Journal, 1965, 1966.
   Marvel, "Exclusive Dealing, JLE, April 1982.
   Mathewson and Winter, "An Economic Theory of Vertical Restraints," RJ, Spring 1984.
   Klein and Murphy, "Vertical Restraints as Contract Enforcement Mechanisms," JB, April 1988.
   Mathewson and Winter, "The Economics of Franchise Contracts, " JLE 10/85.
   Klein and Saft, "The Law and Economcs of Franchise Tying Contracts," JLE 5/85.
   Norton, "An Empirical Look at Franchising," JB April 1988.
   Gilligan, "The Competitive Effects of Resale Price Maintenance" RJ Winter, 1986.
   Rey and Tirole, "The Logic of Vertical Restraints," AER 12/86.

B. Tie-in Selling & Full Line Forcing
   *Burstein, "A Theory of Full Line forcing," *Northwestern University Law Review*, February 1960.
   *Burstein, "The Economics of Tie-in Sales," RES, February 1960 (P).
   Bowman, "Tying Arrangements and the Leverage Problem," *Yale Law Journal*, November 1957.
   R.G.D. Allen, Math. Analysis for Economists, pp. 359-362.
   *S, Ch. 15.
   Telser, "A Theory of Monopoly of Complementary Goods," JB, April 1979.
   Cummings and Ruhter, "The Northern Pacific Case," and Peterman, "The International Salt Case," both JLE, October 1979.
   Adams, W. J. and Yellen, J., "Commodity Bundling and the Burden of Monopoly," QJE, August 1976.

V. Pricing Policy in Imperfectly Competitive Markets

   A. Price Rigidity

      1. Theory
         *Sweezy, "Demand under Conditions of Oligopoly," and companion article by Stigler in RPT (latter, also in S, Ch. 18).
         Carlton, "Contracts, Price Rigidity and Market Equilibrium," JPE, October 1979.
         Carlton, "Market Behavior with Demand Uncertainty and Price Inflexibility," AER September 1978.
         Rotemberg and Saloner, "The Relative Rigidity of Monopoly Pricing," AER, December 1987.

      2. Evidence
         *Means, "Price Inflexibility," *Journal of the American Statistical Association*, 1935.
         *National Bureau of Economic Research, *The Price Statistics of the Federal Government*, pp. 393-412, 419-431.
         *S, Ch. 19.
         *Stigler and Kindahl, *The Behavior of Industrial Prices*, Chs. 1,2,5.
         Means, "The Administered Price Thesis Reconfirmed," AER, June 1972.
         Qualls, "Market Structure and the Flexibility of Price Cost Margins," JB, April 1979.
         Goldstein, "Markup Variability and Flexibility: Theory and Evidence," JB 10/86.
         DePodwin and Selden, "Business Pricing Policies and Inflation," JPE, April 1966.
         Weiss, "Business Pricing Policies and Inflation Reconsidered," JPE, April 1966.
         Weiss, "Stigler, Kindahl and Means on Administered Prices," AER, September 1977.
         Weston and Lustgarten, "Concentration and Wage and Price Changes," in Goldschmid et al. (ed.), *Industrial Concentration: The New Learning*.
         Lustgarten, "Administered Inflation," *Economic Inquiry*, June 1975.
         Lustgarten, *Industrial Concentration and Inflation*, AEI.

Bils, "The Cyclical Behavior of Marginal Cost and Price," AER, December 1987.
Hall, "The Relationship Between P and MC in U.S. Industry," JPE October 1988.

C. Product Durability: Does competition lead to more durable products?
Benjamin and Kormendi, "Interrelationships Between Market for New and Used Goods, " JLE, October 1974.
Swan, "Alcoa: Recycling and Monopoly Power," JPE, February 1980.
*Coase, "Durability & Monopoly, " JLE, April 1972.

VI. Empirical Studies of Market Structure and Its Consequences

A. Measurement of Market Structure.
*S, Ch. 4.
Rosenbluth, "Measurement of Concentration," in NBER.
Scitovsky, "Economic Theory and the Measurement of Concentration, " in NBER.

B. Market Structure in the United States.

1. History
*Nutter, The Extent of Enterprise Monopoly in the U.S.
*Adelnan, "Measurement of Industrial Concentration," in AEA.
Stigler, Five Lectures on Economic Problems, Ch. 5.
Nelson, Concentration in the Marketing Industries of the U.S.
Pashigian, "Market concentration in the U.S. and Great Britain," JLE, October 1968.
*S, Ch. 21.

2. The Role of Mergers
*Markham, "Survey of the Evidence on Mergers, " in NBER.
Nelson, Merger Movements in American Industry.
Weston, The Role of Mergers in the Growth of Large Firms.
McGowan, " International Comparisons of Mergers, " JLE, April 1971.

3. Entry and Firm Growth.
Hymer and Pashigian, "Turnover of Firms as a Measure of Market Behavior, " RES, February 1962.
Peltzman, "Entry in Commercial Banking," JLE, October 1965.
Telser, et al, "Theory of Supply..., " JLE, October 1975.
Hause and DuRietz, "Entry, Industry, Growth,... " JPE August 1984.
Dunne, Roberts and Samuelson, "Patterns of Firm Entry and Exit in U.S. Manufacturing," RJ Winter 1988.
Evans, "The Relationship Between Firm Growth, Size and Age," JIE, 1987.
*Telser, Competition Collusion and Game Theory, Ch. 8.
Burns, "The Competitive Effects of Trust Busting, " JPE, August 1977.
Domowitz Hubbard and Petersen, "Business Cycles and the Relationship between Concentration and Price-Cost Margins," RJ, Spring, 1986.

C. The Effects of Market Structure

   1. On Price Rigidity--See Sec. V. A.2

   2. On Profits: The Role of Concentration

      a. The main findings

         *Bain, "The Relation of the Profit Rate to Industry
            Concentration," QJE, 1951 (P).
         S, Ch. 13.
         *Collins and Preston, Price-cost Margins in Manufacturing.
         Stigler, Capital and rates of Return in Manufacturing.
         *Brozen, "Bain's Concentration and Rates of Return
            Revisited, " JLET October 1971 (P).
         Kilpatrick, "Stigler on the Relationship between Profits
            and Concentration," JPE, May 1968.
         *Weiss, "The Concentration-Profits Relationship and
         Antitrust," in Goldschmid et al. (ed.), Industrial
         concentration: The New Learning. (P)
         *Mann, "Seller Concentration, Barriers to Entry and Rates
            of Return in 30 Industries," RES, August 1966.
         Ornstein, "Concentration and Profits, " JB, October 1972.
         Lindenberg and Ross, "Tobin's q and Industrial
            Organization" JB, January 1981.
         Smirlock et al. "Tobin's q and the Structure-Performance
            Relationship" AER, December 1984.
         Lustgarten, "The Impact of Buyer Concentration, " RES,
            May 1975.

      b. A reinterpretation of the evidence

         Brozen, Merger Concentration and Public Policy.
         *Demsetz, "Industry Structure, Market Rivalry and Public
            Policy," JLE, April 1973 (P).
         *Demsetz, "Two Systems of Belief about Monopoly" in
            Goldschmid, Industrial Concentration: The New Learning.
         Demsetz, The Market Concentration Doctrine, AEI
         *Peltzman, "The Gains and Losses of Industrial
            Concentration, " JLE, April 1977 (P).
         (See also, comments by Lustgarten and Scherer, JLE, April
         1979.)
         Gisser, "Price Leadership and Dynamic Aspects of Oligopoly in
            U.S. Manufacturing" JPE, December 1984.
         Alberts, "Do Oligopolists Earn Non-Competitive Returns",
            AER 9/84.
         Fisher and McGowan, "The Misuse of Accounting Rates of
            Return, " AER 3/83.
         Lustgarten, Productivity and Prices: The Role of
            Concentration, AEI.
         Lynk, "Interpreting Rising Concentration: The Case of
            Beer," JB, 1/84.
         Ravenscraft, "Structure-Profit Relationships. . ." RES,
            2/83.

3. On Profits: The Role of Advertising

   a. Advertising as a Barrier to Entry

   *Comanor and Wilson, "Advertising, Market Structure and
       Performance, " RES, November 1967 (p).
   Comanor and Wilson, _Advertising and Market Power_.
   *Comanor and Wilson, "Advertising and Competition: A Survey,"
       JEL, June 1979.
   Schmalensee, _Economics of Advertising_.
   Strickland and Weiss, "Advertising, Concentration and
       Price Cost Margins," JPE, October 1978.
   Martin, "Advertising, Concentration and Profitability," BJ, Fall
       1979.

   b. Alternative Interpretations

   Telser, "Advertising and Cigarettes," JPE, October 1962.
   Weiss, "Advertising, Profits and Corporate Taxes," RES, November
       1969.
   Peles, "Rate of Amortization of Advertising," JPE, October 1971.
   *Block, "Advertising and Profitability," JPE, March 1974.
   Ayanian, "Advertising and Rate of Return," JLE, October 1975.
   _____, "The Advertising Capital Controversy," JB, 7/83.
   Demsetz, "Accounting for Advertising as a Barrier to
       Entry," JB, July 1979.
   Ornstein, "Industrial Concentration and Advertising
       Intensity, AEI.
   Ferguson, _Advertising and Competition_.
   Nagle, "Do Advertising-Profitability Studies Really Show... ?,
       JLE 10/81.
   Eckard, "Advertising, Competition and Market Share
       Instability," JB, October 1987.

4. On Economic Welfare

   *Harberger, "Monopoly and Resource Allocation," AER, May 1954
       (P).
   Stigler, "The Statistics of Monopoly and Merger," JPE,
       February 1965.
   Schwartzman, "The Burden of Monopoly," JPE, December 1960.
   *Posner, "The Social Cost of Monopoly, " JPE, August 1975.
   Gisser, "Price Leadership and Welfare Losses," AER, September 1986.
   Willner, "Price Leadership and Welfare Losses in U.S. Manufacturing,
       AER, June 1989.

EXAMS AND GRADES

There will be a midterm exam on Tuesday October 31 and a final exam on Tuesday December 12. There are no make-up or other nonscheduled exams for any student for any reason.

Grades depend on your relative standing in the class, not on your absolute score. Your standing in the class will be determined after the final as follows: 1) Your final and midterm exam scores will be divided by the class average on each exam. 2) If your (final/class average) exceeds your (midterm/class average) your midterm is ignored--i.e. your (final/class average) is weighed 100%. 3) If you have done better on the midterm than the final, your (midterm/class average) is weighed 30% and your (final/class average) is weighed 70% to compute your standing. 4) If you do not take the midterm, your final exam score will be multiplied by .95.

If you do not take the final you may petition for a grade of "I" which can be removed the next time I teach the course or, if you obtain consent of the instructor, the next time the course is offered.

Students are welcome to suggest possible exam questions. But, if your question is used, your only reward will be a little more time to think about an answer.

Week (approx.)		Topics to be Covered	Reading List Section
1	I.	Oligopoly Theory	
		A. Cournot	I.B
		B. Bertrand	
		C. Chamberlin	
2	II.	Collusive Methods and When it Pays to Cheat	IB.2
		A. Market Sharing	
	III.	Other Techniques of Imperfect Competition	
3		A. Price Leadership	IB.3
		B. Entry Deterrence	IC
		1. Using Excess Capacity to Deter Entry	IC.2
		C. Predation	IE.
	IV.	Advertising and Non-Price Competition	
		A. Monopolistic Competition	II.A.
5		B. Economics of Information	II.B.
		[Midterm: Tuesday, October 31, 1 hour +]	
6	V.	Vertical Integration: To make or to buy?	III.A.
		A. Theory v. Evidence	
		B. Strategic Motives For Vertical Integration	III.A.3.
		1. The Role of Imperfect Competition	
7-8	VI.	Vertical Integration by Contract	
		A. Retail Price Maintenance	V. A
		B. Exclusive Dealing	
		C. Franchising	
		D. Tie-in Selling and Full-line Forcing	V. B
9-10	VII.	The Empirical Literature	
		A. On Concentration	VI. A,B
		B. On Prices and Profits	VI. C.2
		C. On Advertising	VI. C.3
		D. On the Welfare Effects of Monopoly	VI. C.4
11		[Final: Tuesday, December 12, 2 hours +]	

UNIVERSITY OF CHICAGO
Graduate School of Business

B305/Econ. 380

Mr. Peltzman
Fall, 1989

FINAL EXAM

Answer all questions. Explain each answer. Points are in parentheses. Maximum: 200 points.

(20) I. Explain why a buyer's optimum search strategy may be to set a "reservation" price (a maximum price he/she would be willing to pay) and search until he/she finds a seller asking no more than this price.

(20) II. AlphaBeta Co. produces X from inputs A and B. A is supplied by a monopoly, and B is supplied competitively. Explain how vertical integration can increase the joint profits of Alpha Beta and its input suppliers.

(20) III. In "Advertising as Information," Nelson shows that the Advertising/Sales ratio is

(a) higher for experience goods than for search goods

(b) higher for non-durable experience goods (e.g., beer) than for durable experience goods (e.g., books).

Explain how each of these facts is or is not consistent with Nelson's theory.

(20) IV. "[In oligopolies] higher wages may be without influence on either price or output"

-- P. Sweezy "Demand under Conditions of Oligopoly"

Explain briefly the basis of Sweezy's conclusion.

(20) V. In a recent study of mergers between firms in the same industry, it was found that

a) the profitability of the firms that merged was greater after the merger than their combined pre-merger profitability.

b) the profitability of other firms in the same industry (i.e. those not involved in the merger) declined after the merger.

c) total industry profits increased after the merger.

How could this evidence he used to help interpret the positive correlation between industry profitability and concentration?

(50) VI. You have a patent on two machines, X and Y, which are used by producers of Z. There are two equally numerous types (I and II) of Z-producers. You have no precise information on the value of X's and Y's to these customers. But you believe the following is true.

Type of Buyer	Value of an X	Y
I	High	Low
II	Low	High

(The table says that, e.g., a Type I places an above-average value on X and a below-average value on Y). You are currently renting each machine for $100/month, and each z-producer is renting both an X and a Y.

(35) A. How would you use this information to help decide whether or not to adopt full-line-forcing or tie-in selling?

(15) B. Would your answer to A. change if the table read

Type of Buyer	Value of an X	Y
I	High	High
II	Low	Low

Explain.

(70) VII. XYZ Co. produces a new kind of machine. The value of the machine can be enhanced if retailers provide certain services (demonstrations, appealing displays, etc.) to potential customers. Specifically, XYZ estimates that the demand for the machine will be

 (a) P = 100 - Q if the retail services are provided

and

 (b) P = 50 - Q if the services are not provided

XYZ believes that the only practical way to assure provision of the services is to grant one retailer the exclusive right to sell the machine. There are no marginal costs of producing the machines or of providing the services. But there is a fixed cost of $500 in setting up to provide the services.

(20) A. Explain briefly why XYZ may have to grant one retailer the exclusive right to sell the product in order to assure provision of the services.

(35) B. Assume that, if XYZ, does appoint an exclusive retail agent, it cannot impose any further restrictions on the retail market. XYZ's only remaining choice variable would be set the wholesale price of the machine to its exclusive agent. Given the facts above, will XYZ appoint an exclusive retail agent? Explain.

(15) C. Outline the kind of "further restrictions" that XYZ might wish to impose if it did appoint an exclusive agent.

UNIVERSITY OF CHICAGO
Graduate School of Business

Bus. 305/Econ. 380

Mr. Peltzman
Fall 1988

FINAL EXAM

Answer all questions. Explain each answer. Points are in parentheses.
Maximum: 205 points.

I. (95) Describe each of the following "True," "False" or "Uncertain" and explain your choice.

1. (25) The vertical integration of successive monopolies can be expected to reduce the price of the "downstream" product.

2. (15) A buyer who has spent $50 in search costs to decrease the minimum price of a good by $49 has obviously searched too much and should stop searching. (Assume the buyer seeks 1 unit of the good.)

3. (15) A large seller of a frequently purchased experience good wishes to advertise on several TV programs. All else the same (e.g. the cost of an ad, the size of a program's audience), this advertiser will select programs which cater to different audiences. The reason is that, if the audiences overlap too much, some of the advertising expense will be wasted.

4. (20) Suppose that research and development (R&D) expenses are properly regarded as an investment which produces returns over a long time. However, suppose accountants treat R&D as a current expense--i.e., this year's R&D is deducted from this year's revenues in computing this year's profits. This accounting treatment of R&D will produce a positive correlation between the measured rate of return on assets and the ratio of R&D expenses to assets.

5. (20) One implication of the idea that increased concentration is associated with lower prices is that firms with the largest market share will tend to have the highest rates of return on assets.

II. (20) Here are some data on the share of an industry's output coming from firms of various sizes.

Firm Size Class (% of Industry by Sales)	Share of Industry Output in 1977	1987
0 to 5%	15%	10%
5 to 10%	20	23
10 to 20%	30	35
over 20%	<u>35</u>	<u>32</u>
	100	100

(The first entry under 1977 means that 15% of industry output came from firms whose individual market share did not exceed 5 per cent.)

Use the data and the "survivor technique" to draw a long run average cost curve for a firm in this industry. Explain the drawing.

135

III. (40) Ford Motor Co. produces agricultural equipment. "Ford has been accused of conspiring to shut down Tunis Brothers, a Ford distributor. Tunis charged that Ford's goal was to eliminate competition for another Ford distributor and thereby to boost prices for agricultural equipment.

"Ford said its actions were part of an economically reasonable plan to reorganize dealer locations.

"In a landmark 1986 decision, the U.S. Supreme Court held that the defendant (Ford) will win a case like this if the complaint does not make sense in terms of economic theory." (Quoted material is condensed from a recent story in the Wall Street Journal.)

Outline an argument, based on economic theory, that Ford might use to show that eliminating Tunis as a Ford dealer is "economically reasonable." Be explicit about what you mean by "economically reasonable," and include an nalysis of the effect of Ford's action on prices of agricultural equipment.

IV. (50) Major car rental companies (e.g., Hertz, Avis) offer the following terms "$X per day with Y free miles plus Z¢ per mile for any miles driven in excess of Y." For a typical car, these numbers might be X = $50, Y = 100, Z = 30¢. Assume the marginal cost per mile (m) exceeds zero but is less than Z.

A. (35) Describe the characteristics of car rental demand that would make this price offer more profitable than an alternative such as "$X' per day + m per mile."

B. (15) Recommend a pricing strategy for a potential entrant into the car rental business in light of your answer to A.

UNIVERSITY OF CHICAGO
Graduate School of Business

Bus. 306/Econ. 381 Mr. Peltzman
Economics of Regulation

Reading List and Course Outline

No required text. A packet of readings is available from the bookstore. These readings are preceded with (P) in the reading list. Other recommended readings are denoted (*), and are on reserve in the library.

The course uses economic theory to explain the behavior of regulatory agencies and regulated firms. The history, legislation and institutional organization of the various types of economic regulation are treated only briefly. Background material on these subjects may be found in Kahn, The Economics of Regulation, Phillips, The Economics of Regulation or Wilcox, Public Policies Toward Business. Somewhat more specialized treatments are:

   Garfield and Lovejoy, Public Utility Economics.
   Clemens, Economics and Public Utilities.
   Locklin, Economics of Transportation.
   Neale, The Antitrust Laws of the U.S.
   Gordon, Reforming the Regulation of Public Utilities
   Fisher, Resource & Environmental Economics

If you are unfamiliar with this background material, you should at least sample some of these books.

The following journal and publisher abbreviations are used:

   AER   --American Economic Review
   BJ or RJ --Bell Journal of Economics and Mgt. Science (now RAND Journal)
   ET   --Econometrica
   EA   --Economica
   JLE   --Journal of Law and Economics
   JPE   --Journal of Political Economy
   RES   --Review of Economics and Statistics
   QJE   --Quarterly Journal of Economics
   AEI   --American Enterprise Institute
   BR   --Brookings Institution
   PC   --Public Choice
   JRE   --Journal of Regulatory Economics

I. Introduction

   1. The Classic Case for Economic Regulation

      a. Natural Monopolies
         Troxel, Economics of Public Utilities.

         Lyon and Abramson, Government and Economic Life (chapter on "Public Utilities").

2. The Breakdown of the Classic Case

   (P) Stigler & Friedland, "What Can Regulators Regulate? The Case of Electricity," JLE, Oct. 62.

   * Moore, "The Effectiveness of Regulation of Electric Utility Prices," Southern Econ. Journal, 1970.

   (P) Hilton, "The Consistency of the Interstate Commerce Act," JLE, 1966.

   (Above articles are also cited in subsequent sections.)

   Gray, "The Passing of the Public Utility Concept," in American Economic Association, Readings in the Social Control of Industry.

3. Towards a New Theory of Regulation

   a. Consumer vs. Producer Protection

   (P) Stigler "The Economics of Regulation," BJ, Spring 71.

   (P) Posner, "Taxation by Regulation," BJ, Sp. 71.

   Posner, "Theories of Economic Regulation," BJ, Aut. 74.

   (P) Peltzman, "Pricing in Public and Private Enterprise," JLE, Apr. 71.

   (P) _____, "Towards a More General Theory of Regulation," JLE, Aug. 76.

   (P) Hilton, "The Basic Behavior of Regulatory Commissions," AER, May 72.

   (P) Jordan, "Producer Protection, . . ." JLE, Apr. 72.

   Owen & Braetigum, The Regulatory Game.

   Niskanen, "Bureaucrats and Politicians," JLE, Dec. 75.

   Goldberg, "Regulation and Administered Contracts," BJ, Aut. 76.

   Migué, "Controls v. Subsidies," JLE, Apr. 1977.

   Lee, "A Theory of Just Regulation," AER, Dec. 80.

   * Noll & Joskow, "Regulation in Theory and Practice," in Fromm (ed.) Studies in Public Regulation. (A review of the literature.)

   Noll & Owen, The Political Economy of Deregulation, AEI, 1983.

   * Becker, "A Theory of Competition Among Pressure Groups," QJE, August 1983.

Keeler, "Theories of Regulation and the Deregulation Movement," PC, 1984 (v. 44, n. 1).

Joskow and Rose, "The Effects of Economic Regulation," in Schmalensee and Willig (eds.), The Handbook of Industrial Organization, v. 2.

* Peltzman, "The Economic Theory of Regulation after a Decade of Deregulation," Brookings Papers on Economic Activity, 1989.

II. **Public Utility Regulation: Electricity, Gas, Telecommunication, Broadcasting**

1. The Natural Monopoly Rationale for Regulation (see readings in I. 1)

    a. Evidence on Economies of Scale

    Boiteaux, "Electric Energy: Facts, Problems and Prospects," in J. R. Nelson (ed.) Marginal Cost Pricing in Practice.

    * Nerlove, "Returns to Scale in Electricity Supply," in C. Christ et al., Measurement in Economics.

    Dhrymes & Kurz, "Technology and Scale in Electricity Generation," ET, 1964.

    Sudit, "Additive Non-homogeneous Production Function in Telecommunications," BJ, Aut. 73.

    * Christensen and Greene, "Economies of Scale in the U.S. Power Industry, JPE, July 76.

2. The Welfare Economics of Rate Regulation--what is the "correct" regulated price?

    a. Marginal or Average Cost Pricing

    * Hotelling, "The General Welfare in Relation to Problems of Taxation and Railway and Utility Rates," ET, July 38.

    Coase, "The Marginal Cost Controversy," EA 1946.

    Coase, "The Theory of Public Utility Pricing and Its Application," BJ, Sp. 70.

    Ruggles, "Recent Developments in the Theory of Marginal Cost Pricing," Review of Econ. Studies, 1949-50.

    b. Multipart Pricing and Price Discrimination

    Bonbright, Principles of Public Utility Rates.

    Phillips, Economics of Regulation, ch. 8-11.

Taylor, "The Demand for Electricity," BJ, Sp. 75.

* Panzar and Willig, "Free Entry and the Sustainability of Natural Monopoly," BJ, Sp. 77.

* Baumol and Bradford, "Optimal Departures from Marginal Cost Pricing," AER, June 70.

Braeutigum, "Optimal Policies for Natural Monopolies," in Schmalensee and Willig (eds.) The Handbook of Industrial Organization, v. 2.

c. Peak Load Pricing

Steiner, "Peak Loads and Efficient Pricing," QJE, Nov. 57.

Hirshleifer, "Peak Loads and Efficient Pricing: Comment," QJE, Aug. 58.

Boiteux, "Peak Load Pricing," Journal of Business,, Apr. 60.

Wenders and Taylor, "Experiments in Seasonal-Time-of-Day Pricing of Electricity," BJ. Aut. 76.

Wenders, "Peak Load Pricing", BJ, Sp. 76.

Mitchell, Manning, Acton, Peak Load Pricing.

Acton and Mitchell, "Evaluating Time-of-Day Electric Rates" in Mitchell and Kleindorfer, Regulated Industries and Public Enterprise.

3. The Effects of Regulation and Public Ownership

   a. On Rates

   (P) Stigler and Friedland, "What Can Regulators Regulate?"

   * Moore, "The Effectiveness of Regulation of Electric Utility Prices."

   * Jarrell, "The Demand for State Regulation of Electricity," JLE, Oct. 1978.

   Moore, C. G., "Has Electricity Regulation Resulted in Higher Prices?" Economic Inquiry, June 75.

   Mann, "User Power and Electricity Rates," JLE, Oct. 74.

   (P) Peltzman, "Pricing in Public and Private Enterprise."

   DeAlessi, "An Economic Analysis of Government Ownership," PC, Fall, 74.

Joskow, "Inflation and Environmental Concern: Structural Change in Public Utility Regulation," JLE, Oct. 74.

Fournier and Martin, "Does Government Restricted Entry Produce Market Power? The Market for TV Advertising," BJ, Sp. 83.

Zimmerman, "Regulatory Treatment of Abandoned Property," JLE, Apr. 88.

Mathios and Rogers, "The Impact of Alternative Forms of Regulation on AT&T Long Distance Rates," RJ, Autumn 89.

b. On the Allocation of Resources in Production

(P) Averch and Johnson, "The Behavior of the Firm under Regulatory Constraint," AER, Dec. 62.

Baumol and Klevorick, "Input Choices and Rate of Return Regulation," BJ, Aut. 70.

Spann, "Rate of Return Regulation and Efficiency in Production," BJ, Sp. 74.

Boyes, "An Empirical Examination of the Averch-Johnson Effect," Econ. Inquiry, 3/76.

* Courville, "Regulation and Efficiency in the Electric Utility Industry," BJ, Sp. 74.

Baron and Taggart, "A Model of Regulation under Uncertainty and a Test for Regulatory Bias," BJ, Sp. 77.

Petersen, "An Empirical Test of Regulatory Effects," BJ, Spring 75.

Meyer, R. A., "Publicly Owned v. Privately Owned Utilities," RES, Nov. 75.

Neuberg, L. G., "Two Issues in the Municipal Ownership of Electric Power," BJ, Sp. 77.

Boardman and Vining, "Ownership and Performance: Comparison of Private and State Owned Enterprise," JLE 4/89.

* Hendricks, "Regulation and Labor Earnings," BJ, Aut. 77.
Ehrenberg, The Regulatory Process and Labor Earnings.
Davies, "The Efficiency of Public v. Private Firms," JLE, Apr. 71.

Norton, "Regulation and Systematic Risk: The Case of Electric Utilities," JLE, Oct. 85.

4. Alternatives to Regulation

* Coase, The Federal Communications Commission.

(P) Demsetz, "Why Regulate Utilities?" JLE, 1968.

Williamson, "Franchise Bidding," BJ, Sp. 76.

Schmalensee, The Control of Natural Monopolies, ch. 5.

Schultz, "Conditions for Franchise Bidding in W. Germany", in Mitchell and Kleindorfer, "Regulated Industries and Public Enterprise.

Prager, "Franchise Bidding: The Case of Cable TV," JRE 6/89.

Baumol, Panzar & Willig, Contestable Markets.

Primeaux, "A Reexamination of the Monopoly Market Structure in Electric Utilities," in Phillips, ed., Promoting Competition in Regulated Industries, BR, 1975.

Primeaux, "Determinants of Regulatory Policy toward Competition in Electric Utilities," PC, 1984 (v. 43, n. 2).

Loeb and Magat, "A Decentralized Method for Utility Regulation," JLE, Oct. 1979.

Vogelsang and Finsinger, "A Regulatory Adjustment Process," BJ, Sp. 79.

Beesley and Littlechild, "The Regulation of Privatized Monopolies in the UK," RJ, Autumn 89.

Greenwald and Sharkey, "The Economics of Deregulation of Local Telecommunications," JRE 12/89.

5. Natural Gas and Petroleum

Breyer and MacAvoy, Energy Regulation by the Federal Power Commission.

MacAvoy, Price Formation in Natural Gas Fields.

MacAvoy, "The Regulation Induced Shortage of Natural Gas," JLE, Apr. 71.

_____ and Pindyck, Price Controls and the Natural Gas Shortage, AEI.

* Helms, Natural Gas Regulation, AEI.

Kitch, "Regulation of the Field Market for Natural Gas," JLE Oct. 68.

142

Erickson & Spann, "Supply Response in a Regulated Industry: The Case of Natural Gas," BJ, Sp. 71.

Mitchell, *Federal Energy Administration Regulation*, AEI.

Smith, Bradley and Jarrell, "Studying Firm-Specific Effects of Regulation: Oil Price Regulation," RJ Winter 1986.

III. Transportation Regulation
  A. Surface Freight
    1. The Origins of Regulation

    a. The Interstate Commerce Act.

    (P) Hilton, "The Consistency of the Interstate Commerce Act."
    * MacAvoy, *The Economic Effects of Regulation: The Trunkline Railroad Cartels* . . .

    * Kolko, *Railroads & Regulation*.

    Gilligan, Marshall, Weingast, "Regulation and the Theory of Legislative Choice: The Interstate Commerce Act of 1887," JLE 4/89.

    Prager, "Using Stock Price Data to Measure the Effects of Regulation: The Interstate Commerce Act," RJ, Summer 89.

    b. Are Railroads a Natural Monopoly?

    (P) Spann & Erickson, "The Economics of Railroading," BJ, Aut. 70.

    * Keeler, "Railroad Costs Returns to Scale and Excess Capacity," RES, May 74.

    Harris, "Economies of Traffic Density in Rail Freight," BJ, Aut. 77.

    2. The Effects of Regulation and Deregulation

    a. Railroads

    * Meyer, et al., *The Economics of Competition in Transport Industries*.

    * Friedlaender, *The Dilemma of Frieght Transport Regulation*.

    National Bureau of Economic Research, *Transportation Economics*, (see esp. articles by Nelson and Roberts).

    Garrod and Miklius, "Captive Shippers and the Success of Railroads in Capturing Monopoly Rent," JLE, Oct. 87.

Robinson & Tomes, Union Wage Differentials in the Public & Private Sector. Journal of Labor Economics, Jan. '84.

Friedlaender, "The Social Costs of Railroad Regulation," AER, May 71.

Winston, "Welfare Effects of ICC Regulation Revisited," BJ, SP 81.

(P) Boyer, "Minimum Rate Regulation and the Railroad Problem," JPE, June 1977.

Boyer, "Equalizing Discrimination in Transport Rate Regulation", JPE, Apr. 81.

Levin, "Allocation in Surface Freight Transportation," BJ, Spring 1978.

Levin, "Railroad Rates, Profitability and Welfare Under Deregulation," BJ, SP 81.

Levin, "Regulation Barriers to Exit and Investment Behavior in Railroads," in Fromm Studies in Public Regulation.

Dougan, "Railway Abandonments and the Theory of Regulation", PC, 1984 (v. 44, n. 1).

MacDonald, "Competition and Rail Rates for Corn, Soybeans and Wheat," RJ Sp. 87.

MacDonald, "Railroad Deregulation: Effects on Grain Transportation," JLE 4/89.

* McFarland, "The Effects of U.S. Railroad Deregulation..." JRE 9/89.

b. Trucking

(P) Sloss, "Regulation of Motor Freight Transportation," BJ, Aut. 70.

* Moore, Freight Transportation Regulation, AEI.

Moore, "Deregulating Surface Freight Transportation," in Phillips (ed.), Promoting Competition in Regulated Markets, BR.

_____, "The Beneficiaries of Trucking Regulation," JLE. Oct. 78.

Kim, "The Beneficiaries of Trucking Regulation Revisited." JLE April '84.

* Rose, "Labor Rent Sharing and Regulation: The Trucking Industry," JPE, Dec. 87.

Rose, "The Incidence of Regulatory Rents in the Motor Carrier Industry," RJ, Aut. 85.

Moore, Trucking Regulation, AEI.

Friedlaender and Spady, Freight Transport Regulation.

MacAvoy, Regulation of Entry and Pricing in Truck Transportation, AEI.

Breen, "The Monopoly Value of Household Goods Carrier Operating Certificates," JLE, Apr. 1977.

Frew, "The Existence of Monopoly Profits in the Motor Carrier Industry," JLE, Oct. 81.

Daughety, "Regulation and Industrial Organization," JPE,, Oct. 84.

Schipper, Thompson and Weil, "Disentangling Interrelated Effects of Regulatory Change: Motor Carrier Deregulation," JLE 4/87.

B. Airlines

Caves, Air Transport and Its Regulators.

Keyes, Federal Control of Entry into Air Transportation.

(P) Keeler, "Airline Regulation and Market Performance," BJ Aut. 72.

* Jordan, Airline Regulation in America.

* Douglas and Miller, Economic Regulation of Domestic Air Transport.

Douglas and Miller, The CAB's Domestic Passenger Fare Investigation, BJ Sp. '74.

Gronau, "Effect of Travel Time on the Demand for Transportation, JPE, Mar. '70.

De Vaney, "The Effect of Price and Entry Regulation on Airline Output and Efficiency," BJ, Sp. 75.

CAB Practices and Procedures, U.S. Senate Subcte. on Administrative Practice, Cte. on Judiciary, 1975.

Eads, "Competition in the Airline Industry," in Phillips, ed., Promoting Competition in Regulated Markets.

MacAvoy, *Regulation of Passenger Fares and Competition among Airlines*, AEI.

* Bailey, Graham and Kaplan, *Deregulating the Airlines*.

Graham and Sibley, "Efficiency and Competition in the Airline Industry," BJ, Sp. 83.

Spiller, "The Differential Impact of Airline Regulation on Individual Firms," JLE, 10/83.

Morrison and Winston, *The Economic Effects of Airline Deregulation*, BR.

Morrison and Winston, "Empirical Implications and Tests of Contestability," JLE 4/87.

Moore, "U.S. Airline Deregulation: Its Effects on Passengers, Capital and Labor," JLE, 4/86.

Bailey and Williams, "Sources of Economic Rent in the Deregulated Airline Industry," JLE, Apr. 88.

C. Miscellaneous

Kitch, "The Regulation of Taxicabs," JLE, Oct. 71.

Eckert, "The Los Angeles Taxi Monopoly," *Southern Cal. Law Review*, 1970.

_____, and Hilton, "The Jitneys," JLE, Oct. 72.

Pashigian, "Consequences and Causes of Public Ownership of Urban Transport," JPE, Dec. 76.

Keeler and Small, "Optimal Peak Load Pricing on Urban Expressways," JPE, Feb. 77.

Smith, "Franchise Regulation: An Economic Analysis of State Restrictions on Automobile Distribution", JLE Apr. 82.

IV. Environmental Protection

A. Externalities and the Rationale for Regulation

Pigou, *The Economics of Welfare*, Pt. II, Ch. 9.

Turvey, "On Divergence between Social and Private Cost," EA 1963.

(P) Coase, "The Problem of Social Cost," JLE, 1960.

Demsetz, "When Does the Rule of Liability Matter?" J. of Legal Studies, 1972.

Baumol and Oates, The Theory of Environmental Policy, pt. I.

Lave and Seskin, "Acute Relationships Among Daily Mortality, Air Pollution and Climate," in Mills, ed., Economic Analysis of Environmental Problems.

Fischer, Resources and Environmental Economics, Ch. 6.

B. Implementation of Regulation

* Dales, Pollution, Property, and Prices.

* Kneese and Bower, Managing Water Quality: Economics and Technology.

(P) Kneese, "Environmental Pollution Economics and Policy," AER, May 71.

Ridker, Economic Costs of Air Pollution: Studies in Measurement.

Ridker and Hemming, "The Determinants of Residential Property Values," RES, May 71.

Baumol and Oates, Theory of Environmental Policy, pt. II.

Oates and Baumol, "Instruments for Environmental Policy," in Mills, Economic Analysis of Environmental Problems.

Harrison, Who Pays for Clean Air?

Siegan, "Non-zoning in Houston," JLE, Apr. 70.

Rueter, "Externalities in Urban Property Markets," JLE, Oct. 73.

Peskin, Portney, Kneese, Environmental Regulation and the U.S. Economy (discusses current policy issues).

Maloney and McCormick, "A Positive Theory of Environmental Quality Regulation," JLE, Apr. 82.

Maloney and Brady, "Capital Turnover and Marketable Pollution Rights," JLE, 4/88.

Leone and Jackson, "The Political Economy of Federal Regulatory Activity: Water Pollution," in Fromm, editor, Studies in Public Regulation.

Graves and Krumm, Health and Air Quality, AEI.

White, Regulation of Air Pollution from Motor Vehicles, AEI.

Pashigian, "Effect of Environmental Regulation on Optimal Plant Size," JLE, April '84.

> *   _____, "Environmental Protection: Whose Self Interests are being Protected?" Econ. Inquiry, 10/85.

V. Consumer Protection: Safety and Fraud

> Nelson, "Advertising as Information," JPE, July-Aug. 74.
>
> *   Klein and Leffler, "The Role of Market Forces in Assuring Contractual Performance", JPE, Aug. 81.
>
> Schmalensee, "Advertising and Product Quality", JPE, Jun. 78.
>
> (P) Akerlof, "The Market for Lemons," Quarterly J. of Econ., Aug. 70.
>
> (P) Darby and Karni, "Free Competition and the Optimal Amount of Fraud," JLE, Apr. 73.
>
> Grossman, "The Informational Role of Warranties and Private Disclosure about Product Quality", JLE, Dec. 81.
>
> Oi, "The Economics of Product Safety," BJ, Sp. 73.
>
> Epple and Raviv, "Product Safety . . .," AER, Mar. 1978.
>
> Leland, "Quacks, Lemons and Licensing," JPE, Dec. 79.

a. Effects of Regulation in Specific Industries

1. Finance and Securities

> (P) Stigler, "Public Regulation of the Securities Markets," J. of Business, Apr. 64.
>
> (See also articles by Friend and Herman, Robbins and Werner, and reply by Stigler in J. of Bus., Oct. 64.)
>
> (P) Benston, "Required Disclosure and the Stock Market," AER, Mar. 1973.
>
> (P) Jarrell, "The Economic Effects of Federal Regulation of the Market for New Security Issues", JLE, Dec. 81.
>
> *   Simon, "The Effect of the 1933 Securities Act," AER 6/89.
>
> Schwert, "Public Regulation of National Securities Exchanges: A Test of the Capture Hypothesis," BJ, Sp. 77.
>
> Horwitz and Kolodny, "Line of Business Reporting," BJ, Aut. 1977.
>
> Tinic and West, "The Securities Industry Under Negotiated Rates." BJ, Sp. 80.
>
> Jarrell, "Change at the Exchange: The Causes and Effects of Deregulation," JLE, Oct. '84.

Stoll *Regulation of Security Markets*.

Crafton, "The Effects of Usury Laws," JLE, Apr. 80.

Barth, "Benefits and Costs of Legal Restrictions in Personal Loan Markets," JLE, 10/86.

Haddock and Macey, "Regulation on Demand: A Private Interest Model with an Application to Insider Trading Regulation," JLE, Oct. 87.

Ippolito, R., "The Regulatory Effect of ERISA," JLE, 4/88.

2. Advertising

   Peltzman, "The Effect of FTC Advertising Regulation", JLE, Dec. 81.

   Benham, "The Effect of Advertising on the Price of Eyeglasses," JLE, Oct. 72.

   Bond, "A Direct Test of the Lemons Model: Used Pickup Trucks," AER, Sept. 82.

3. Health Care and Pharmaceuticals

   * Kessel, "Price Discrimination in Medicine", JLE, Oct. 58.

   Benham and Benham, "Regulating Through the Professions," JLE, Oct. 75.

   Haas-Wilson, "The Effect of Commercial Practice Restrictions: The Case of Optometry," JLE, 4/86.

   Baily, M. N., "R and D Costs and Returns: The U.S. Pharmaceutical Industry," JPE, Jan. 72.

   (P) Peltzman, "An Evaluation of Consumer Protection Legislation: The 1962 Drug Amendments," JPE, Sept. - Oct. 73.

   Peltzman, "The Health Effects of Mandatory Prescriptions," JLE, 10/87.

   Grabowski, *Drug Regulation and Innovation*, AEI.

   Grabowski and Vernon, The Regulation of Pharmaceuticals, AEI.

   * Leffler, "Physician Licensure," JLE, Apr. 78.

   Noether, "The Effect of Policy Changes on the Supply of Physicians," JLE, 10/86.

Shepard, "Licensing Restrictions and the Cost of Dental Care," JLE, Apr. 78.

DeVany, Gramm et al. "The Impact of Input Regulation: the U.S. Dental Industry," JLE, Oct. 82.

Sloan and Steinwald, "Effects of Regulation on Hospital Costs," JLE, Apr. 80.

Cone and Dranove, "Why did States Enact Hospital Rate-setting Laws?" JLE 10/86.

4. Product and Workplace Safety

Peltzman, "The Effects of Automobile Safety Regulation," JPE, Aug. 75.

Arnould and Grabowski, "Auto Safety Regulation," BJ, Sp. 81.

Gaston and Caroll, "Occupational Restrictions and Quality of Service Received," Southern Economic Journal, Apr. 1, 1981.

Viscusi, "The Impact of OSHA," BJ, Sp. 79.

* Viscusi, "The Impact of OSHA Regulation, 1973-83" RJ Winter 1986.

Viscusi, "Consumer Behavior and the Safety Effects of Regulation," JLE, Oct. 85.

Schneider, Klein, Murphy, "Governmental Regulation of Cigarette Health Information", JLE, Dec. 81.

Jarrell & Peltzman, "The Impact of Product Recalls on the Wealth of Sellers", JPE, June 85.

Borenstein and Zimmerman, "Market Incentives for Safe Commercial Airline Operation," AER 12/88.

Neumann and Nelson, "Safety Regulation and Firm Size: Effects of the Coal Mine Health and Safety Act of 1969," JLE, Oct. 82.

* Staten and Umbeck, "Information Costs and Incentives to Shirk: The Air Traffic Controllers," AER, 12/82.

Crandall and Lave, The Scientific Basis of Health and Safety Regulation, BR, '81 (case studies of Air Bags, Saccharin, cotton dust, etc.).

Viscusi, "The Lulling Effect of Safety Regulation," AER May '84.

Thomas, "Revealed Bureaucratic Preference: Priorities of the CPSC," RJ, Sp. 88.

Bartel and Thomas, "Predation through Regulation: The Wage and Profit Effects of OSHA and EPA," JLE, 10/87.

5. Food and Beverage

Kwoka, "Pricing under Federal Milk Market Regulation," Economic Inquiry, July 1977.

Federal Milk Marketing Orders, AEI.

Ippolito and Masson, "Social Cost of Milk Regulation," JLE, Apr. 78.

Smith, "An Analysis of State Regulation of Liquor Store Licensing," JLE, Oct. 82.

Ulrich, Furtan and Schmitz "The Cost of a Licensing System: An Example from Canadian Prairie Agriculture," JPE 2/87.

* Gardner, "Causes of U.S. Farm Commodity Programs," JPE 4/87.

6. Insurance

Munch and Smallwood, "Solvency Regulation in Insurance," BJ, Sp. 80.

Ippolito, "Price Regulation in Auto Insurance," JLE, Apr. 80.

VI. International Trade

Bhagwati and Srinivasan, "Revenue Seeking: A Generalization of the Theory of Tariffs," JPE, 12/80.

Brock and Magee, "The Economics of Special Interest Politics: Tariffs," AER, 5/78.

Pincus, "Pressure Groups and Tariffs," JPE, 8/75.

Hillman, "Declining Industries and Political Support Protectionism," AER, 12/82.

Godek, "Industry Structure and Redistribution through Trade Restrictions," JLE, 10/85.

Marvel and Ray, "The Kennedy Round: Evidence on the Regulation of International Trade," AER, 3/83.

Marvel and Ray, "Intraindustry Trade: Sources and Effects on Protection," JPE, 12/87, 1278-1291.

Exam and Term Paper

Your grade will be based on a final exam and term paper. The paper will account for 35 percent of the grade. It is recommended that the paper be a replication and/or extension of past studies of the causes or effects of regulation, such as those on the reading list. However, any paper topic relevant to the subject matter of the course is acceptable. The paper should contain results of empirical work you have conducted. Please discuss the paper with me before you begin working on it. Each student will have available a limited amount of time on the university's computer and the GSB's computer. (Use of this time may be arranged in W309.)

The final exam will be given on Wednesday, March 14 from 2 p.m. to 4 p.m. There will be no make-up or other nonscheduled exam for any student for any reason. If you do not take the final exam, or hand in your paper before the end of the quarter, you may petition for a grade of "I", which can be removed by taking the exam the next time the course is offered or when you complete the paper.

You will, however, be charged interest for late papers: all papers are graded on a scale $A = 4$, $B = 3$, etc. If you submit your paper late, your numerical grade will be divided by $\left(1 + .015\sqrt{t}\right)$ where t = number of days from the end of the quarter to the day you submit your paper.

The prerequisites for the course are Bus. 300 and Bus. 370 (or Econ. 300) or equivalent. However, knowledge of basic statistics, including interpretation of multiple regression analyses, will be helpful.

Name_____

UNIVERSITY OF CHICAGO
Graduate School of Business

B306/Econ. 381   Mr. Peltzman
                                                      Winter 1990

FINAL EXAM

Answer all questions in the space provided. Do not use blue books. Explain each answer. Points are in parentheses. Maximum: 200 points.

(40) I. There are two types of customers for natural gas, Residential and Industrial, with the following demands

$P_x = 30 - X$, X = Industrial gas consumption
$P_y = 24 - Y$, Y = Residential gas consumption

A single gas pipeline can serve both customer groups. Or separate, somewhat smaller lines can be built for each type. Assume that the only costs involved in serving customers is the fixed cost of building the pipeline. These costs are as follows:

1. $328 for a single pipeline to serve both groups

2. $180 for a separate line to serve either the industrial or residential markets.

Here are some useful additional facts.

1. The maximum total expenditures by residential customers is $144 (at $P_y = 12$); the maximum expenditure by industrial customers is $225 (at $P_x = 15$).

2. The "Ramsey prices" are $P_x = 10$, $P_y = 8$

(10)   A. Give a very brief definition, in plain English, of Ramsey prices.

(15)   B. Are Ramsey prices sustainable against the threat of entry? Explain.

(15)   C. Use the facts to make an argument for restricting entry into natural gas distribution.

153

(40) II. An economist has estimated that efficient peak-load electricity prices for Baltimore Gas and Electric Co. would be as follows.

Actual prices are in [ ]

Customer Class	Prices /KWH Peak	Off Peak
Residential	27¢ [8¢]	4¢ [8¢]
Industrial	16 [6]	4¢ [6]

(20) a. Explain briefly how the peak load prices would be more efficient than the actual prices.

(20) b. Explain why a regulatory agency might rationally resist adopting a peak load structure like the one listed above.

(40) III. Discuss the plausible effects of deregulation of the airline industry on each of the following.

(10) a. The average load factor.

(15) b. The difference between load factors on long distance v. short distance flights.

(15) c. The average time required for a round trip, as measured by the total hours elapsed between leaving and returning home.

6 Name _____

(20) IV. A proposal to re-regulate railroad rates has been introduced in the U.S. Congress. The major support for this proposal comes from shippers of coal over long hauls. Explain why long haul coal shippers might favor regulation of railroad rates.

(30) V. In the diagram at right, the curve labeled (1) is the marginal benefit of air pollution to a factory. (2) shows the marginal damage of pollution to nearby homeowners. Assume there are well defined rights to clean air and that there are no transaction costs. Use the letters (which define areas) in the diagram to describe as precisely as you can the Coasian bargain that would be made if:

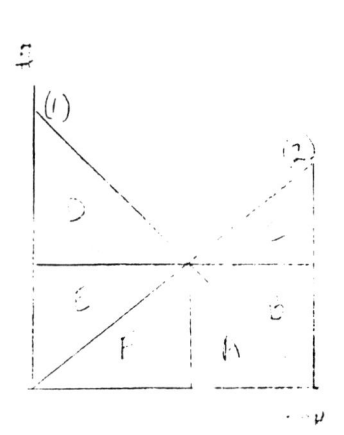

(15) A. The factory owned all rights to use of clean air.

(15) B. The homeowners owned all rights to clean air.

(30) VI. Explain why consumers who are uncertain about product quality buy "too many" low quality goods. Then discuss how a government enforced minimum quality standard would affect consumer welfare.

Name _____

UNIVERSITY OF CHICAGO
Graduate School of Business

Bus. 306/Econ. 381   Sam Peltzman
                                                      Winter, 1989

FINAL EXAM

Answer all questions in the space provided. Do not use blue books. Print your name on each page. Explain each answer, except where otherwise indicated. Points are in parentheses.

I. Describe each of the following "True", "False" or "Uncertain" and explain your choice briefly.

(15) 1. All else the same, an unexpected increase in demand leads to a smaller price increase in a regulated industry than in an unregulated industry.

(15) 2. Unless there are precisely defined and cheaply enforced rights to "clean air," private bargaining will not lead to the efficient amount of clean air.

(10) 3. Producer groups are more likely to bribe politicians than consumer groups.

(15) 4. The reorganization of the airline industry into "hub-and-spoke" networks (i.e. flights or originate or terminate at a central city--the hub--where passengers may take connecting flights to outlying cities) is a consequence of deregulation.

(10) 5. All else the same, the per-capita amount of services provided by doctors and auto mechanics should be greater in areas with high population turnover than in areas with stable populations.

II. Explain briefly how reduced regulation of the railroad industry could be expected to affect each of the following

(10) (a) (P_i/P_j) where P = a freight rate
                            i = a manufactured good (e.g. cars)
                            j = a bulk commodity (e.g. coal)

(10) (c) Ton Miles carried/Miles of Track

(10) (b) The average distance carried per ton of freight

Name _____

III. (± 45) XYZ Edison Co. produces electricity with inputs of K and L. XYZ is subject to a maximum rate-of-return on K = s and faces prices of w and r for L and K respectively. Assume

1) s always > r
2) s is always bending
3) The amount of L is fixed

For each event listed below fill in the table with the symbol which best describes the prediction implied by the Averch-Johnson model. Use these symbols

+ = the variable will increase
- = the variable will decrease
0 = the variable will not change, or there is no clear prediction about the direction of change.

Do NOT explain your choices. Each correct entry is worth 5 points; each incorrect entry is worth -5; no entry = 0.

EVENT:	AMOUNT of K	MARGINAL PRODUCT of K	XYZ'S PROFITS
a) s is reduced			
b) r increases			
c) w increases			

Name _____

IV. (25) Up to 1975, commission rates for transactions on the New York Stock Exchange were regulated by a government agency. The regulation was abolished in 1975. A recent study of the effects of deregulation concludes that since 1975 rates per share have increased for small transactions while rates on large transactions have declined.

Use this post-deregulation history and a theory of politically optimal regulation to fill-in the diagram at right: Show what the cost function probably looks like and explain its connection to the different rate patterns emerging under regulation and deregulation. You may assume that stock brokerage is structurally competitive.

COST PER SHARE

NUMBER OF SHARES TRADED

158

V. (50) ABC Co. has two machines which generate pollution, an old one and and a new one. Each would generate 60 units of pollution if the pollution is uncontrolled. The machines have the following pollution control cost functions

$C_{OLD} = X^2$

$C_{NEW} = \frac{1}{2} X^2$, where

C = total cost of pollution control

X = units of pollution controlled.

(The <u>marginal</u> control cost functions are shown in the diagram.)

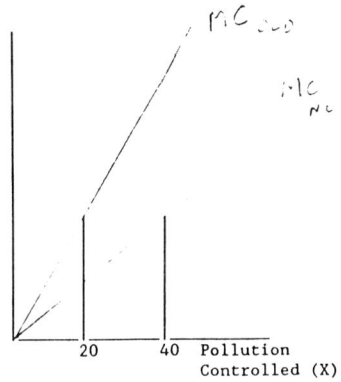

Assume that the Environmental Protection Agency (EPA) requires: X = 20 for the old machine, and X = 40 for the new machine. Both machines are profitable given these requirements.

Now EPA proposes a new rule that puts a <u>total</u> control requirement of X = 60 on ABC which can be met in any way the firm chooses (e.g., ABC could meet the new requirement by shutting down one of the machines).

Describe as precisely as you can the firm's optimal response to the new rule.

UNIVERSITY OF CHICAGO
Graduate School of Business

B306/Econ. 381

Mr. Peltzman
Winter, 1987

FINAL

Answer all questions. Explain all answers. Points are in parentheses.
Maximum: 140 points.

(75) I. Describe each of the following "True", "False" or "Uncertain" and explain your choice.

(10) 1. A law requiring sellers to provide "free" information about product quality will improve consumer welfare.

(10) 2. For natural monopolies, marginal-cost-pricing-plus-subsidies is more efficient than average-cost pricing.

(10) 3. If two groups are both politically successful, the smaller group is likely to have higher per-capita campaign contributions.

(15) 4. A regulated industry's profit function is $\pi = f(p)$, and p^*, π^* is the current regulatory equilibrium. Then a technological change changes $f(p)$ to $g(p)$. The new profit function has these properties:

$g(p^*) = \pi^*$ -- i.e. p^* still $\rightarrow \pi^*$

$g'(p) > f'(p)$ -- a \$1 increase in p generates more π than before.

The technological change implies a new regulatory equilibrium with higher prices and higher profits.

(15) 5. If the price of fuel increases, electric utilities regulated according to a fair rate-of-return standard will tend to use less fuel intensive technologies.

(15) 6. A predictable effect of airline deregulation has been an increase in the proportion of passengers who place relatively low values on flight frequency and ready availability of a seat at a specific time.

(15) II. Since minimum price regulation of railroads was weakened in 1980, there has been considerable growth of "piggyback" rail traffic, in which a loaded container is shipped by rail between two cities and trucks perform the local pickup and delivery of the container. Explain the connection between the change in regulation and the growth of "piggyback" traffic.

(20) III. Assume that marginal and average costs of pollution control are greater for existing plants than for new plants. As the politically appointed head of the EPA you can impose any required level of control on any plant, but you cannot impose pollution taxes or allow plants to trade pollution "rights". Also, you cannot change the air/water quality, standards to be achieved by pollution control. Outline your regulatory strategy and provide a brief rationale for it.

(30) IV. You value a "good" used car at $1000 and a "bad" used car at $500. A specific car is offered to you at $600, and you believe that it is equally likely to be good or bad.

    (10) 1. What is the most you would pay for a test that can determine whether the car is good or bad?

    (20) 2. Suppose there is a horizontal long run supply of good used cars at a price of $600 and a horizontal long run supply of bad used cars at a price of $500. Also assume that the cost of the test described above exceeds what you (or any other used car buyer) is willing to pay. Outline briefly an argument that the government should nevertheless require such a test to be performed.

UNIVERSITY OF CHICAGO
Graduate School of Business

Business 306/Econ. 381   Mr Peltzman
                                                                Winter, 1986

FINAL EXAM

Answer all questions. Explain each answer. Points are in parentheses.
Maximum: 200 points.

(60) I. Explain briefly each of the following concepts, and describe the
          regulatory context to which the concept applies.

          1. Ramsey pricing
          2. Sustainability of natural monopoly against entry
          3. Value of service pricing
          4. Asymmetric information
          5. Contestable markets

(30) II. You are the head of an agency which regulates prices of the X
          industry. By law, each X producer is a local monopoly.
          Production of X uses inputs A and B. A is supplied by a
          monopoly; B is supplied by a constant cost competitive industry.
          Suppliers of both A and B are organized politically, but you
          have no authority to regulate prices of those inputs directly. You
          must select one of the following rules to apply to rate
          applications from X producers:

          1. Target revenues of X producers shall be a target multiple of
             their expenditures on A.

          2. Target revenues of X producers shall be a target multiple of
             their expenditures on B.

          Which rule is most consistent with your political survival? Why?

(49) III. There are two politically-relevant groups in a city: Residents and
          Automobile drivers. Automobiles emit pollutants which cause harm
          to Residents. Both groups are organized politically, but it is
          prohibitively costly for them to deal with each other outside the
          political arena. There are currently no restrictions on automobile
          pollution, and the marginal damage from pollution exceeds the
          marginal benefit.

          (20) 1. Explain why this marginal condition is insufficient to
                  imply that an efficient long-run response to auto
                  pollution requires some restriction of pollution.

          (20) 2. Suppose that some restriction of pollution is efficient
                  and that the city is considering the following.

(a) a constant per unit tax on auto pollutants.

(b) a transferable right to emit a limited amount of pollutants to be given to each auto owner.

Discuss the potential advantages and disadvantages of each pollution control mechanism.

(30) IV. In many airline markets there is currently a large spread of prices: typically there is a "standard" fare with no restrictions and a variety of "discount" fares with restrictions on e.g. how far in advance payment must be made, which days of the week the trip can be made, etc. The spread of prices today is wider than the spread of prices under regulation.

Based on your knowledge of both the economics and regulation of air transportation, defend the proposition that the <u>long-run equilibrium</u> response to deregulation implies a wider spread of fares in the same market. Describe the types of fare restrictions which would be consistent with your argument and the types that would be inconsistent with it.

V. Before 1975 minimum stock brokerage commissions on the New York Stock Exchange were set by negotiation between a cartel of exchange members and a regulatory agency (the SEC). Then, and now, the general pattern of brokerage commission rates could be summarized in the following formula

$$C = A + B \cdot N, \text{ where}$$

C = commission, in dollars, for a particular transaction
N = number of shares involved in the transaction
A, B = constants

In 1975, rates were deregulated, and subsequently most brokerage firms raised A and decreased B.

What inferences can you draw from this history about (a) the technology of the brokerage industry, (b) the response of the SEC to that technology before 1975, and (c) changes in the extent of non-price competition following deregulation.

Massachusetts Institute of Technology
Alfred P. Sloan School of Management
50 Memorial Drive
Cambridge, Massachusetts 02139

Robert S. Pindyck
Mitsubishi Bank Professor
of Applied Economics

Professor Robert S. Pindyck
E52-454 (x6641)

15.013 -- INDUSTRIAL ECONOMICS FOR STRATEGIC DECISIONS

FALL 1989

This subject is designed to provide a working knowledge of the analytical tools of industrial economics that bear most directly on the strategic decisions that firms must make. The kinds of decisions that will be of interest to us include pricing, investment in new production capacity, output, advertising, the introduction of new products, brands, and quality variations, and investments in R&D. Our emphasis will be on the way firms interact strategically. Industrial structure, strategic interactions among rival sellers, and strategies for deterring entry will be covered with a game-theoretic orientation and with the use of case material.

Students taking this course should have a good background in microeconomics (specifically, course 15.011 or its equivalent), and also some background in corporate finance, especially capital budgeting.

The following books will be used in the course, and can be purchased at The Coop:

W. Adams, editor - The Structure of American Industry, 7th edition, New York: Macmillan, 1986; referred to as Adams below.

M. E. Porter - Competitive Strategy, New York: Free Press, 1982; referred to as Porter below.

In addition, a Xeroxed set of readings and HBS cases should be purchased from Graphic Arts, which is in the basement of the Sloan Building.

Grading in this course will be based on a Midterm Exam and a Final Exam (both in-class, and together counting for about half of the grade), two memoranda, each limited to no more than five pages in length (and together counting for about a quarter of the grade), and your performance in a semester-long strategic oligopoly game (also counting for about a quarter of the grade). Finally, class participation will also be taken into account when assigning grades.

15.013 Fall '89

The memoranda will involve the analysis of a particular industry from the point of view of an established firm, a potential entrant, or some other interested party. The first memorandum will analyze the structure and behavior of the industry, and the second will address strategic prospects, opportunities, and problems. (It is important to begin thinking soon about a topic for the memoranda, and it may be helpful to read Appendix B in *Porter* while doing so.)

Dates to Remember

Mon., September 25 -	Trial play of strategic oligopoly game.
Mon., October 2 -	First real play of strategic game. For the rest of the semester, game will be played every Monday.
	ALSO:
	Hand in 1-page note on industry and viewpoint.
Mon., October 9 -	Holiday, NO CLASS
Mon., October 23 -	Turn in Memo #1 (on structure and conduct).
Mon., October 30 -	Mid-Term Exam
Mon., December 4 -	Turn in Memo #2 (on prospects and problems).
Mon., December 11 -	Final Exam
Wed., December 13 -	Debriefing, and results of strategy game.

15.013 Fall '89   Course Outline: Page 3

15.013 - INDUSTRIAL ECONOMICS FOR STRATEGIC DECISIONS
TENTATIVE OUTLINE AND READING LIST

1. INTRODUCTION: SOURCES AND USES OF MARKET POWER
   (About 2 classes.)

   Introduction to the course. Nature and sources of market power. The interaction of firms as a source of and limit to market power. Use of market power to capture consumer surplus. How intertemporal production constraints affect pricing and market power - the learning curve.

   R. Pindyck, "The Measurement of Monopoly Power in Dynamic Markets," Journal of Law and Economics, April 1985. (Read pp. 193-202, 207-213.) [CN #1]

   "DuPont in Titanium Dioxide" [HBS #9-385-140]

2. THE STRUCTURAL ANALYSIS OF INDUSTRY   (About 4 or 5 classes.)

   An analysis of the key dimensions of market structure that both create and limit opportunities for market power, and that affect rivalry among firms and profit levels. Scale economies, learning effects, and network externalities. The importance of "being first." The role of information in determining market structure. How can these dimensions be measured, what conditions determine their existence and importance, and what are their implications for strategy?

   A. Elements of Market Structure

      Porter, Chapters 1, 2, & 7.

      "Rockwell International." [HBS #9-383-019]

      "The Oil Tanker Shipping Industry in 1983." [HBS #9-384-034]

      "The U.S. Bicycle Industry in 1974." [HBS #9-382-030]

      Elzinga, "The Beer Industry," Chapter 6 in Adams.

   B. Information, Product Quality, and Market Structure

      G. Akerlof, "The Market for 'Lemons': Quality Uncertainty and the Market Mechanism," Quarterly Journal of Economics, August 1970. [CN #2]

      M. Spence, Market Signalling, Chapters 2 & 3. [CN #3]

      R. Schmalensee, "Product Differentiation Advantages of Pioneering Brands," American Economic Review, 1982. [CN #4]

15.013 Fall '89   Course Outline: Page 4

3. **ANALYSIS OF STRATEGIC BEHAVIOR -- GAME THEORY AND MARKET MODELS** (About 4 classes.)

    Introduction to simple game theoretic models of oligopolistic behavior, and development of tools and insights useful for strategic analysis. The meaning of "rational" behavior when the actions of others affect your payoffs. Conditions that can facilitate or limit oligopolistic coordination. Explicit versus implicit bargaining, and the meaning of "bargaining power." The use of promises, binding commitments, threats, and retaliations. The role of reputation and the importance of credibility. Decision making with asymmetric information, and the role of uncertainty.

    A. Game Theoretic Models of Oligopolistic Pricing and Output

        Review Chapters 12 and 13 of R. Pindyck and D. Rubinfeld, Microeconomics.

        R. Axelrod, "The Emergence of Cooperation among Egoists," American Political Science Review, 75, 306-318. [CN #5]

        A. Dixit, "Recent Developments in Oligopoly Theory," American Economic Review, May 1982. [CN #6]

    B. Conditions Affecting Oligopolistic Coordination

        F. M. Scherer, Industrial Market Structure and Economic Performance, Chapters 6 & 7. [CN #7]

        Airline Pricing Series (to be handed out in class).

        "General Electric vs. Westinghouse in Large Turbine Generators" [HBS 9-380-128].

4. **STRATEGIC INTERACTIONS AMONG RIVAL SELLERS** (About 3 or 4 classes.)

    How strategic behavior, together with elements of industry structure, combine to determine prices, output levels, and profits. The organization and behavior of cartels. Dominant firms. Signalling. The ways in which firms can compete along price and non-price lines.

    A. Cartels In Action

        R. Pindyck, "Cartel Pricing and the Structure of the World Bauxite Market," Bell Journal of Economics, Autumn 1977. [CN #8]

        J. V. Koch, "The Intercollegiate Athletics Industry," Chapter 10 in Adams.

15.013 Fall '89   Course Outline: Page 5

- B. <u>Dominant Firms and Collusive Practices</u>

    W. Adams & H. Mueller, "The Steel Industry," Chapter 3 in <u>Adams</u>.

- C. <u>Signals and Moves</u>

    <u>Porter</u>, Chapters 4 & 5.

    "Polaroid-Kodak" and "Polaroid-Kodak Addendum."
    [HBS #9-376-266, 9-378-165]

- D. <u>Non-Price Rivalry</u>

    W. Adams and J. Brock, "The Automobile Industry," Chapter 4 in <u>Adams</u>.

    S. C. Salop and D. T. Scheffman, "Raising Rivals' Costs," <u>American Economic Review</u>, May 1983. [CN #9]

5. STRATEGIC BEHAVIOR THAT AFFECTS STRUCTURE   (About 4 classes.)

The ways in which the strategic behavior of firms can affect the structure of an industry. Methods of discouraging potential entrants. Methods of inducing existing competitors to exit. Pricing, capacity expansion, and brand proliferation. The strategic implications of decisions involving buyers and suppliers. The costs and benefits of vertical integration.

- A. <u>Deterrence via Pricing, Predation, and Capacity Expansion</u>

    <u>Porter</u>, Chapters 15 & 16.

    - B. Yamey, "Predatory Price Cutting: Notes and Comments," <u>Journal of Law and Economics</u>, 1972. [CN #10]

    - A. Dixit, "The Role of Investment in Entry-Deterrence," <u>The Economic Journal</u>, March 1980. [CN #11]

    "Wal-Mart Stores' Discount Operations" [HBS 0-387-018]

- B. <u>Deterrence Along Non-Price Dimensions</u>

    - R. Schmalensee, "Entry Deterrence in the Ready-to-Eat Breakfast Cereal industry," <u>Bell Journal of Economics</u>, 1978. [CN #12]

    F.M. Scherer, "The Breakfast Cereal Industry," Chapter 5 in <u>Adams</u>.

15.013 Fall '89　　　　　　　　　Course Outline: Page 6

C. Suppliers, Customers, and Vertical Integration

Porter, Chapters 6 & 14.

"Note on Supplying the Automobile Industry." [HBS 9-378-219]

B. G. Katz, "Territorial Exclusivity in the Soft Drink Industry," Journal of Industrial Economics, September 1978. [CN #13]

6. INVESTMENT DECISIONS AND STRATEGIC OPTIONS (About 2 or 3 classes.)

A. Investment with Entry and Exit

Briefly review Chapters 6, 8, 9, 10, 11, 20, and 21 of Brealey and Myers, Principles of Corporate Finance.

"The Disposable Diaper Industry in 1974." [HBS #9-380-175]

B. Investment and Options

R. Pindyck, "Irreversibility, Uncertainty, and Investment." (Read Sections 1 and 2, skim the rest.) [CN #14]

D. Siegel, J. Smith, & J. Paddock, "Valuing Offshore Oil Properties with Option Pricing Models," Midland Corporate Finance Journal, 1987 [CN #15]

7. R&D, INNOVATION, AND INDUSTRY EVOLUTION (About 3 classes.)

Determinants of firm growth and industry evolution. The role of R&D. The race to innovate. Making the R&D investment decision: strategic and non-strategic aspects. Sleeping patents, and the decision to adopt a new innovation. The decision to license a patent. Forecasting the evolution of market structure.

A. Investments in R&D, and the Value of Patents

R. Gilbert & D. Newbery, "Preemptive Patenting and the Persistence of Monopoly," American Economic Review, June 1982. [CN #16]

C. Shapiro, "Patent Licensing and R&D Rivalry," American Economic Review, May 1985. [CN #17]

G. Mitchell & W. Hamilton, "Managing R&D As A Strategic Option," Research & Technology Management, 1988 [CN #18]

B. Growth and Evolution

Porter, Chapter 8.

"The Chain Saw Industry in 1978," (and "Addendum"). [HBS #9-379-176, 177]

ROBERT S. PINDYCK
Sloan School of Management
Massachusetts Institute of Technology

15.013 - Industrial Economics
for Strategic Decisions

MIDTERM EXAM

(Monday, October 30, 1989)

[64] 1. Decide whether each of the following is <u>true, false, or uncertain</u>, and give a <u>brief but clear explanation</u> of your answer. (Most of the credit will be given for the explanation!) [8 points each.]

(a) You are planning to enter the oil tanker industry, but you know that demand for tankers is subject to large and unpredictable fluctuations. Therefore you would be better off leasing tankers from other firms, rather than buying tankers of your own.

(b) The demand for Rockwell International's water meters is very inelastic because it is difficult for people to reduce their consumption of water.

(c) The cost of bauxite is a small fraction of the total cost of producing aluminum, so bauxite demand is very inelastic. However, the International Bauxite Association could not raise the price of bauxite above a certain limit because to do so would encourage cheating and make it impossible to sustain a collusive agreement.

(d) Many consumers of breakfast cereals enjoy variety, and therefore buy different cereals from time to time. This reinforces the "first mover advantage" of new brands, and helps existing companies deter entry.

(e) Massport has chosen Worcester as the most likely site for a new airport to relieve congestion at Logan. Should the airport be built, there will be a need for one, but probably only one, new luxury hotel in Worcester. You announce that you plan to build such a hotel in Worcester, and to make the announcement credible, you purchase a choice piece of land close to the downtown area. You can expect this to deter entry by other hotel companies.

(f) During the early 1980's some automobile companies introduced warranties that were much more extensive than the standard 12 month/12,000 mile warranty. A more extensive warranty can be an effective signal of product quality.

(g) After General Electric published its pricing book and announced that it would sell to all customers at the published price (book price times a multiplier), it also instituted a "price protection" clause. This clause facilitated coordination with Westinghouse.

(h) A high price is a signal of high quality.

170

15.013 Midterm Exam   October 30, 1989
                                                                Page 2

[36] 2. You play the following bargaining game against an opponent. You
         move first and must make an offer - a dollar amount between $0 and
         $25. Denote your offer by A1. Your opponent can accept or reject
         this offer. If she accepts, you receive A1 and she receives
         ($25 - A1).

         If your offer is rejected, your opponent makes a counter offer,
         which we denote by B2, and again a dollar amount between 0 and
         $25. You can accept or reject the offer. If you accept, you get
         .83(25 - B2) and your opponent gets .83xB2. (The .83 is a
         "discount rate" applied to each round there is disagreement.)

         If you reject B2, you make an offer between 0 and $25, denoted by
         A3. If your opponent accepts the offer, you get (.83)(.83)xA3,
         and your opponent gets (.83)(.83)(25 - A3). If your opponent
         rejects A3, the game ends with each of you getting
         (.83)(.83)(.83)($10) = $5.72.

         Assume that there is no uncertainty in anyone's mind about the
         payoffs, and each of you is risk neutral, out to maximize expected
         payoff. <u>What offer should you make for A1? Should you expect the
         offer to be accepted? Does it matter who goes first in this game</u>?
         Provide a clear explanation/analysis for your answers.

                                                                     171

ROBERT S. PINDYCK
Sloan School of Management
Massachusetts Institute of Technology

15.013 - Industrial Economics
for Strategic Decisions

FINAL EXAM

(Monday, December 11, 1989)

[40] 1. Decide whether each of the following statements is <u>true, false, or uncertain</u>, and give a <u>brief but clear explanation</u> of your answer. (Most of the credit will be given for the explanation.) [8 points each.]

(a) Many airlines have <u>frequent flyer programs</u>, in which free tickets and other benefits are awarded in return for specified amounts of cumulative miles flown. Such programs can serve to increase the monopoly power of the airlines that offer them.

(b) Firm A produces memory chips which it sells in a competitive market. Among its customers is Firm B, which uses the chips to produce a specialized computer. Firm B is a monopoly producer of this computer. There is no uncertainty about costs or demand, and no potential economies of scale or scope. If Firms A and B merge, total profits will rise, and the price of the computer will fall.

(c) Predatory pricing is uneconomical. It is better to buy up a competing firm rather than force it out of the market by drastically cutting your own prices.

(d) The value of a firm is the present value of all of its expected future profits. The riskier is the firm's business, the higher is the risk premium that must be added to the discount rate when computing this present value, and hence the lower is the value of the firm.

(e) Your firm and four other construction companies are bidding for a construction project. The lowest bid will win the contract. Before bidding, each firm independently estimates the cost of completing the project. The true cost is unknown, and all estimates are subject to (a mean zero) error. [That is, if the true but unknown cost is C, your estimate is $\tilde{C} = C + \epsilon$, where the estimation error ϵ has an expected value of zero.] Your engineers estimate the cost to be $10 million, and you feel that an additional $1 million should be allowed for a reasonable profit. If you bid $11 million and win the contract, your expected profit is $1 million.

[12] 2. We have seen that P&G and Kimberly-Clark, the two largest producers of disposable diapers, compete agressively in R&D, spending large amounts of money each year to try to improve product quality and shave production costs. The two firms are in

15.013 Final Exam
December 11, 1989
Page 2

a repeated prisoners' dilemma; if they could somehow agree to spend less money on R&D, they would both earn higher profits. In some respects the situation is similar to that in the water meter industry - the same firms competing for many years, and stable demand growth. Why is it so much harder to resolve the prisoners' dilemma in the case of diapers?

[18] 3. In what ways does territorial exclusivity in licensing to bottlers increase the profits of soft drink syrup producers? In what ways does it benefit consumer welfare? In what ways does it harm consumer welfare?

[30] 4. Suppose 8 brands of breakfast cereal are positioned evenly around a unit circle that represents the space of product attributes. (Hence the brand density is 8 per unit of product space.) Competition is local (i.e., only with the nearest brands), and brands cannot be repositioned. The cost of production for each brand is:

$$C(q) = F + vq$$

where F is a fixed cost. The market price, P, exceeds variable cost, v. Given F, v, and P, each brand is currently profitable. In fact, even if there were as many as 12 brands, each would be profitable, but with more than 12 brands, none would be profitable.

[6] (a) Suppose an entrant introduces one new brand, for a total of 9 brands. (i) What will be the brand density for the new brand? (ii) Will the new brand be profitable? Explain briefly.

[8] (b) Suppose the fixed cost, F, were zero. How would your answers to (a) change? Explain briefly.

[8] (c) How would your answers to (a) change if the fixed cost, F, were not zero, but brands could be repositioned costlessly?

[8] (d) Given that there are fixed costs and repositioning is difficult, how do you explain the fact that existing cereal companies continually introduce new brands?

Boston College
Department of Economics

Industrial Organization

Prof. Steve Polasky
Carney 333
x3696

Ec. 353
Fall 1988

Texts: The required readings for this course are contained in two sources: a) Martin, <u>Industrial Economics: Economic Analysis and Public Policy</u>, 1988, and b) a coursepack of readings containing a collection of articles. The coursepack can be purchased either in class or in the economics department office in 131 Carney. You are also expected to have daily access to <u>The Wall Street Journal</u>. We will occasionally refer to articles as illustrations or examples of the material that we discuss in class.

Course Requirements: 5 Problem Sets 20%
Midterm 35%
Final 45%

It is important to hand in problem sets. The best way to learn economics is by working out problems. Past semesters have shown a strong relationship between doing problem sets and final grades. You may work in groups to complete the problem sets (and in fact are encouraged to do so) but you must write up and hand in your own paper. No problem sets will be accepted after the answers to the problem set have been handed out.

If your grade on the final is much better than your grade on the midterm, the grade on the midterm will be given less weight. Class participation will count favorably for borderline cases. Any question on grading will be handled by regrading the entire test or problem set. The midterm is tentatively scheduled for October 27th. The final is on December 17th at 9 a.m.

1. Introduction and Brief Review of Microtheory
   A. Overview
      Martin Chapter 1
   B. Review of Intermediate Micro: Competition and Monopoly
      Any Intermediate Micro text chapters on competition and monopoly.
      Examples: Browning and Browning– Chap. 9 & 11; Varian–
      Chap. 22,23 &25.

2. Competition versus Monopoly: An Appraisal
   Martin Chapter 2
   Scherer, Industrial Market Structure and Economic Performance,
      2nd ed.,1980, 9–28
   Leibenstein, "Allocative Efficiency vs. X-Efficiency," American
      Economic Review, June 1966
   Stigler, "The Xistence of X-efficiency," American Economic
      Review, March 1976

3. Introduction to Antitrust Policy
   Martin, Chapter 3 and Chapter 18: 500– 519

4. Theory of the Firm, Mergers and Takeovers
   Martin Chapters 9 and 10
   Shleifer and Vishny, "Value Maximization and the Acquisition Process,"
      Journal of Economic Perspectives, Winter 1988
   Scherer, "Corporate Takeovers: The Efficiency Arguments,"
      Journal of Economic Perspectives, Winter 1988

5. Oligopoly and Collusion
   A. Introduction to Game Theory
      Davis, Game Theory: A Nontechnical Introduction, Chap 1, Chap 5:
         75–119
   B. Oligopoly
      Eaton, "Oligopoly", Chap 12: 1–30
      Polasky, "Notes on Oligopoly"
      Polasky, "Notes on the Hotelling Model of Spatial Competition"
   C. Collusion
      Martin Chapter 6
      Salop, "Practices that (Credibly) Facilitate Oligopoly Co-ordination,"
         in Stigliz and Mathewson (ed.), New Developments in the
         Analysis of Market Structure, 1986

6. Entry and Exit
   A. Potential Competition: Entry, Deterrence and Contestability
      Martin Chapter 4
         Dixit, "Recent Developments in Oligopoly Theory," American Economic Review, May 1982
         Baumol, "Contestable Markets: An Uprising in the Theory of Industrial Structure," American Economic Review, March 1982, 1–8
      "Too Many Cereals for the FTC," Business Week, March 20, 1978. (Reprinted in Watson and Getz, Price Theory in Action, 1981)
   B. Price Discrimination and Predatory Pricing
      Martin Chapters 15 and 16
         McGee, "Predatory Price Cutting: The Standard Oil (NJ) Case," The Journal of Law and Economics, October 1958

7. Non-Price Competition: Advertising, Quality, Durability
   A. Advertising
      Martin Chapter 11
         Nelson, "Advertising as Information," The Journal of Political Economy, July 1974, 729–734, 749–752
         Dixit and Norman, "Advertising and Welfare," Bell Journal, Spring 1978, 1–6
   B. Quality
         Akerlof, "The Market for Lemons: Quality Uncertainty and the Market Mechanism", Quarterly Journal of Economics, 1970.
         Polasky, "Notes on Product Durability and Planned Obsolescence."

8. R&D, Innovation and Patents
      Martin Chapter 12
         Kamien and Schwartz, Market Structure and Innovation, 1982, 1–19
         Hirshleifer, "The Private and Social Value of Information and the Reward to Inventive Activity," American Economic Review, 1971

Boston College
Department of Economics

Ec. 353
Industrial Organization

Steve Polasky
Fall 1988

Midterm

Answer all of the following questions to the best of your ability. Be as specific and as clear as possible. The points for each problem are given. Notice that the problems at the end of the midterm are weighted more heavily. Be sure to give yourself time to work on these problems. One good way to insure that you will have plenty of time is to focus your answers on the early questions to exactly what is asked. Most of these questions can be answered in a short amount of time if you are focused. Good luck.

1. (6 points) Define allocative efficiency. Explain why a monopolist will not be allocatively efficient.

2. (6 points) Define Nash Equilibrium. Find all Nash Equilibria for the following game.

	L	R
U	5, 7	7, 8
D	12, 3	6, 5

3. (10 points) Define X-efficiency. Explain why Leibenstein thinks it exists and why Stigler thinks that it does not exist.

4. (10 points) Explain the difference between a Per Se Rule and a Rule of Reason. Which rule was applied in the Trans-Missouri Freight case? Does the application of this rule to this case make good economic sense? Explain why or why not.

5. (12 points) Suppose that upon announcement of a merger or takeover attempt, that the stock price of the target company rises.
   a) Explain how this might be taken as evidence that the merger or takeover will lead to greater efficiency.
   b) Explain why this evidence might not reflect an efficiency gain (Give at least two different reasons).

6. (20 points) Suppose that you are the oil minister for Saudi Arabia and are responsible for setting Saudi oil policy. Demand for oil is given by: $P(Q) = 120 - Q$, where Q is measured in barrels of oil. Assume that costs of producing oil in OPEC countries, including Saudi Arabia, is zero. Assume that costs of producing oil in Non–OPEC countries is $10 per barrel (AC = MC = $10). Non–OPEC producers produce 20 barrels as long as price remains above their production costs and they shutdown otherwise. For this question you may assume that OPEC consists of Saudi Arabia, Kuwait, Iraq, and Iran. (There are actually many more members.)

a) Given that price is above $10, what is the profit maximizing quantity and price for OPEC? How much profit does OPEC make?

b) The oil minister for Kuwait claims that OPEC would make more profit by lowering price and forcing non–OPEC producers to shutdown. Prove whether this argument is correct or not.

c) Suppose that other members of OPEC exceed their quotas and produce 70 barrels of oil regardless of price. What is Saudi Arabia's profit maximizing quantity to sell? What is the resulting market price for oil?

d) After the last OPEC meeting, no agreement was made to force members to cut back on their over–production. Suppose that all members of OPEC think that the cartel agreement is dead. Set up, **but do not solve**, the profit maximizing problem for Saudi Arabia if all OPEC members behave as Cournot oligopolists.

7. (12 points) In industry X, price is currently $50. There are constant average and marginal costs of production of $10 (AC=MC=$10). Demand is given by: $P(Q) = 90 - 2Q$.

a) Find the deadweight loss in this industry.

b) Suppose that the demand curve where unknown. What assumption(s) did Harberger make to get around this problem? Explain why these assumption(s) might lead to over or under–estimates of the deadweight loss.

(The exam continues on the next page)

8. (24 points) The game tree given below represents a "takeover game." The current management makes a decision on whether to be hard-working or lazy. Next, a raider can decide to attempt a takeover or to not attempt a takeover. The game ends if there is not a takeover attempt. If there is a takeover attempt, the current management must decide whether to accept the takeover bid, or to instigate a poison pill and fight the takeover. If management chooses the poison pill, then the raider decides whether to withdraw the attempt or to takeover even though they will set off the poison pill.

  a) Find the credible Nash equilibrium to this game.
  b) Define the notion of "threat." Give an example of a threat that can be made in this game that would change the outcome.
  c) Define poison pill (or give an example of one). Can it be in current shareholders interest to have a poison pill in the corporate charter? Explain.
  d) Define golden parachute (or give an example of one). Can it be in current shareholders interest to have a golden parachute in the corporate charter? Explain.
  e) Explain why managers do not necessarily maximize profits.
  f) Will takeovers force managers to maximize profits? Why or why not.

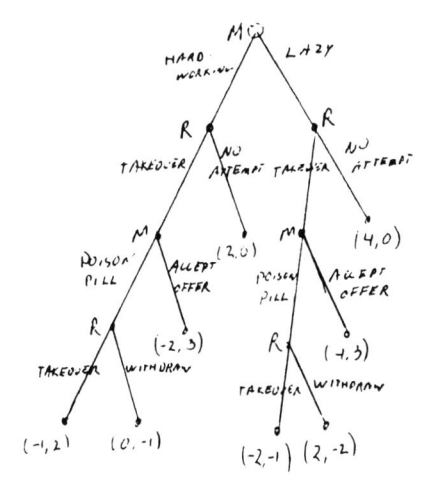

Boston College
Department of Economics

Ec. 353
Industrial Organization

Steve Polasky
Fall 1988

Final Exam

In your answers be as specific and as clear as possible. Please be organized and make sure that your answers are relevant to the question asked. Show your work on the numerical problems. Good luck.

SECTION I: Answer the following question.

1. There is an industry composed of two firms that behave as Cournot oligopolists. There is no possibility of entry. The industry demand curve is given by: $P(Q) = 24 - Q$, where Q is total industry quantity and P is price. Initially, each firm has constant average and marginal cost production of $6 (AC=MC=$6).

   a) Set up the profit for function for firm 1, as a function of its own output, q_1, and of the other firm's output q_2.

   b) Solve for the reaction function for firm 1 (and for firm 2). Solve for the Cournot level of output for each firm.

   c) Solve for the level of profit for each firm.

   d) Now suppose that firm 1 can take an action that will raise firm 2's marginal and average costs to $12 per unit (for example by causing higher input prices or labor costs). Assume that firm 1's costs remain at $6 per unit. Solve for the Cournot level of output for each firm.

   e) Given the level of costs as in part (d), solve for the level of profits for firm 1.

   f) Are the profits that firm 1 earns higher or lower than before its rivals costs were raised? Explain why this result occurs.

SECTION II: Answer 3 out of 4 questions in this section.

2. Assume that a cartel has been formed in an industry that contains two firms. Assume that there is no possibility of entry. If both firms cooperate with a collusive agreement they will each earn profits of $50 per period. If firm A cheats on the agreement while firm B cooperates, then firm A will earn $75 in that period and firm B will earn $0. If both firms cheat they will each earn $20 that period. Write out the payoff matrix for this game.

a) Suppose this game is repeated twice. Suppose that player B can commit to a strategy of cooperating in round 1, and in round 2 will play whatever player A did in round 1 (so, for example, if player A cheated in round 1 player B will cheat in round 2). Will this strategy deter cheating by player A? Explain.

b) If this game were to extend beyond two periods, is it more or less likely that firms can deter cheating? Explain.

c) Suppose that player B can instantly detect what player A is doing and can immediately respond to what player A does. So, if player A cheats in a round so will player B. If player A cooperates in a round so will player B. Will this strategy keep player A from cheating? Explain.

d) Explain how one of the facilitating practices talked about by Salop would decrease the time to detection.

e) How else can firms support collusive outcomes?

3. A Swedish car manufacturer faces relatively elastic demand at home and relatively inelastic demand in the United States. Specifically, the home demand curve is given by: $Q_s = 12 - P_s$, where Q_s is the quantity of cars in Sweden and P_s is the price in Sweden. The US demand curve is given by: $Q_{us} = 20 - P_{us}$, where Q_{us} is the quantity of these cars in the US and P_{us} is the price in the US. Suppose production occurs at a constant marginal cost of $6. Assume that price is the strategic variable for the firm. (Note: for realism, all dollar figures are really in thousands of dollars).

a) What price should the company charge US consumers? What price should it charge to Swedish consumers?

b) Suppose that if it possible for Yuppies from the United States to travel to Sweden, purchase cars in Sweden, and transport them back to the US for $2. Because of this, price can not differ between the two markets by more than $2. Write down the single profit expression over the two markets for the car company in this case where the US price, P_{us}, is $2 more than the Swedish price, P_s.

c) What price should the car company charge now in the US?

4. Nelson, in his article on advertising, and Akerlof, in his article on "The Market for Lemons," are concerned with situations in which the firm has full information about the product but the consumer does not.
   a) Describe Akerlof's argument about what happens in the used car market.
   b) Describe Nelson's argument about how advertising conveys information to the consumer.
   c) Discuss why these two papers come to such different results about how the market functions when consumers lack full information.

5. There is an ongoing debate in economics about whether firms would have incentives to take predatory actions to force exit or deter entry of rival firms.
   a) Summarize the arguments stating that predatory actions will not be undertaken by profit maximizing firm.
   b) Summarize the arguments that state that predatory actions will at times be undertaken by profit maximizing firms.
   c) What should antitrust laws be in regards to pricing decisions by firms? Specifically, should firms be allowed to charge different prices in different markets, and should firms be allowed to charge prices below cost? Explain.

Boston College
Department of Economics

Ec. 853
Fall 1989

Steve Polasky
333 Carney
x3696

Industrial Organization I

Course Requirements: Midterm 25%
Paper 25%
Final 50%

The midterm is tentatively scheduled on October 24 and the final on December 18. The first deadline for the paper will be November 9. I will read all of the papers during the following week and make suggestions. You will then "revise and resubmit" the paper by the last day of class, which is December 12. There will also be several problem sets to help you work through the material. These will not be graded. I do, however, urge you to work through them carefully as I think this is the way that you really learn economics.

Texts: J. Tirole (1988), The Theory of Industrial Organization.
E. Rasmusen (1989), Games and Information: An Introduction to Game Theory.
(optional) F.M. Scherer (1980), Industrial Market Structure and Economic Performance, 2nd Edition.
(optional) Schmalensee, R. and Willig, R., Eds. (1989), The Handbook of Industrial Organization.

Reading List
(*Indicates required reading, +indicates suggested reading)

1. Perfect Competition, Monopoly and Efficiency

    A. Simple Theory of Perfect Competition and Monopoly (Review)
    +Varian, H. (1987), Intermediate Microeconomics, Chapters 18–25.
    +Varian, H. (1978), Microeconomic Analysis, Chapters 1, 2.

    B. Market Structure and Market Performance.
    *Tirole, Introduction, and Chapter 1, 65–72.
    *Scherer, Chapter 2.
    Scherer, Chapters 3, 4, 17.

C. Extensions of the Monopoly Model: Price Discrimination, Non-Linear Pricing and Durable Goods
   *Tirole, Chapters 1, 72–92, and Chapter 3.
   *Bulow, J. (1982), "Durable Goods Monopolists," Journal of Political Economy, 314–332.
   Phlips, L. (1981), The Economics of Price Discrimination.

2. Theory of the Firm, Vertical and Horizontal Integration

   A. The Theory of the Firm
      *Tirole, Chapter 0.
      *Williamson, O. (1973), "Markets and Hierarchies: Some Elementary Considerations," American Economic Review, 316–325.
      Jensen, M. and Meckling, W. (1976), "Theory of the Firm: Managerial Behavior, Agency Cost, and Ownership Structure, The Journal of Financial Economics, 305–360.
      Arrow, K. (1974), The Limits to Organization.
      Holmstrom, B. and Tirole, J. (1987), "The Theory of the Firm," in The Handbook of Industrial Organization.

   B. Contracts, Incentives, and Agency Theory
      *Rasmusen, Chapters 6–7.
      *Hart, O. and Holmstrom, B. (1987), "The Theory of Contracts," in Bewley, T. (ed.), Advances in Economic Theory, Fifth World Congress.
      *Laffont, J. J., and Tirole, J. (1988), "The Dynamics of Incentives Contracts," Econometrica, 1153–1175.
      *Grossman, S. and Hart, O. (1986), "The Costs and Benefits of Ownership: A Theory of Lateral and Vertical Integration, Journal of Political Economy, 691–719.
      Bamberg, G. and Spremann, K., eds. (1987), Agency Theory, Information, and Incentives.

   B. Takeovers
      *Grossman, S. and Hart, O. (1980), "Takeover Bids, the Free Rider Problem and the Theory of the Corporation," Bell Journal, 42–64.
      *Shleifer, A. and Vishny, R. (1986), "Greenmail, White Knights, and Shareholders' Interest, Rand Journal, 293–309.
      *Stein, J. (1988), "Takeover Threats and Managerial Myopia", Journal of Political Economy, 61–80.
      Journal of Economic Perspectives (1988), "Symposium on Takeovers."

C. Vertical Integration
   *Tirole, Chapter 4.
   *Schmalensee, R. (1973), "A Note on the Theory of Vertical Integration," Journal of Political Economy, 442–449.

3. Oligopoly and Game Theory: Strategic Competition

   A. An Introduction to Game Theory with Applications to Static Oligopoly
      *Rasmusen, Chapters 1–3.
      *Tirole, Chapters 5 and 11.
      Friedman, J. (1986), Game Theory with Applications to Economics.
      Luce, R.D. and H. Riaffa (1957), Games and Decisions.
      Shubik, M. (1984), Game Theory in the Social Sciences.
      +Schelling, T. (1960), The Strategy of Conflict.

   B. Dynamic Oligopoly, Collusion and Repeated Games
      *Tirole, Chapter 6.
      Scherer, Chapters 6–8.
      *Shapiro, C. (1986), "Theories of Oligopoly Behavior," in The Handbook of Industrial Organization.
      *Domowitz, I., Hubbard, G., and Petersen, B. (1987) "Oligopoly Supergames: Some Empirical Evidence on Prices and Margins," The Journal of Industrial Economics, 379–398.
      *Green, E. and Porter, M. (1984), "Non-Cooperative Collusion under Imperfect Price Information," Econometrica, 87–100.
      *Abreu, D. (1988), "On the Theory of Infinitely Repeated Games with Discounting," Econometrica, 383–396.
      Fudenberg, D. and Maskin, E. (1986) "The Folk Theorem in Repeated Games with Discounting or with Incomplete Information," Econometrica, 533–554.
      Axelrod, R, (1984), The Evolution of Cooperation.

   C. Product Differentiation
      *Tirole, Chapter 7.
      Scherer, Chapter 14.
      *D'Aspremont, C. Gabszewicz, J., and Thisse, J. (1979), "On Hotelling's 'Stability of Competition'," Econometrica, 1145–1150.
      *Thisse, J.F. and Vives, X. (1988), "On the Strategic Choice of Spatial Price Policy," American Economic Review, 122–137.
      *Salop, S. (1979), "Monopolistic Competition with Outside Goods," Bell Journal, 141–156.

   D. Games with Asymmetric Information.
      *Rasmusen, Chapter 5.
      *Tirole, Chapter 9.

*Polasky, S. (1989), "Information Acquisition and Revelation in an Oligopolistic Exhaustible Resource Market," Boston College Working Paper.

*Riordan, M. (1985), "Imperfect Information and Dynamic Conjectural Variations," Rand Journal, 41–50.

*Kreps, D. and Wilson, R. (1982), "Reputation and Imperfect Information," Journal of Economic Theory, 253–279.

*Fershtman, C. and Judd, K. (1987), "Equilibrium Incentives in Oligopoly," American Economic Review, 927–940.

Kreps, D. and Wilson, R. (1982), "Sequential Equilibria," Econometrica, 863–894.

Dasgupta, P. and Maskin, E. (1986), "The Existence of Equilibria in Discontinuous Economic Games, I: Theory," Review of Economic Studies, 1–26.

Dasgupta, P. and Maskin, E. (1986), "The Existence of Equilibria in Discontinuous Economic Games, II: Applications," Review of Economic Studies, 27–41.

4. Entry and Deterrence

*Tirole, Chapter 8.

*Dixit, A. (1982), "Recent Developments in Oligopoly Theory," American Economic Review – Papers and Proceedings, 12–17.

*Gilbert, R. (1989), "The Role of Potential Competition in Industrial Organization," Journal of Economic Perspectives, 107–127.

*Aghion, P. and Bolton, P. (1987), "Contracts as Barriers to Entry," American Economic Review, 388–401.

*Milgrom, P. and Roberts, J. (1983), "Limit Pricing and Entry Under Incomplete Information," Econometrica, 443–460.

*Salop, S. and Scheffman, D. (1983), "Raising Rivals' Costs, American Economic Review – Papers and Proceedings, 267–271.

5. R&D and Innovation

*Tirole, Chapter 10.

Scherer, Chapters 15–16.

Schumpeter, J., Capitalism, Socialism, and Democracy, Chapters 5, 8.

*Dixit, A. (1988), "A General Model of R&D Competition and Policy," Rand Journal, 317–326.

*Loury, G. (1979), "Market Structure and Innovation," Quarterly Journal of Economics, 395–410.

*Spence, A.M. (1984), "Cost Reduction, Competition, and Industry Performance," Econometrica, 101–121.

*Gilbert, R. and Newbery, D. (1982), "Preemptive Patenting and the Persistence of Monopoly," American Economic Review, 514–526.

*Fudenberg, D. and G. Tirole (1985), "Preemption and Rent Equalization in the Adoption of New Technology," Review of Economic Studies, 383–401.

*Katz, M. and Shapiro, C. (1986), "Technology Adoption in the Presence of Network Externalities," Journal of Political Economy, 822–841.

*Katz, M. and Shapiro, C. (1987), "R&D Rivalry with Licensing or Imitation, American Economic Review, 402–420.

Nelson, R. and S. Winter (1982), An Evolutionary Theory of Economic Change.

Kamien, M. and N. Schwartz (1982), Market Structure and Innovation.

6. Product Selection, Quality, Advertising and Signalling.

*Tirole, Chapter 2.

*Rasmusen, Chapters 8–9.

*Cho, I–K and Kreps, D. (1987),"Signalling Games and Stable Equilibria, Quarterly Journal of Economics, 179–221.

*Ackerlof, G. (1970) "The Market for Lemons: Qualitative Uncertainty and Competition Equilibrium," Quarterly Journal of Economics, 488–500.

Kihlstrom, R. and Riordan, M. (1984), "Advertising as a Signal," Journal of Political Economy, 427–450.

*Milgrom, P. and Roberts, J. (1986), "Price and Advertising Signals of Product Quality," Journal of Political Economy, 796–821.

*Dixit, A. and V. Norman, "Advertising and Welfare," Bell Journal, 1–17, 1978.

Nelson, P. (1974), "Advertising as Information," Journal of Political Economy, 729–754.

Boston College
Department of Economics

Ec 853
Industrial Organization I

Steve Polasky
Fall 1989

Midterm

1. a) Briefly explain how including a dilution factor in the corporate charter can increase a shareholder's expected returns.
   b) Briefly explain how seemingly myopic behavior on the part of managers can increase shareholder returns.
   [Note: I am looking for a quick, intuitive, explanation of the main mechanism(s) that drive these results. Answers to each part need be no longer than a short paragraph.]

2. Suppose there are N firms in an industry and that each has constant marginal costs of $c per unit: $C_i(q_i) = cq_i$, where C_i is the total cost of production for firm i and q_i is the level of production for firm i. The industry inverse demand curve is:

$$P(Q) = a - bQ, \text{ where } Q = \sum_{i=1}^{N} q_i.$$

   a) Set up the maximization problem for firm i. Solve for firm i's reaction function.
   b) Solve for firm i's Cournot equilibrium level of output. (Hint: it might be easier to first find the industry level of output.) How much profit does firm i make in equilibrium?
   c) Now suppose that one of the N firms is selected to be a Stackelberg leader and allowed to move first. All the other N−1 firms play simultaneously, after the leader plays. Let $Q_{-L}(q_L)$ represent the output of all follower firms as a function of q_L, the leader's output. Solve for the function $Q_{-L}(q_L)$. Use this expression to write the profit maximization problem for the Stackelberg leader.
   d) Solve for the equilibrium level of output for the Stackelberg leader and for a Stackelberg follower.
   e) Suppose that the goal of the government is to maximize total surplus. If it were in the government's power to regulate the industry such that it could let one firm commit to a level of output prior to other firms' commitments, would it wish to do so? In other words, does total surplus increase in the Stackelberg equilibrium as compared to the Cournot equilibrium? Explain.

3. A consumer needs two things to listen to music using compact disk technology: i) a compact disk player and ii) compact disk(s). Let consumer i have the following utility function for compact disks: $U_i = a_i q_i - q_i^2/2 - A - pq_i$, where A equals the price of a compact disk player, p is the price of a compact disk, and q_i is the number of disks that consumer i buys. A consumer also has the option of not purchasing a compact disk

player or compact disks, in which case their utility is 0. Assume that compact disk players cost $C to make (per unit) and that each disk can be made for a cost of $d.

a) Set up the profit maximization problem for a monopolist that sells both compact disk players and compact disks and faces identical consumers ($a_i = a_j$ for $j \neq i$). What is the individual rationality constraint in this case? What is the incentive compatibility constraint?

b) Solve for the monopolist's profit maximizing A and p.

c) Suppose that there are many different types of consumers ($a_i \neq a_j$ for $j \neq i$). Using graphs or words, explain why a monopolist that is restricted to setting a single p and a single A for all individuals will not set prices in an efficient manner and will fail to capture all surplus generated by consumption.

d) Now suppose that there is again only one type of consumer but that firm 1 makes compact disk players and that firm 2 makes compact disks.

   i) If firm 1 gets to set its price for compact disk players first, how much will it charge for a compact disk player? What will firm 2 charge for the compact disks?

   ii) Now suppose that firm 2 gets to set its price for compact disks first. How much will it charge for compact disks? How much will firm 1 charge for compact disk players?

Boston College
Department of Economics

Ec 853
Industrial Organization I

Steve Polasky
Fall 1989

Final Exam

Please answer all of the following questions. In your answers be as clear and as specific as possible. The exam is meant to take about two hours, however, you may have up to three hours to complete the exam. Good luck.

1. (10 points) Explain how a contract between a firm and its customers can be used as a barrier to entry. How is the analysis changed when the firm has more information about the probability of entry than do customers?

2. (15 points) Both Green and Porter (1984) and Rotemberg and Saloner (1986) try to explain how collusion is supported in a repeated game context. Explain how collusive outcomes are supported in each model. If the Green and Porter model of collusion is correct, what pattern of prices would one expect to see over time? If the Rotemberg and Saloner model of collusion is correct, what pattern of prices would one expect to see over time. Does either pattern appear to be empirically valid?

3. (10 points) Suppose there is an exhaustible resource with fixed stock size S. Demand for the resource in each of two time periods is a constant elasticity demand curve:
$$P(Q_t) = Q_t^{-\beta} \quad (0<\beta<1)$$
Assume that there are no costs of production. Assume that the discount factor on second period sales is δ.
   a) Suppose the industry is a monopoly. Solve for the profit maximizing extraction path. At what rate do prices increase?
   b) Now let there be two firms in the industry each with half of the stock. Solve for the Cournot–Nash equilibrium extraction path for each firm.
   c) How does the industry extraction path for part (b) compare with that of part (a)? Explain the intuition for your results.

4. (20 points) Suppose there are two firms with homogeneous products that compete in an industry with no possibility of entry by any other firm. Firm i (i=1,2) chooses quantity, q_i, simultaneously with the other firm in order to maximize its profit. Industry demand can be either high or low. Let demand in state i be given by: $D_i = A_i - Q$, i = L,H. Each state occurs with probability of 1/2. Cost of production is c per unit for each firm. Suppose that firm 1 knows what state of the world exists at the time it is called upon to play but firm 2 does not.

a) Suppose that firm 1 can make information available to firm 2 prior to play. Solve for the ex ante expected profits for firm 1 if it makes information available.

b) Suppose that firm 1 keeps information about demand private. Solve for the ex ante level of profit when it keeps its information private.

c) Given the chance to sign a contract to release information prior to learning the true state of demand would the firm want to release information to the other firm?

d) Suppose that there was no possibility to make a binding agreement to release information prior to finding out the state. Suppose there is, however, an opportunity to release information about the state of demand after it is learned. What would be the outcome for this game. Would firm 1 reveal information or not? Explain.

5. (25 points) Suppose there are two firms with homogeneous products that compete in an industry with no possibility of entry by any other firm. Let q_i represent the output of firm i, i = 1,2. Let demand in the industry is given by:

$$P(Q) = a - Q \quad (a > 0)$$

where Q is total industry output, $Q = q_1 + q_2$. The cost of production for firm 1 is a function of how much it spends on R&D and how much it produces:

$$C_1(R_1,q_1) = \frac{c_1}{R_1} q_1 - dR_1$$

Firm 2 has a simple cost function (no possibility of R&D):

$$c_2(q_2) = c_2 q_2.$$

a) Suppose that firm 1 gets to commit to a level of R&D before the firms get to commit to quantities. Setup the second stage profit maximization problem for each firm and solve for the Cournot–Nash equilibrium quantities for each firm as a function of R_1.

b) With linear demand and constant marginal cost (as in this problem) profit for a firm equals quantity squared ($\Pi_i = q_i^2$). Using this fact, show how the square of the optimal amount of R&D (R_1^{*2}) at the first stage is related to q_1. (Note: solving for the explicit value for R_1^* is a real mess. However, the relation between R_1^{*2} and q_1 is fairly clean.)

c) Now suppose that the R&D decision is taken simultaneously with the quantity decision by each firm. Solve for the optimal level of R_1^{*2} as a function of q_1. (Again do not solve for the explicit value of R_1^*)

d) Using the results from parts (b) and (c), show whether R_1^* greater when the firm gets to commit to R&D prior to quantity commitment or greater when the firm commit to R&D at the same time as they commit to quantity. Explain the intuition for your result.

e) Suppose instead of quantity competition, the firms produced imperfect substitutes and competed with prices. Does the comparison made above still come out the same or would the results be reversed? Explain.

Boston College
Department of Economics

Ec 853
Industrial Organization I

Steve Polasky
Fall 1989

Problem Set 1

The following problems run the range from fairly easy to fairly challenging (though I realize that difficulty should be measured by the problem doer rather than the problem maker). In addition to the problem here, you should also look at problems in Tirole as they are very good questions.

1. You are in charge of selling a passion fruit wine cooler in the Boston area. You have done a marketing study and have targeted two areas to sell your wine cooler. These areas are: i) Studentia, a low rent neighborhood made up of students and derelicts, and ii) Newtonia, an upscale neighborhood where everyone drives Volvo station-wagons. In Studentia you decide to market your product as "Boondoggle Farms Wine Drink." Demand for the "Drink" is $P(Q) = 1.00 - .01Q$. In Newtonia you market your product as "Parisian Passion, The Unique Wine Cooler." Demand for "Passion" in Newtonia is: $P(Q) = 10.2 - .10Q$. The cost of making the wine cooler is constant at $.20.
   a) What price should you set in each market in order to maximize profit?
   b) What price would you set if there were no way to price discriminate?
   c) Does social surplus increase or decrease with price discrimination? Is this a general conclusion?
   d) With linear demand and constant marginal cost, show whether allowing third degree price discrimination always increases, always decreases, or has an ambiguous effect on total surplus.

2. Dizzyworld is an amusement park with lots of rollercoaster rides. A typical individual has a demand for rollercoaster rides of $P(Q) = 10 - Q$. Assume that the marginal cost of providing rollercoaster rides is $2. If Dizzyworld can set a two-part tariff, what price should they set for the gate fee and what price should they set per ride?

3. Suppose that Monolith Industries Inc. is the only producer of product "X". The cost of providing a unit of "X" is $4 (MC = AC = $4). The demand for product "X" is: $P = 24 - Q$.
   a) If Monolith can not price discriminate, how much output will it sell? What price will it charge? How much profit will it make? How much consumer surplus will there be?
   b) If this were a perfectly competitive industry, how much output would be sold? What would the price be? How much profit would firms make? How much consumer surplus would there be?

c) Now assume that Monolith can undertake perfect price discrimination. How much output will be sold? How much profit will the firm make? How much consumer surplus will there be?

d) Rank monopoly, perfect competition, and price discriminating monopoly in terms of how much total social surplus (sum of consumer surplus plus profit) is generated.

4. Suppose a durable goods monopolist faces linear demand: $P(Q_t) = a - Q_t$, $t = 1,2$, and has constant marginal costs of c per unit. Assume that there is no discounting between periods.

   a) Solve for profit maximizing production plan for the monopolist if it can commit to period 1 and period 2 production before any sales or production take place.

   b) Suppose that the monopolist can not pre-commit to period 2 production. Solve for the profit maximizing plan in this case. By how much does profit decrease in this case versus profit in case (a).

   c) Why is the plan in part (a), the "optimal plan," "time inconsistent/subgame imperfect"?

5. A monopolist faces two types of customers. Each customer of type i has a demand curve for the monopolist's product given by: $P(q) = a_i - q$, for $i = 1,2$, where q is quantity purchased. Assume that $a_1 < a_2$. The proportion of type 1 customers in the population is λ, and the proportion of type 2 customers is $1-\lambda$. (Normalize population size to be 1.) The monopolist has constant returns to scale in production and can produce each unit of the good at a cost of $c. Assume that the monopolist may charge a "two part tariff" of the form: $T(q) = G + pq$.

   a) If the monopolist can discriminate between the two groups, find the optimal two-part tariff to charge each group.

   b) Now suppose that the monopolist can not observe customer type.

   i) Find the optimal two-part tariff if the monopolist wishes to sell to both groups.

   ii) Find the necessary condition for the monopolist to wish to sell to both groups. What would be the outcome if this condition fails to hold?

   c) Show geometrically how much profit the monopolist loses when it can not discriminate between groups of customers (assume that the monopolist wishes to sell to both groups). Show how much social surplus is lost in the case when the monopolist can not discriminate between groups. Is the loss in social surplus greater or less than the loss in profit? Explain.

6. In Tirole, you should look at exercises in Chapter 1 and Chapter 3.

Boston College
Department of Economics

Ec 853
Industrial Organization I

Steve Polasky
Fall 1989

Problem Set #2

1. Problems 1 and 2 in Tirole, Chapter 0 (Theory of the Firm).

2. Suppose that managers can either work hard (H) or be lazy (L). The cost to the manager of working hard is $c(H) = h$, while the cost of being lazy is $c(L) = 0$. Assume that the profit of the firm can either be high (Π_2) or low (Π_1). If the manager works hard, then $\text{Prob}(\Pi_2) = x$; $\text{Prob}(\Pi_1) = 1-x$. If the manager is lazy, then $\text{Prob}(\Pi_2) = y$; $\text{Prob}(\Pi_1) = 1-y$. (Assume that $0 < y < x < 1$). The shareholders of the company have the rights to any profit from the firm and agree to pay the manager a wage (w), which can be dependent upon the observed profit but not on the unobserved level of effort. Shareholders are risk neutral. Managers have a utility function $U(w)$, where $U' > 0$ and $U'' < 0$, i.e., managers are risk averse. Assume that the managers could achieve $U(w_0) = k$ at another firm.
   a) Set up the principal and agent problem.
   b) What is the individual rationality constraint? What is the incentive compatibility constraint?
   c) Show that the optimal solution to this problem could be achieved if the shareholders only want the managers to be lazy.
   d) Show that the optimal solution could be achieved if the mangers where risk neutral.
   e) Show that the solution when the shareholders want the managers to work hard and managers are risk averse will not be a Pareto efficient solution (i.e., a second best not a first best solution to the problem).

3. At Sure-King Corp. profits are a linear function of managers' effort level (e) and of a random variable (ε): $\Pi(e,\varepsilon) = e + \varepsilon$. Owners of Sure-king are risk neutral and care only about the profits net of wage payments to managers. Managers are paid a wage w, which can be a function of profits (but can not be a function of effort because effort is unobservable.) Let the wage contract be restricted to a linear contract: $w(\Pi) = a\Pi + b$. Let the utility function of managers be $U(w(\Pi)-c(e)) = (w(\Pi)-c(e))^\alpha$, $0<\alpha\leq 1$. Assume that managers dislike working hard and that there disutility (measured in dollar terms) is: $c(e) = \dfrac{e^2}{2}$. Assume that the managers can attain a utility level K if they work outside the firm.
   a) Solve for the optimal level of effort and of risk sharing (first best solution).
   b) Solve the principal and agent problem in the case when $\alpha=1$. Is the solution optimal?
   c) What happens in the case when $\alpha<1$? Demonstrate why the solution to the principal-agent problem in this case will be suboptimal.

4. The government wishes to construct a new defense system (SDI: Super Ditch Interuptor, a giant trench across southern Arizona and New Mexico to prevent terrorist infiltration of the US). The government will award the project to the lowest bidder in a sealed bid auction. Assume there are N firms that could build the project. The costs for completing the project for any firm are $c_i = d_i + x + e$, where d_i = minimum costs of completing the project for firm i, x = the amount that costs are above minimum costs, and e = a random cost component that can not be known until after the project has been undertaken. The amount that costs exceed the minimum by can be controlled by a firm through increasing vigilance, h_i, so $x = x(h_i)$. Assume that the government is risk neutral and that all firms are risk averse, though each firm's attitudes towards risk differs. The government does not observe any of the components of c, only the total cost after the firm has completed the project.

The government awards contracts of: $ac_n + (1-a)b_n$, where b_n is the low bid and $0 < a < 1$. This is a form of contract that allows for higher or lower payment depending upon the actual costs of the project.

a) Set up the objective function for a firm.
b) Set up the objective function for the government.
(Be sure to indicate what the choice variables are for a firm and for the government.)
c) Discuss the problems the government might have in getting the project completed in an efficient manner.

5. Consider a competitive industry consisting of a large number of firms both actual and potential. Each firm has the following cost structure: $C(q,K) = \frac{q^2}{K} + rK$, where C is total cost, K measures investment in fixed plant and equipment, q is the firm's total output flow and r is the rental rate on captial. Regard K as fixed in the short run but variable in the long run. Let n be the number of active firms in the industry. Suppose that demand for the industry's output is linear: $P(Q) = a - bQ$.

a) For given capacity K, find the minimum efficient scale of operation for a firm in this industy.
b) For given output q, find the cost minimizing investment in fixed plant and equipment.
c) For a given number of firms, n, each with capacity K, find the short run industry equilibrium.
d) Assuming (n,K) as above, find the short run industry equilibrium. Indicate in terms of the parameters (r,a,b) and the industry structure (n,K) whether firms are making or losing money in the short run.
e) Find the long run average cost function for firms in this industry, and the long run industry equilibrium price and level of production. What is the total industry investment in fixed plant at this long run equilibrium? What can you say about industry structure (i.e., n and K) in long-run equilibrium? Describe how adjustments are made form the short to the long run.
f) Suppose that, starting from a situation of long-run equilibirium, demand grows unexpectedly (a is larger than before). Suppose there is a significant lag in new firms entering this industry, and incumbent firms have a cost advantage over new entrants.

Describe how industry structure would evolve over time. What would happen if r were a declining function of the level of profitability of the enterprise (through internal financing). Could the competitiive structure of the industry be jeopardized under these circumstances?

Boston College
Department of Economics

Ec 853
Industrial Organization I

Steve Polasky
Fall 1989

Problem Set #3

1. In the game of chicken you can either play gutsy (G) or flinch (F). If you can make the other flinch while not flinching yourself you gain 6 while the other gets 0. If you both flinch you both get 2. If you both play gutsy then you both lose −2. Find all Nash equilibria for this game.

2. Prove that in a bimatrix game if a constant is added to the payoffs of the rows player in one of the columns then the set of Nash equilibria is unchanged. What is the corresponding statement for the columns player?

3. In Newtonia all individuals are identical. They all earn income (Y_i) and can spend their income on public parks (p_i) and Volvo stationwagons (v_i). The price of each good is 1. There are N people in Newtonia.

   a) If each person's utility function is $U_i(P,v_i) = P^a v_i^{1-a}$, where P = provision of public parks = sum of all p_i, find the utility maximizing amount of spending on Volvos and public parks by each individual.

   b) What is the socially optimal provision of public parks and of Volvos? How does this compare with the choice made by individuals?

   c) Now suppose that $U(P,v_i) = .5P + v_i$. What is the choice made by the utility maximizing individual. What is the socially optimal choice? (Hint: is this an interior solution or a corner solution?)

   d) Why does individual choice lead to a different outcome than the socially optimal outcome?

4. Prove that a dominant strategy equilibrium is a Nash equilibrium.

5. Nature deals a card to player 1. The card has a 50% probability of containing $20 and a 50% probability of containing $10. Player 1, after seeing the card, has two options:

   i) reveal the card to player 2, and play matching pennies with player 2. If 2 fails to match it, 2 pays 1 the amount on the card, otherwise nothing happens.

   ii) does not reveal the card and challenges 2 to guess the card. If 2 fails she pays 1 the card's value, otherwise nothing.

   a) Draw out the extensive form of this game.

b) Solve for the subgame perfect Nash equilibrium in this game by using backward induction.
c) How much would you have to pay 2 (assuming risk neutrality) in order to induce her to play?

6. Suppose that duopolists produce a product for which there is a linear demand curve: $P(Q) = a - bQ$. Suppose that all firms have marginal costs of production that are constant at c per unit.
   a) Solve for the Cournot equilibrium.
   b) Show that the resulting equilibrium price satisfies: $\frac{p-c}{p} = H/\varepsilon$, where $H = \sum_{i=1}^{n} s_i^2$ is the Herfindahl index of concentration, and ε is the price elasticity of demand.
   c) Show that the Cournot equilibrium is a Nash equilibrium for some game.
   d) Solve for the Stackelberg outcome. (Let firm 1 be the Stackelberg leader.) Show that the Stackelberg outcome is a Nash equilibrium for some game. How does the "Stackelberg game" differ from the "Cournot game?"
   e) Solve for the cartel solution. Assume that the firms split the profits of the cartel 50–50. Show that the cartel outcome is not a Nash equilibrium (i.e., show that a firm can always make more profit by cheating on the agreement).
   f) What is the Bertrand equilibrium?
   g) Suppose that $P(Q) = 1 - Q$, cost of production are zero, and that each firm has production constraints of 1/2. Find the maximum and minimum price that we would see in Bertrand competition.
   h) Rank in terms of profit for a firm the following outcomes: Cournot, Bertrand, Stackelberg leader, Stackelberg follower, Cartel member (assuming an equal sharing rule). Does this ranking hold in general?
   i) Rank in terms of social welfare the following outcomes: Cournot, Bertrand, Stackelberg, Cartel. Does this ranking hold in general?

7. Keep all of the assumptions of problem 6 except that now suppose that firm 1 has costs per unit of c_1 and firm 2 has costs of production of c_2. Assume that $c_1 < c_2$.
   a) Solve for the Cournot equilibrium
   b) Solve for the Bertrand equilibrium.
   c) What would a cartel solution involve in this case (assume that side payments among cartels members can be made).
   d) Define $\Delta c = c_2 - c_1$. Suppose that firm 1 can take measures to decrease their costs by Δc. If they are in Cournot competition how much is this worth to

them? By how much does social surplus increase? Is the change in profits or social surplus greater? Give an intuitive explanation of your answer.

e) Answer the same questions as in part (d) if instead of Cournot competition we have Bertrand competition.

8. Find the N-firm Cournot-Nash equilibrium for an industry that has a demand curve of $P(Q) = (Q)^{-b}$, and each firm has a constant marginal cost of production c.

9. Assume that there are two firms (X,Y) in an industry that produces a homogeneous good. Industry demand is given by $P = a - bQ$. Marginal cost is c for both firms.

a) Solve for the Cournot output of each firm, and the level of profit for each firm.

b) Suppose that one firm decides to "split" and now becomes two firms (Y: Y,Z). Solve for the new Cournot equilibrium. What happens to the profit of the firm that split (i.e., profit of Y+Z). What happens to the profit of firm X? Explain why profit either increases or decreases for the "splitting" firm.

Boston College
Department of Economics

Ec 853
Industrial Organization I

Steve Polasky
Fall 1989

Problem Set #4

1. Assume there are two firms that produce a homogeneous good. Let the market demand curve be: $P = 14 - Q$. Each firm's costs are $C(q_i) = 2q_i$.

    a) Assume that firm 2 chooses a quantity knowing the quantity that firm 1 has chosen, and that firm 1 knows this. What is the Nash equilibrium in this game?

    Forcing firm 2 to choose q_2 knowing q_1 is just like letting firm 1 precommit to a quantity choice. With this interpretation of the game, it seems reasonable to question why firm 1 had this oppportunity while firm 2 did not. Assume there is really a two-stage game being played. In the first stage, the firms simultaneously decide whether or not to precommit to a quantity, and if so, which quantity. Then, in the second stage, the firms play the following game. If they have both precommitted, trade takes place at the market clearing price. If neither firm has chosen to precommit, the standard Cournot game is played. If one firm has precommitted while the other has not, the game played is the analogue to the game played in part (a). To simplify, assume that the firms have only three possible moves in the first stage. They may commit to a quantity of 4, to a quantity of 6, or they may choose not to commit.

    b) Find the subgame perfect Nash Equilibrium if the firms choose pure strategies in the first stage of the game.

2. In industry X, there is a Cournot duopoly with no threat of entry. Firm 1 has constant per unit costs of $c_1 = 12$. Firm 2 can have either high constant per unit costs, $c_2^H = 24$, or low constant per unit costs, $c_2^L = 12$. Assume that each outcome occurs with a 50% probability. Firm 2 knows whether it has high or low costs prior to making its production decision. There are no fixed costs for either firm. The inverse industry demand curve is: $P(X) = 72 - X$, where $X = x_1 + x_2$, and x_1 and x_2 are the quantities produced by firms 1 and 2 respectively.

    a) Suppose that firm 2 can reveal information about its true costs to firm 1 and that firm 1 can verify the information. Find the ex ante expected profit for firm 2 when it reveals its information.

    b) Find the ex ante expected profit for firm 2 when it keeps its information about costs private.

    c) Is it better for firm 2 to reveal its cost information or to keep the information private? Give some economic intuition that helps to explain your result.

3. Assume that there are two firms and two time periods. In the first period, firm 1 is a monopolist. Firm 2 decides whether to enter the market in the second period. If firm

2 enters there is Cournot competition in the second period. If firm 2 does not enter, firm 1 remains a monopolist in period 2. The discount factor between period 1 and 2 is δ. Firm 1 can be of two types: a high cost firm (H) with probability x, or a low cost firm (L) with probability (1−x). Let $M^t(q_1)$ = the per period profit to the monopolist of type t (t= H,L) when they play quantity q_1. Assume, for now, that the monopolist can either produce q_1^H, the profit maximizing output for a monopolist of type H, or q_1^L, the profit maximizing output for a monopolist of type L. Let $D_1^t(q_1,q_2)$ = the per period profit to firm 1 when firm 1 is of type t, firm 2 enters and the firms engage in Cournot competition, where q_1 is the output of firm 1 and q_2 is the output of firm 2. Define $D_2^t(q_1,q_2)$ in a similar fashion.

a) Show what conditions are necessary for there to exist a pooling equilibrium in this game. Explain.

b) Show what conditions are necessary for there to exist a separating equilibrium in this game. Explain.

c) Now suppose that the monopolist is not restricted to q_1^H, or q_1^L in the first period but may produce any quantity it desires. Show how this would change the necessary conditions for the separating equilbrium to exist.

4. Blockbuster Films distributes movies to theaters. Assume that movie-goers will see the movie once (and only once) if the price of the movie is below their reservation price, otherwise they will not see the movie. They may see the movie in period 1 (first-run), or in period 2 (second-run). Movie-goers are either: i) Trendies, who have a high reservation price for first-run movies (P_t) but have a lower reservation price for second-run movies ($\delta_t P_t$; $0 < \delta_t < 1$); and ii) Cheapskates, who have reservation price P_c for first run movies ($P_c < P_t$), but do not have any discount for seeing second-run movies. Assume that the proportion of the population that are trendies is λ (Normalize total population size to be 1). Assume there are no costs to film distribution and that the firm does not discount revenue received in the second period.

a) State the conditions on prices for first-run and second-run movies (P_1 and P_2) that will make trendies choose to go see the movie in the first period and cheapskates to see the movie in the second period (Separating). Given that this is the strategy that Blockbuster wants to pursue, what are the profit maximizing prices, P_1 and P_2?

b) State the conditions on prices for first-run and second run movies that will make both groups see the movie in period one (Pooling). Given that this is the strategy that Blockbuster wants to pursue, what are the profit maximizing prices, P_1 and P_2? Is it ever more profitable for Blockbuster to set prices to get the Pooling outcome rather than the Separating outcome? If so, for what parameter values is this true?

c) State the conditions on prices for first-run and second run movies that will make only trendies see the movie (Exclusive). Given that this is the strategy that Blockbuster wants to pursue, what are the profit maximizing prices, P_1 and P_2? Is it ever more profitable for Blockbuster to set prices to get the Exclusive outcome rather than the Separating outcome? If so, for what parameter values is this true?

5. Polo Springs and Belmo Springs each sell spring water to consumers in Yuppieville. Each firm can magically produce spring water for no cost (it naturally bubbles out of the ground). Polo, has a demand curve: $X(P_x, P_y) = a - (1/2)P_x + cP_y$, where P_x is the price of Polo water and P_y is the price of Belmo water, $a > 0$, $c > 0$. Belmo has a demand curve given by $Y(P_x, P_y) = \alpha - (1/2)P_y + \gamma P_x$, $\alpha > 0, \gamma > 0$. Assume that $\gamma c < (1/2)$.

a) Solve for the equilibrium prices set by a Stackelberg leader and a Stackelberg follower.

b) Let $a = 40$, $\alpha = 40$, $c = 0.25$, and $\gamma = 0.25$. Does the Stackelberg leader or follower make more profit in this model? Explain the intuition for this result.

U

Northwestern University
Professor Robert Porter
Andersen Hall 1-326
491-3491

Economics C-49
The Structure of American Industry
Fall 1988

Course Description:

    This is a one quarter introduction to industrial organization for advanced undergraduates. Students are assumed to be familiar with the material covered in Economics C-10. The attached list of topics describes the material to be covered in this course.

Text:

    The required text for this course is by Stephen Martin, "Industrial Economics: Economic Analysis and Public Policy," Macmillan, 1988. In addition, you may wish to purchase Walter Adams (editor), "The Structure of American Industry," 7th edition, Macmillan, 1986. This book is a compilation of case studies of some prominent American industries. Both books are on reserve at the library.

Course Requirements:

    There will be four or five problem sets, a mid-quarter exam and a final. The final is officially scheduled for Tuesday, December 13, 9:00 to 11:00 AM. The approximate weighting scheme for the final grade will be:

Problem Sets	20%
Mid-quarter Exam	30%
Final Exam	50%

Any student who does not hand in the problem sets or take either exam will not receive credit for the course.

Economics C-49, Fall 1988, page two

Readings:

Class discussion will proceed through the following topics more or less as listed. There are no precise dates for particular topics.

1. Introduction
     Martin, Chapters 1 and 3

2. Producer Theory (Review)
     Martin, Chapter 2

3. Perfect Competition and Monopoly
     Martin, Chapter 2
     Adams, Chapter 1

4. Oligopoly and Monopolistic Competition
     Martin, Chapter 5

5. Market Power and Welfare
     Martin, Chapters 2 and 3

6. Collusion
     Martin, Chapter 6

7. Advertising and Product Differentiation
     Martin, Chapters 8 and 11

8. Barriers to Entry
     Martin, Chapters 4 and 16

9. Price Discrimination
     Martin, Chapter 15

10. Vertical Integration and Mergers
     Martin, Chapters 9 and 10

11. Vertical Pricing and Restrictions
     Martin, Chapter 17

12. Technological Innovation
     Martin, Chapter 12

13. The Role of International Trade
     Martin, Chapter 13

The case studies in Adams are pertinent for many of these topics.

Economics C-49
The Structure of American Industry
Homework #1

Consider a competitive industry in which each firm uses a single input x, which is purchased at a price of w, to produce an output q, which is sold at a competitive price of p. Each firm of type i is endowed with an amount θ_i of an input which cannot be purchased in any market. For example, it may represent the efficiency of the corporate structure. There are 3 types of firms, so i can equal 1, 2 or 3. Firms of different types have different amounts of this input, so $\theta_1 \neq \theta_2$ for example. A firm with θ units of the untraded input faces a production function $q = \sqrt{x\theta}$.

(a) Show that the total cost of producing q units of output is wq^2/θ, for a firm with θ units of untraded input.

(b) What is the firm's cost minimizing demand function for x? Is this input strongly normal (i.e., does it use more x if it produces more)? This demand will be a function of q, w and θ.

(c) Find the firm's profit maximizing output, which we will denote by q^*. Describe how q^* varies as p, w and θ vary.

(d) Show that $\hat{\theta}$, the endowment of the "marginal firm", is zero. Why doesn't this depend on input or output prices?

(e) Suppose that $\theta_1 = 1$, $\theta_2 = 2$ and $\theta_3 = 3$, and that there are 100 firms of each type. Compute the industry supply function, which should depend on p and w.

(f) The industry demand function if $D(p) = 1-p$. Compute the equilibrium price, denoted by p^e. This should just depend on w.

(g) Compute the industry demand function for the input x at the equilibrium price you computed in part (f).

Economics C-49
The Structure of American Industry
Homework #2

1. Do problem 5-1, on page 130 of Martin.

2. Let q_1 and q_2 denote the outputs of two duopolists. Let the market demand function be $p = 200 - 2(q_1 + q_2)$ and their total cost functions be $C_1(q_1) = 20q_1$ and $C_2(q_2) = q_2^2$

    (a) Determine the competitive price, output levels and profits.

    (b) Determine the Cournot/Nash price, output levels and profits.

    (c) Determine the collusive price, output levels and profits.

3. Consider an industry with two firms which produce the same product. Let q denote the output of firm i, for i = 1, 2 and let $Q = q_1 + q_2$.

    The industry demand curve is given by:

    $$p(Q) = 1/Q.$$

    where p is the price of the product. Each firm's total cost function is $C(q) = cq$. Firms choose output levels to maximize single period profits.

    (a) Find the symmetric Cournot equilibrium.

    (b) When the two firms choose their Cournot equilibrium outputs, what will the value of the Lerner index be?

ROBERT PORTER
Economics C-49
The Structure of American Industry
Midquarter Examination
November 2, 1988

The is a one hour exam. Budget your time carefully. Don't answer any questions that have not been asked. Remember to write your name on each examination booklet. There is no choice, so remember to answer all questions. The three questions will have equal weighting in the grading.

1. Identify or describe briefly each of the following:
   (a) Lerner index
   (b) Minimum efficient scale
   (c) Conjectural variation
   (d) decreasing returns to scale
   (e) 4-firm concentration ratio

2. (a) Suppose that the Justice Department must decide whether to approve a merger that would convert a competitive but inefficient industry into a monopolistic but efficient producer. What factors should the Justice Department take into account? Indicate possible welfare trade offs in a clearly labelled diagram.
   (b) Suppose that an economic study of a particular industry has determined that some, but not all, firms earned higher rates of return than the national average, and that larger firms tended to earn higher economic profits than smaller firms. Furthermore, at any point in time, different firms tended to charge identical prices, and firms changed prices concurrently. Do either or both of these facts necessarily imply that the firms in the industry have behaved noncompetitively, so that antitrust action is warranted?

3. Consider an industry with a linear demand function: $p = 100 - 2Q$, where p denotes price and Q denotes the total quantity of the product being considered. There are four firms in the industry, each with the same total cost function:

   $$C(q_i) = 20 + (q_i)^2 \quad , \quad i = 1, 2, 3, \text{ or } 4,$$

   where q_i is the output of firm i. Thus $Q = q_1 + q_2 + q_3 + q_4$.

   (a) Suppose that all four firms are competitive price takers; i.e., they ignore the effect of their own output on the market price p. What is the supply function of a typical firm? I.e., how much will each supply given a price p?
   (b) Compute the industry supply function.
   (c) Compute the equilibrium price.
   (d) Show that the profit of each firm is positive in equilibrium.

Economics C-49
The Structure of American Industry
Homework #3

1. Consider a symmetric triopoly in which firms produce a homogeneous product for which the demand curve is:

    $$P = 30 - 2(q_1 + q_1 + q_3).$$

    where q_i denotes the output of firm i. Each firm as a constant marginal cost of 6, and no fixed costs. The firms behave noncooperatively, and the industry is initially at a Cournot equilibrium.

    (a) Find the symmetric Cournot equilibrium output, and show your work.

    (b) Do any two firms in the industry have an economic incentive to merge, thereby creating a duopoly? (Hint: Compare the profits of two of the triopolists with those of one of the duopolists.)

2. Suppose that the state government has decided to grant a monopoly to sell gasoline along I-294, and that only two firms are competing for this right. The monopoly is worth $R in present discounted value terms to the firm that gets it. The government agency which awards this monopoly right is subject to lobbying pressure, and each firm must decide how much money to spend on lobbying. Let E_i denote the dollar amount of lobbying expenditures for firm i (where i is 1 or 2). Let P_i denote the probability that firm i obtains the monopoly. This probability is determined by the firm's fraction of total industry lobbying expenditures. Assume that $P_i = 0$ if $E_i = 0$. (If a firm spends nothing, it will not get the right.)

    (a) What is the probability that firm 1 wins if only it spends money on lobbying? What is the probability that each firm wins if they spend equal amounts?

    (b) The expected value of the monopoly for a firm is the probability of winning multiplied by the present value of the monopoly. Each firm maximizes its expected profit, which is the expected value of the monopoly minus its expenditure on lobbying. Write the expression for the expected profit for firm i in terms of the notation given above.

    (c) Think of this competition as a one period game with two players who must select their lobbying expenditures independently. Find the Nash equilibrium levels of E_1 and E_2. (Hint: The equilibrium expenditure levels will be the same for each firm, and these equilibrium levels will depend on R.)

    (d) What fraction of the discounted value of the monopoly (R) will be spent on lobbying by the two firms?

Economics C-49

The Structure of American Industry
Homework #4

1. (a) Suppose that a car dealer has a local monopoly in selling Toyotas. It pays $w to Toyota for each car that it sells, and charges each customer $p. Its demand curve is given by Q = 10-p. What is the profit maximizing price? (This will be a function of w.) If p is set at this level, how many cars will it sell? What will its profits be?

   (b) Now consider Toyota's problem. If it charges w per car to its dealer, it can calculate how many cars the dealer will buy (as we did in part (a)). This gives a demand function for Toyota as a function of w. Suppose it costs Toyota $2 to produce each car (the units here are thousands of dollars). What is the profit-maximizing choice of w? What will Toyota's profits then be? What price will its dealer then charge? What are the resulting dealer profits?

   (c) Now suppose Toyota operates the dealership, eliminating the intermediate step of selling to the dealer. It sells cars to customers at a price p, and each costs two to produce. Final demand remains Q = 10 - p. What is the profit-maximizing choice of p? What profits will Toyota get?

   (d) Compare the profits of Toyota in (c) with the joint profits of Toyota and the dealer in (b). Are customers better off (in terms of the price they pay) when Toyota runs the dealership?

2. Suppose that a film distributor is trying to sell two films to two theaters. The theaters value the films as follows:

   Old Orchard would pay $80 for a Clint Eastwood movie and $25 for a Woody Allen film.

   Evanston would pay $70 for Clint Eastwood and $30 for Woody Allen.

   Once the film is made, the distributor bears no costs in providing copies of these films to the theaters.
   Derive the maximum profit the distributor can earn if the films are sold separately. Show that block booking, in which the two movies are sold as part of one package, is a more profitable strategy.

ROBERT PORTER
Economics C-49
The Structure of American Industry
Final Examination
December 13, 1988

This exam is two hours long. Approximate times are given for each of the 5 questions. Grades will be proportional to these times. Be sure to answer <u>every</u> question, and to define <u>all</u> notation you introduce. Collusion, if detected, will be punished. Good luck!

1. (15 minutes) Identify or describe <u>briefly</u> each of the following:

    (a) Herfindahl index
    (b) contestable market
    (c) vertical integration
    (d) block booking
    (e) FTC

2. (20 minutes) Briefly answer each of the following:

    (a) Why might a cartel (or collusive arrangement) be unstable in a static (one period) world, and yet be stable in a dynamic setting, where firms compete over a long time horizon?

    (b) List five possible ways in which a consumer could try to infer the quality of a good she is considering buying. Suppose that the true quality is not observable until after the good is bought.

3. (15 minutes) Carefully explain when it may be profitable for a firm to build excess capacity, that is productive capacity which it never actually uses, when it faces a threat of potential entry into its market.

4. (25 minutes) Assume duopolists face a demand curve given by $p = 8-Q$, where $Q = q_1 + q_2$, and the firms have identical costs functions with fixed costs of 3 and average variable costs of 2 per unit.

    (a) Write the profit function for each firm.
    (b) Derive the reaction function for each firm.
    (c) Find the Cournot equilibrium quantities, price and profits. Show your work.
    (d) Illustrate the reaction functions and the Cournot equilibrium in a graph.

PLEASE TURN OVER

5. (25 minutes) Suppose consumers are evenly distributed along a street that is one mile long. Each consumer will buy one unit from the closest firm, and so each firm's demand equals its share of the consumers. Firms sequentially choose locations along the street, and relocation is prohibitively costly. There is free entry into this market. Thus, firm 1 decides whether and where to locate, followed by firm 2, etc., until no further firm wishes to enter.

Assume all firms charge a price of $12, pay a fixed cost of $2 if they enter and have variable costs equal to $4 times their market share, so $C(q) = 2 + 4q$ if q is their market share.

(a) What is the market share of a firm that just breaks even?

(b) How many firms will actually enter in the sequential location equilibrium, and where will they locate?

(c) Do all firms earn zero profits in equilibrium? Compute the profits for each firm.

G

Prof. Robert Porter
Andersen Hall 1-326
491-3491
                 Northwestern University
                     Economics D-50-3
                    Industrial Organization
                        Spring 1990

    This is the third quarter of the graduate industrial organization sequence. Students are assumed to be familiar with the material covered in Economics D-50-1 and 2. There is no required text, although the following books are available for purchase:

    Jean Tirole, The Theory of Industrial Organization, MIT, 1988.

    Timothy Bresnahan and Richard Schmalensee, editors, The Empirical
        Renaissance in Industrial Economics, Basil Blackwell, 1987.

    David Kreps, A Course in Microeconomic Theory, Princeton, 1990.

The Tirole text provides an up-to-date discussion of many topics in theoretical industrial organization. Renaissance is a collection of empirical articles from a recent Journal of Industrial Economics symposium. The Kreps book is a new micro text, and it includes a very useful discussion of relevant game-theoretic concepts. In addition, the following is a valuable, but expensive, reference:

    Richard Schmalensee and Robert Willig, editors, Handbook of Industrial
        Organization, 2 volumes, North-Holland, 1989.

This is a recent installment in the North-Holland Handbook series, and consists of 26 chapters on various aspects of industrial organization and regulation. Copies of chapters relevant to this course will be made available. Other books you may wish to consult include:

    William Baumol, John Panzar, and Robert Willig, Contestable Markets and
        the Theory of Industry Structure, Harcourt Brace Jovanovich, 1982.

    Dennis Carlton and Jeffrey Perloff, Modern Industrial Organization, Scott
        Foresman, 1990.

    James Friedman, Oligopoly Theory, Cambridge, 1983.

    James Friedman, Game Theory with Applications to Economics, Oxford,
        1986.

    Morton Kamien and Nancy Schwartz, Market Structure and Innovation, 1982.

    Richard Nelson and Sidney Winter, An Evolutionary Theory of Economic
        Change, Harvard, 1982.

    Steven Salop, editor, Strategy, Predation and Antitrust Analysis,
        Federal Trade Commission, 1981.

F. M. Scherer and D. Ross, <u>Industrial Market Structure and Economic Performance</u>, 3rd edition, Houghton Mifflin, 1990.

George Stigler, <u>The Organization of Industry</u>, Irwin, 1968.

George Stigler and James Kindahl, <u>The Behavior of Industrial Prices</u>, National Bureau of Economic Research, 1970.

Joseph Stiglitz and Frank Mathewson, editors, <u>New Developments in the Analysis of Market Structure</u>, MIT, 1986.

Lester Telser, <u>Theories of Competition</u>, North-Holland, 1988.

The attached syllabus indicates the topics I intend to discuss. I will try to limit the amount of reading to one paper per lecture. The papers selected are not all "classics", but they do illustrate the strengths and weaknesses of various approaches.

Grading will be based on several problem sets and a final exam. The Tirole book also contains a number of worthwhile exercises, together with answers.

Class discussion will proceed through the following topics more or less as listed. There are no precise dates for particular topics.

I. Dynamic Models

  D. Abreu, "Extremal equilibria of oligopolistic supergames," JET 6/86, 191-225.

  D. Abreu, D. Pearce and E. Stacchetti, "Optimal cartel equilibria with imperfect monitoring," JET 6/86, 251-269.

  W. Brock and J. Scheinkman, "Price setting supergames with capacity constraints," RESTUD 7/85, 371-382.

  J. Friedman (1983), Chapters 5 and 7.

  D. Kreps (1990), Chapter 14.

  D. Kreps and M. Spence, "Modelling the role of history in industrial organization and competition," in G. Feiwel, editor, <u>Issues in Contemporary Microeconomics and Welfare</u>, 1985, 340-378.

  D. Levhari and L. Mirman, "The great fish war: An example using a dynamic Cournot-Nash solution," BJE Spring 1980, 322-334.

  C. Shapiro, "Theories of oligopoly behavior," <u>Handbook</u>, Vol. 1, Chapter 6.

  J. Tirole (1988), Chapters 6 and 11.

D50-3, Spring 1990, page three

II. Econometrics of Markets with Imperfect Competition

O. Ashenfelter and D. Sullivan, "Nonparametric tests of market structure: An application to the cigarette industry," *Renaissance*, 113-128.

T. Bresnahan, "Competition and collusion in the American automobile industry: The 1955 price war," *Renaissance*, 87-112.

T. Bresnahan, "Empirical studies of industries with market power," *Handbook*, Vol. 2, Chapter 17.

T. Bresnahan and P. Reiss, "Do entry conditions vary across markets?" (with discussion), BPEA:Micro 1987, 833-881.

T. Bresnahan and P. Reiss, "Empirical models of discrete games," mimeo, Stanford, 1989. (forthcoming, J. Econometrics)

R. Gilbert and M. Lieberman, "Investment and coordination in oligopolistic industries," RJE Spring 1987, 17-33.

R. Hall, "The relationship between price and marginal cost in U.S. industry," JPE 10/88, 921-947.

J. Panzar and J. Rosse, "Testing for "monopoly" equilibrium," *Renaissance*, 73-86.

R. Porter, "A study of cartel stability: The Joint Executive Committee 1880-1886," BJE Autumn 1983, 301-314.

D. Scheffman and P. Spiller, "Geographic market definitions under the U.S. Department of Justice Merger Guidelines," JLE 4/87, 123-147.

R. Schmalensee, "Econometric diagnosis of competitive localization," IJIO 3/85, 57-70.

R. Schmalensee, "Inter-industry studies of structure and performance," *Handbook*, Vol. 2, Chapter 16.

III. The Size Distribution of Firms: Theory

C. Holt, "A dynamic model of competitive industry structure with learning by doing," mimeo, Virginia, 1988.

B. Holmstrom and J. Tirole, "The theory of the firm," *Handbook*, Vol. 1, Chapter 2.

H. Hopenhayn, "A dynamic stochastic model of entry and exit to an industry," mimeo, Stanford, 1989.

B. Jovanovic, "Selection and evolution of industry," EM 5/82, 649-670.

R. Lucas, "Adjustment costs and the theory of supply," JPE 8/67, 321-334.

R. Lucas, "On the size distribution of business firms," BJE Autumn 1978, 508-523.

J. Panzar and R. Willig, "On the comparative statics of a competitive industry with inframarginal firms," AER 6/78, 474-478.

E. Prescott and J. Boyd, "Dynamic coalitions, growth, and the firm," in E. Prescott and N. Wallace, editors, Contractual Arrangements for Intertemporal Trade, 1987, 146-160.

E. Prescott and M. Visscher, "Organization capital," JPE 6/80, 446-461.

R. Rob, "Learning and capacity expansion in a new market under uncertainty," mimeo, Pennsylvania, 1988.

J. Tirole (1988), Chapter 0 ("The theory of the firm").

IV. The Size Distribution of Firms: Empirics

V. Chetty and J. Heckman, "A dynamic model of aggregate output supply, factor demand and entry and exit for a competitive industry with heterogeneous plants," J. Econometrics 10/86, 237-262.

T. Dunne, M. Roberts and L. Samuelson, "Patterns of firm entry and exit in U.S. manufacturing," RJE Winter 1988, 495-515.

T. Dunne, M. Roberts and L. Samuelson, "The growth and failure of U.S. manufacturing plants," QJE 11/89, 671-698.

D. Evans, "The relationship between firm growth, size, and age: Estimates for 100 manufacturing industries," Renaissance, 197-211.

D. Evans, "Tests of alternative theories of firm growth," JPE 8/87, 657-674.

D. Evans and B. Jovanovic, "An estimated model of entrepreneurial choice under liquidity constraints," JPE 8/89, 808-827.

B. Hall, "The relationship between firm size and firm growth in the U.S. manufacturing sector," Renaissance, 213-236.

A. Pakes, "Mueller's Profits in the Long Run," RJE Summer 1987, 319-332.

A. Pakes and R. Ericson, "Empirical implications of alternative models of firm dynamics," mimeo, Yale, 1990.

D50-3, Spring 1990, page five

V. Research and Development

T. Bresnahan, "Measuring the spillovers from technical advance: Mainframe computers in financial services," AER 9/86, 742-755.

W. Cohen, R. Levin and D. Mowery, "Firm size and R&D intensity: A re-examination," Renaissance, 173-195.

M. Gort and S. Klepper, "Time paths in the diffusion of product innovations," EJ 9/82, 630-633.

Z. Griliches, "Patents: Recent trends and puzzles" (with discussion), BPEA:Micro 1989, 291-330.

Z. Griliches, A. Pakes and B. Hall, "The value of patents as indicators of inventive activity," in P. Dasgupta and P. Stoneman, editors, Economic Policy and Technological Performance, 1987, 97-124.

A. Jaffee, "Technological opportunity and spillovers of R&D: Evidence from firms' patents, profits, and market value," AER 12/86, 984-1001.

B. Jovanovic and G. MacDonald, "Competitive diffusion," mimeo, NORC, 1988.

M. Kamien and N. Schwartz (1982).

R. Levin and W. Cohen, "Empirical studies of invention and innovation," Handbook, Vol. 2, Chapter 18.

M. Lieberman, "The learning curve and pricing in the chemical processing industries," RJE Summer 1984, 213-228.

R. Nelson and S. Winter (1982).

S. Oster, "The diffusion of innovation among steel firms: The basic oxygen furnace," BJE Spring 1982, 45-56.

A. Pakes, "Patents as options: Some estimates of the value of holding European patent stocks," EM 7/86, 755-784.

J. Reinganum, "The timing of innovation: Research, development, and diffusion," Handbook, Vol. 1, Chapter 14.

J. Tirole (1988), Chapter 10.

VI. Auctions

O. Ashenfelter, "How auctions work for wine and art," JEP Summer 1989, 23-36.

D. Graham and R. Marshall, "Collusive bidder behavior at single-object second-price and English auctions," JPE 12/87, 1217-1239.

K. Hendricks and R. Porter, "An empirical study of an auction with asymmetric information," AER 12/88, 865-883.

K. Hendricks, R. Porter and B. Boudreau, "Information, returns, and bidding behavior in O.C.S. auctions: 1954-1969," <u>Renaissance</u>, 147-172.

P. McAfee and J. McMillan, "Auctions and bidding," JEL 6/87, 699-738.

P. Milgrom, "Auction Theory," in T. Bewley, editor, <u>Advances in Economic Theory: Fifth World Congress</u>, 1987, 1-32.

P. Milgrom, "Auctions and bidding: A primer," JEP Summer 1989, 3-22.

J. Riley, "Expected revenues from open and sealed bid auctions," JEP Summer 1989, 41-50.

R. Wilson, "A bidding model of perfect competition," RESTUD 10/77, 511-518.

R. Wilson, "Strategic analysis of auctions," mimeo, Stanford, 1990. (forthcoming, Handbook of Game Theory).

Economics D-50-3
Industrial Organization
Problem Set #1
Spring 1990

1. Show that the Cournot-Nash equilibrium in a homogeneous product industry is not industry profit maximizing in general.

2. Consider a two stage duopoly game in which the firms make simultaneous entry decisions in the first stage and simultaneous output decisions in the second stage. Let $e_i = e$ denote a decision to enter by firm i, and let $e_i = n$ denote a decision to not enter. If the first stage decision is to not enter, then the firm's output must be zero in the second stage. A firm that chooses to enter can then produce 0, 1, or 2 units in the second stage. The relationship between firms' outputs and profits, in the event that they enter, is given in the figure below, where the left hand number in each pair of numbers is the profit for firm one. If either firm decides not to enter, it earns a profit of 1.5 from the best alternative use of its capital in some other market.

	$x_2 = 0$	$x_2 = 1$	$x_2 = 2$
$x_1 = 0$	0,0	0,3	0, 4
$x_1 = 1$	3,0	2,2	1, 1
$x_1 = 2$	4,0	1,1	-2,-2

When a game is represented in extensive form, a player's decision rule specifies the player's action for each of that player's information sets.

(a) Depict the extensive form for the two stage described above and specify a possible decision rule for player 1 (any decision rule will do).

(b) Find a subgame perfect Nash equilibrium for the two stage game described above. Explain.

(c) Are there any Nash equilibrium pairs of decision rules for this two stage game which are not subgame perfect? Explain.

3. Consider a duopoly in an industry which exists for two periods. The demand curve in the industry in period t (for t = 1,2) is given by

$$P_t = k/Q_t,$$

where P_t is the price in period t and Q_t is the total output produced in that period. There is therefore a constant demand elasticity of minus one.

In the first period, the firms have identical constant unit costs of c. In the second period, the firms again have constant unit costs, now equal c exp($-bQ_1$). The firms have lower costs in the second period because of learning, but all learning spills over so your competitor learns as much as you do from your output. Assume $c > bk/4$, and that c, b, and K are all positive. The interest rate is zero. The firms compete by choosing quantities. Finally, consumers cannot buy the good in period 1 for consumption in period 2.

(a) Solve for the closed loop or subgame perfect Nash equilibrium.

(b) Solve for the symmetric open loop equilibrium, in which firms choose their first and second period outputs simultaneously, taking as given their competitor's first and second period outputs. Compare and contrast your answer to that in part (a).

(c) How would a positive interest rate have influenced these two solutions? Why is there a difference?

(d) What would the closed loop equilibrium be with price competition?

4. Consider a two period duopoly pricing game. The firms can choose one of three prices in each period, corresponding to collusion (C), Bertrand (B), and price war (W) levels. Their payoffs in each period, when firm i charges P_i, are given by:

	$P_2 = C$	$P_2 = B$	$P_2 = W$
$P_1 = C$	4, 4	0, 5	-1, 5
$P_1 = B$	5, 0	2, 2	-1, 1
$P_1 = W$	5, -1	1, -1	0, 0

The ordered pairs correspond to the first and second firm's payoffs, respectively. Characterize the set of subgame perfect pure strategy Nash equilibria of this game, and the Pareto optimal (from the standpoint of the firms) elements of this set.

5. Consider two quantity setting firms which are engaged in an oligopoly supergame. In any period, they face the inverse demand curve $p = 3 - Q$, where Q is industry output, and pay constant unit costs of one dollar per unit of output. Assume that firms can observe the quantity choices of their rival with a one period lag.

   a. Suppose that both firms discount profits at the same rate r. Show that if $r < 8/9$, then the symmetric joint profit maximizing output vector is supportable as a noncooperative equilibrium by simple trigger strategies. Assume that punishments entail reversion to static noncooperative output levels.

   b. For cases where r exceeds 8/9, solve for the most profitable symmetric quantity vector that is supportable by simple trigger strategies.

   c. Now suppose that r is between 8/9 and one. Suppose that, rather than employing simple trigger strategies, firms follow more complicated strategies. They continue to produce at joint profit maximizing outputs, but follow a reversion by each producing one unit for one period. If either firm fails to produce one unit in a "punishment period", then the next period is also a punishment period.
   Show that these strategies are subgame perfect, and that they yield higher equilibrium payoffs than those calculated in part (b).

6. Consider a repeated two person prisoner's dilemma game, in which the payoffs in each period are as follows: if both players cooperate then each receives a payoff of 5; if both defect then they receive a payoff of only zero; if one defects and the other cooperates then the defector receives a payoff of 6 and the cooperator receives minus one. The players do not discount future payoffs. Each period, there is a 10 per cent chance that the game will end, if it has not ended already.
   Suppose that players choose their intended strategies on each round, passing their instructions to a referee for implementation. The referee then implements those intentions "noisily": If told to play a noncooperative strategy, the referee plays this strategy with probability .9, but plays cooperatively with probability .1. If told to play cooperatively, the referee does so with probability .8 and plays noncooperatively with probability .2. Players know which instructions they sent and, at the end of each round, the referee's implementation of both strategies is revealed to both players. But players don't know what instructions their opponent sent.
   Assume that the random ending of the game in any round and the referee's random implementations of strategies are independently distributed random events.

   a. Prove that it is a Nash equilibrium for players to always send instructions to play noncooperatively. What is the expected payoff to the players in this equilibrium?

b. Suppose players adopt the strategy: Instruct the referee to play cooperatively until either player fails to cooperate (in terms of the implemented strategy), and thereafter instruct the referee to play noncooperatively. Is this an equilibrium? If so, what are the expected payoffs to the players in this equilibrium?

c. Suppose players adopt the strategy: Instruct the referee to play cooperatively until either player fails to cooperate. Then instruct the referee to play noncooperatively for N periods. Then instruct the referee to play cooperatively again, until the next incident of noncooperation. For which N is this an equilibrium? For the smallest such N, what are the expected payoffs to the players in this equilibrium?

d. Now suppose the referee is less capricious - instructions to act noncooperatively are followed with probability .95 and those to act cooperatively are followed with probability .9. Redo parts (a), (b) and (c).

Economics D-50-3
Industrial Organization
Problem Set #2

1. In a competitive industry, shifts in the demand curve identify the market supply curve. We are all familiar with the proposition that "there is no supply curve for a monopolist," since observed price and quantity do not lie on the monopolist's marginal cost function. The question is, how could observed market information on price, quantity, and supply- and demand-shift variables be used to identify the parameters of the unobserved marginal cost function? For simplicity, assume linear functions:

   Cost: $MC = a_0 + a_1 q + a_2 w$

   Demand: $p = b_0 + b_1 q + b_2 I$

   where a and b are parameter vectors, w is the wage rate (or a vector of factor prices), I is income (or a vector of demand-shift variables), p is price, q is quantity, and MC is marginal cost.

   In answering the question posed above, you should specify the stochastic elements for the demand and/or marginal cost equations. You may assume that the monopolist is risk neutral. Be specific about whether the monopolist's decision is made before or after the random elements are observed, and how this affects whether the system of equations to be estimated is identified.

2. It has been proposed that an econometrician could distinguish between a monopolist and a competitive firm by examining time series on revenues, factor prices, and other relevant exogenous variables, and econometrically estimating

$$H = \sum_{i=1}^{m} \partial \ln R / \partial \ln w_i,$$

where R is revenues, and w_i is the price of factor i (for $i = 1, 2, \ldots m$).

   (a) Suppose that factor prices are exogenous. Show that $H = 1$ for a competitive firm, and that $H < 0$ for a monopolist.

   (b) Suppose instead that labor is the only factor of production, and that bilateral bargaining has resulted in a contract in which the number of workers is fixed over time, and their wages adjust so that a fixed fraction of total revenues accrue to labor. Show that, if the firm is a monopolist, $H = 1$, if wages are incorrectly taken to be exogenous. (Hint: Suppose that revenues are determined by the function $R(q,z)$, where q is output and z is an exogenous variable which is observed by the firm and its workers, but not by the econometrician.)

Economics D-50-3
Industrial Organization
Problem Set #3

1. Consider a homogeneous oligopoly of N firms with a linear inverse demand curve, $p = A - BQ$, where A and B are positive. Define $S(N-i)$ to be the sum of the output of firms 1 to N-i inclusive, and let $S(0)$ be zero. The index i for any firm indicates its position in a Stackelberg hierarchy: firm 1 is the leader and chooses its output first, firm 2 chooses second, taking $S(1)$ as given, etc. Hence, firm i chooses ith, taking $S(i-1)$ as given. There are no production costs.

   (a) Solve for the subgame-perfect outputs of firms N-2, N-1, and N as functions of $S(N-3)$, $S(N-2)$, and $S(N-1)$, respectively.

   (b) If $N = 3$, use the results in part (a) to determine the firms' outputs as functions of A and B.

   (c) Show that, for any N, each firm's output is twice as large as that of the firm following it in the hierarchy.

2. Consider an industry with an arbitrary distribution of firm sizes, each firm producing the same good and each drawing on the same technology and paying the same factor prices.

   (a) Suppose that the industry is in a Cournot equilibrium. What must the shape of the common marginal cost schedule be? What restrictions, if any, must be placed on market shares if this is to be a stable equilibrium, i.e., if marginal revenue is to intersect marginal cost from above for each firm?

   (b) Now suppose that the industry is in Bertrand equilibrium. What must the shape of the common cost function be if existing firms have different levels of output?

3. Consider an economy of I individuals, where I is large but finite.

The utility function common to all the I agents is

$$\sum_{j=1}^{J} x(i,j)^{\gamma} \qquad \text{where} \quad 0 < \gamma < 1,$$

and where J is the number of commodities (to be determined endogenously). Here $x(i,j)$ is the amount of commodity j consumed by individual i. The technology for producing good j is

$$y(j) \leq n(j) \qquad \text{where} \quad y(j) = \sum_{i=1}^{I} x(i,j)$$

and where $n(j)$ is the number of workers allocated to producing good j. The manager of technology j is the residual claimant, receiving the difference between the revenues earned on good j and the wage bill. Each technology must have one manager. Thus,

$$I = \sum_{j=1}^{J} n(j) + J.$$

An individual can choose whether to manage a technology or to be employed by someone else. The numeraire is the wage, so all workers have income one. Given the prices selected by the firms, they choose consumption levels of J goods to maximize utility subject to their budget constraints.

Manager j's income equals her receipts $p(j)y(j)$, less wage payments $n(j)$. Managers also choose consumption bundles to maximize utility subject to their budget constraints.

(a) Determine the equilibrium value of J, when managers choose Nash equilibrium prices, and compare this to the value of J which maximizes the welfare of this society.

(b) Determine how the equilibrium and optimal firm sizes change as I varies.

Economics D-50-3
Industrial Organization
Problem Set #4

1. Suppose that N firms are competing to develop a particular technological innovation. The first to succeed, if any, will receive $V, the value of a patent on the innovation. The others receive nothing for their efforts. Model this problem as a one period noncooperative game in which each firm i chooses its expenditure on research E_i. Denote total industry research expenditure by E. Further assume that:

   (i) The probability that the ith firm is the first to develop the innovation is given by $E_i/(1 + E)$.

   (ii) Each firm maximizes its expected profits.

   (iii) $V > 1$.

   (a) If there were only one firm, what would be its optimal expenditure?

   (b) In the general case of N firms, find the symmetric Nash equilibrium expenditure.

   (c) What happens to each firm's equilibrium expenditure, and to total industry expenditures, as N becomes infinitely large? Explain your answer.

   (d) Now assume that V is a prize from the government. If the social value of the innovation is W, then what monetary award V should the government offer to stimulate the socially optimal amount of research? How does the award V depend on the number of firms which are allowed to compete for the prize?

2. In recent years, there has been increasing interest in the economic consequences of allowing firms competing in the same industry to engage in joint ventures, e.g., to build a plant as a joint venture, and to divide the net revenues between the firms in a preassigned way.

   Consider a homogeneous product duopoly initially in Cournot equilibrium. The inverse market demand function is $p = 1 - Q$, and both firms have constant marginal costs of c. There are no fixed costs. Suppose that because of the joint venture, the jointly operated new plant could produce output at a constant marginal cost of w, where $w < c$. Assume that the firms can precommit that the new plant will produce an output of 2Q, and that the costs and revenues of the joint venture will be split equally between the duopolists.

   Consider the following two alternatives:

   (i) The firms can make a binding agreement that they will not produce any output from their old plants (which had marginal costs of c).

D50-3, Spring 1990
Problem Set #4

2.(con.) (ii) The firms cannot make a binding agreement to not produce from their old plants. In this case, they will choose Nash equilibrium output levels from their old plants, taking the precommitted quantity from the joint venture as given.

For each of these two alternatives, determine:

(a) whether the duopolists will find it profitable to engage in the joint venture; and, if so,

(b) the quantity that will be produced by the joint venture;

(c) the quantity each firm will produce from its old plant (for alternative (ii) only);

(d) whether the product price increases or decreases, relative to the initial Cournot equilibrium; and

(e) whether social surplus (measured by the change in consumers' and producers' surplus) increases or decreases, relative to the initial equilibrium.

3. Suppose an industry has inverse demand $p_t = D(Q_t)$ for $t = 1, 2, 3, \ldots$ Assume that $QD(Q)$ is concave and that D is decreasing. Suppose that a firm's production costs in period t are proportional to its output, with proportionality constant c_t. Assume that cumulative <u>industry</u> production experience reduces production costs, according to:

$$c_{t+1} = g(E_t), \quad \text{where } E_t = Q_t + dE_{t-1} \text{ for } 0 < d < 1,$$

where g is decreasing and strictly convex. Assume $E_0 = 0$. There is a constant interest rate, denoted r.

(a) Specify the program a monopolist would solve. Specify the necessary conditions for an optimal steady state, in which price and quantity are constant.

(b) Consider the subgame perfect Markov equilibrium, where N firms noncooperatively choose outputs, contingent solely on cumulative industry production experience. Specify necessary conditions which a steady state must satisfy in equilibrium.

(c) Does one of the market structures above necessarily dominate the others? If so, why? If not, how might you determine which is preferred? (Specify your welfare criterion. Assume that a lump sum tax in the amount of the present discounted value of profits can be imposed on the firms and distributed in equal shares to the identical consumers.)

Economics D-50-3
Industrial Organization
Problem Set #5

1. Suppose that N film exhibitors are going to bid for the exclusive rights to show "Rambo IV". The value to exhibitor i of showing this movie is R(i), where R(i) exceeds R(i+1) for all i ≥ 1. Each exhibitor will earn w if it shows some other movie, where R(N) exceeds w.

    The bids take the form of a percentage of the exhibitors' receipts, say b(i) for exhibitor i, so that if i wins with a bid of b(i) it must pay the producer b(i)R(i), and its net receipts are R(i) - b(i)R(i).

    What is the Nash equilibrium of this bidding game? (Which firm wins in equilibrium and what is its bid?)

2. Suppose that two risk neutral firms wish to bid for a government oil lease. Sealed bids are solicited, and the lease is awarded to the high bidder at a price equal to its bid. Ties are decided by the flip of a coin. Firm 1 makes its bid with the advance knowledge of whether the lease is worth $0 or $1, but firm 2 bids with no prior information, in the sense that it ascribes equal prior probabilities to these two events. Each firm bids to maximize its expected payoffs, given the bidding strategy of the other firm.

    (a) Are there any pure strategy Nash equilibria? If so, characterize them. If not, why not?

    (b) Suppose that each firm adopts a mixed strategy, i.e., a strategy that assigns a probability distribution over a range of possible bids. In a Nash equilibrium, will the range of bids that are made with positive probability be the same for each bidder?

    (c) Find a pair of Nash equilibrium (mixed) bidding strategies. (Hint: In equilibrium, a bidder cannot increase expected profit by altering the probability distribution of its bids. The informed firm will only make a positive bid if the value of the lease is $1. The uninformed firm will only make a positive bid if its expected payoff is nonnegative, so its bid cannot exceed the expected value of the lease (1/2).)

3. Consider a sealed bid, first price auction with two bidders. The object being sold is worth v(i) to bidder i. Both v(1) and v(2) are positive and less than one. Each bidder knows her own value, but not the other's. Each bidder knows only that the other's value is a random draw from the uniform distribution on (0,1).

    The rules of the auction are that the high bid wins, and the winner pays an amount equal to her bid. Thus, if bidder 1 wins with a bid b, her monetary payoff is v(1) - b.

3.(con.) Both bidders are risk averse with the same von Neumann-Morgenstern utility function, which exhibits constant relative risk aversion of $1 - \lambda$, where $0 < \lambda < 1$. The common utility function, therefore, is $u(w) = w^\lambda$.

  (a) Compute the symmetric Nash equilibrium bidding strategies.

  (b) How could the rules of the auction (described in the second paragraph) be altered so that the equilibrium bids equal the values, i.e., so that $b(i) = v(i)$ in equilibrium? Explain.

4. Suppose that N risk neutral agents participate in a sealed bid, second price auction. Therefore, individual bids are not observed by the other participants until after the bidding is closed, the object is awarded to the highest bidder, and that bidder pays the amount bid by the second highest bidder. Assume that the agents know their own valuation of the object, but know only the probability distribution of the valuations of other agents. Further, assume that these valuations are known to be positive with probability one, and that they are independently and identically distributed with continuous density over a closed interval.

   Derive the symmetric Nash equilibrium bidding strategies (where equilibrium bids are expressed as functions of own valuations) of the agents involved in this auction game.

5. Consider an independent private values auction with two bidders. Person 1 values the object at A+B. Person 2 values it at B+C. The values A, B and C are independently and uniformly distributed on [0,1]. Each bidder knows his or her own valuation, but person 1 only knows the value of the sum A+B while person 2 only knows the value of the sum B+C.

   Compute Nash equilibrium bidding strategies for the two bidders for each of the following three auction formats:

   (i) A sealed bid auction, in which the highest bidder wins the object and pays his or her bid.

   (ii) A second price sealed bid auction, in which the highest bidder wins the object but pays only the second highest bid.

   (iii) A sealed bid auction in which both bidders pay their bid, regardless of who wins, and the highest bidder is awarded the object.

UNIVERSITY OF PENNSYLVANIA

Economics 135, Industrial Organization Professor Andrew Postlewaite
Fall, 1989 McNeil 467, x8-7350

Text: *The Theory of Industrial Organization* by Jean Tirole, MIT Press, 1988

On reserve at Van Pelt:

Industrial Market Structure and Economic Performance by F. M. Scherer, Rand McNally, 1980.

Economic Theory of the Industry by Michael Waterson, Cambridge Press, 1984

Industrial Organization: Theory, Evidence and Public Policy by Kenneth Clarkson and Roger Miller, McGraw Hill, 1982.

    The purpose of this course is two-fold. First, this course is a topics course in industrial organization. Industrial organization is not the study of how to organize industry or to organize anything else. Rather it is the study of firms and industries to understand better how they operate and what the consequences would be of various changes that they might be subjected to. The second purpose of this course is to provide advanced economic students with an understanding about modern economics: why we should be interested in the analysis of particular economic problems and how such analysis is done. In class, we will devote most of our time to theoretical models that are meant to analyze a variety of problems. We will not spend as much time in class on case studies and empirical tests of such models. This emphasis should most emphatically not lead you to underestimate the value of such work. Rather, most of the case studies can be read without too much difficulty without help from me; the theoretical models will be new to many of you and will generally be more difficult. The theoretical models also give a more realistic view of what further work in economics would be like.

    The models we study are abstract models requiring some analytic skills. It is assumed that everyone in the course is familiar with calculus. We will not use calculus all the time and we will not draw on any advanced techniques, but knowledge of, and ability to do, rudimentary differentiation and integration are expected.

    Grading The grades in the class will be based primarily on two exams to be given in class during the semester. The second exam will count slightly more than the first. In addition, I will use class participation to determine grades in marginal circumstances.

The following is a tentative outline of the topics we will cover and the reading associated with the topics. With high probability the topics will be modified as we progress. It is impossible to determine precisely the amount of time we will discuss each topic at the beginning of the course. I will regularly let you know the material we will be covering in upcoming classes.

1. Overview

2. Perfect Competition, Monopoly, and Welfare, Section 1

3. Oligopoly Theory, Section 5

    a. Game theory I, Section 11.1, 11.2
    b. Cournot-Nash Equilibrium
    c. Cournot-Nash Equilibrium with Entry
    d. Stakelberg Equilibria
    e. Bertrand Equilibria
    f. Game theory II, Section 11.3
    g. Dynamic Oligopoly, Section 6

4. Monopolist Competition, Section 7

    a. Chamberlain's Theory
    b. Hotelling's Spatial Model

5. Entry Barriers and Deterrence, Section 8

    a. Contestability, Section 8.1
    b. Limit Pricing
    c. Game Theory III, Section 11.4, 11.5
    d. Milgrom-Roberts Limit Pricing, Section 9.4
    e. Predation and Reputation, Section 9

6. Research and Development

    a. Patents and the Incentive to Innovate, Section 10.1
    b. Patent Races, Section 10.2

7. Advertising and Marketing, Section 2

    a. Product Quality and Consumer Information, Section 2.3
    b. Advertising as a Signal, Section 2.6

ECONOMICS 631
INDUSTRIAL ORGANIZATION

University of Michigan
Professor Salant
Fall, 1989

Readings: The textbook for the course is Jean Tirole's <u>The Theory of Industrial Organization</u>, which is available at Ulrichs and elsewhere. Additional required readings are contained in a coursepack available at Dollar Bill.

In addition to these readings, I have placed supplementary (of interest but not required) material in Foster library.

Office Hours: I will be available Fridays from 1:30 to 3:00 or by appointment in:

254 Lorch Hall
764-2370 (office)

Examinations: There will be a final examination from 1:30-3:30 on December 20. In addition, there will be a take-home mid-term handed out on Wednesday, October 25. To receive credit, students must return the exam at the start of class on the following Monday.

Departures from Schedule: There will be no class on Wednesday, November 22.

Seminars: The regular time for the IO seminar is Thursday from 3:30-5:00. Other IO presentations are scheduled for the Theory seminar on Friday 3:30-5:00. Announcements for both seminars are posted on the bulletin board next to the mail-box room. Seminar papers are available in Foster library several days before the presentation.

Students are invited (but certainly not required) to attend seminar presentations. I will call attention to those of particular interest or relevance to the course. For example: on Friday September 15 in the Theory seminar, Larry Samuelson will be presenting a paper related to the second section of your reading list entitled "The Normal Form Suffices: Von Neumann and Morgenstern were right!"

READINGS

* indicates supplementary reading (recommended but not required)

You are *not responsible* for the material in the supplements following the Tirole chapters unless it is specifically assigned.

1. **Price Discrimination** (3 weeks)
   The first week will summarize the theory, which is well-surveyed in the Tirole text. In the case of second-degree discrimination note carefully the information available to the seller and the implicit restrictions on his strategies. Can he extract all the surplus? How does his maximized profit change a) if he is unrestricted in the strategies he can use, b) if he is restricted to make a single offering, c) if he can offer a menu of alternatives (two-part tariffs versus other menu items), or d) a sequence of such menus. The second week will explore real-world examples of discrimination. Examples of third-degree price discrimination: South African gold sales to the IMF, navel orange sales to the fresh and concentrate markets, journals to individuals and institutions, and reciprocal dumping. Examples of second-degree price discrimination: franchise fees as two-part tariffs and menus of health insurance plans offered to Federal employees.

   a. Theory

   i. Tirole--Preface, Introduction, Ch. 1, Ch. 3 plus p.153-4 and 160-2

   ii. Loeb-Magat

   iii. Bagnoli-Salant-Swierzbinski

   b. Application

   i. Lenard and Mazur

   ii. Krugman, p.25-32

   iii. Tirole--Ch.4

   iv. Besanko-Sappington, p.1-12

   v. Unger, "Largest Competitive Health Program Faces a Crisis"*

2. **Game Theory** (1 week)
   The emphasis here will be on fundamentals: extensive and normal form representations, strategies, elimination of weakly dominated strategies, Nash equilibrium, and subgame perfection. Games of incomplete information (signaling) and supergames will be discussed later in the course in the contexts in which they arise.

   a. Surveys

   i. Kreps (Palgrave essay)

   ii. Van Damme (Palgrave essay)

      iii. Dixit

      iv. Tirole--Ch. 11 (stop after section 4)

  b. Experimental

      i. Cooper, DeJong, Forsythe, and Ross

  c. Historical

      i. Daniel Ellsberg, "The Theory and Practice of Blackmail"*

      ii. Kuhn/Waldegrave (1713)

3. *Static Oligopoly* (2 weeks)
Nash equilibrium with price or quantity as the strategic variable. Cases of interest: substitutes or complements, homogeneous goods or differentiated products. Emphasis on existence and uniqueness of pure- strategy equilibria. Famous examples of non-existence of such equilibria: Bertrand plus fixed costs, Bertrand with capacity constraints (or increasing marginal costs), and nonconcave payoff functions.

  a. Overview

      i. Tirole--Ch. 5

      ii. Shapiro, Sections 1 and 2

      iii. Daughety--Introduction

  b. Uniqueness

      i. Gaudet and Salant

  c. Implicit Optimization

      i. Bergstrom and Varian

  d. Strategic Substitutes but Complements in Demand

      i. Chari and Jones, "A Reconsideration of the Problem of Social Cost: Free Riders and Monopolists"*

4. *Multi-Stage Games Under Complete Information* (3 weeks)
Strategic moves and tactical responses. The necessity that the strategic move be both observable and costly to reverse.

  a. Comparative Statics

      i. Dixit

      ii. Gaudet and Salant

b. Use in Multi-Stage Games (Changes in Decision Variables Exogenous to Subgames)

      i. Shapiro, Section 4

      ii. Tirole, p.21-34

   c. Export Subsidies

      i. Krugman, p.32-41

      ii. Brander-Spencer

   d. Entry Deterrence

      i. Tirole--Ch. 8

      ii. Dixit

      iii. Judd

5. *Cartels* (2 weeks)
   The focus is on three topics: the determinants of membership in the cartel, the collective choice of quotas, and the effectiveness of penalties against production in excess of the quota (cheating).

   a. Formation

      i. Farrell-Shapiro*

      ii. Review Merger Application in Gaudet-Salant (4aii above)

   b. Collective Choice

      i. Cave-Salant

      ii. Salant

   c. Enforcement

      i. Tirole--Ch. 6

      ii. Shapiro, Section 3

      iii. Farrell-Maskin, "Renegotiation in Repeated Games" *

6. *Predation* (1.5 weeks)
   This section constitutes a very brief introduction to a few prominent games of incomplete information in IO. The solution concepts used include: Bayesian Nash equilibrium, perfect Bayesian equilibrium, sequential equilibrium, and trembling-hand perfect equilibrium (in both the normal form and the agent-normal form).

a. Economic Analysis

    i. Tirole--Ch. 9

    ii. Ordover-Saloner

    iii. Milgrom-Roberts, "Informational Asymmetries, Strategic Behavior, and Industrial Organization"*

    iv. Roberts, "Battles for Market Share"*

b. Refinements of Nash Equilibrium under Imperfect/Incomplete Information

    i. Tirole--remainder of Ch. 11

    ii. Salant-Rest, "Litigation of Questioned Settlement Claims..."*

    iii. Van Damme

    iv. Harris

    v. Ramey

University of Michigan
Prof. Salant
Fall, 1989

631 Mid-term

1. Arbitrage and Third Degree Price Discrimination

Consider the following game between a monopolist producer and two arbitrageurs. The three players act independently. The monopolist sets a price in each of two markets (P_1 and P_2). Two arbitrageurs observe these prices and then each simultaneously sets prices in market 2 (P_a and P_b). The three players must satisfy whatever demand arises at the quoted prices.

Denote the demand by final users in the two markets as $D_i(m_i)$ where m_i is the price a final user pays in market i and $i = 1, 2$. A final user in market 1 must pay $m_1 = P_1$ since no arbitrageur sells in that market. But a final user in market 2 must pay $m_2 = \min(P_2; P_a; P_b)$. In the event that more than one seller charges the lowest price in market 2, assume that the induced demand is divided equally among the lowest price sellers.

Assume that the monopolist can produce at constant marginal cost c (and zero fixed cost). Assume the monopolist can deliver to market 1 at no additional charge but must incur a transport cost of t_m per unit shipped to deliver to market 2. Assume the two arbitrageurs have identical transport costs, t per unit, for shipping items to market 2 and that such goods have to be acquired in market 1 at the market price of $m_1 = P_1$. The two transport costs (t and t_m) may be equal or, alternatively either one may be strictly larger than the other.

Assume that $(P_2 - c)D_2(P_2)$ is strictly concave and that, in the absence of arbitrageurs, unconstrained 3rd degree price discrimination would lead the firm to charge a price in market 2 which exceeds the price in market 1 by more than t.

a. For any given P_1 and P_2, under what circumstances will the arbitrageurs be active (i.e. buy in market 1 and sell in market 2)?

b. For those P_1 and P_2 which induce the arbitrageurs to be active, what price would each charge in market 2 in the Nash equilibrium of the subgame which follows?

c. Under what circumstances (relationship of t and t_m) will the arbitrageurs be inactive in the play of the subgame perfect equilibrium?

d. Under what circumstances will the arbitrageurs be active in the play of the subgame perfect equilibrium?

e. Answer part a of problem 4 in "Practice Problems: Price Discrimination" located in the last section of your coursepack. Think of the Swedish market as market 1 and the U.S. market as market 2. It is assumed in the question explicitly that $t = 2000$ and implicitly that $t_m = 0$. That is, interpret the problem as assuming that the Swedish manufacturer has no production facilities in the U.S. but can ship cars from Sweden to the U.S. costlessly.

f. Revise your answer to e if $t_m = 3000$ but all other data remain unchanged.

1

g. In intertemporal extraction problems, markets 1 and 2 are, respectively, the current market and next year's market. Assume the monopolist can extract at constant marginal cost.

It is typically assumed that if the monopolist wishes to sell in market 2, he leaves oil *in the ground* until he needs it. Hence, the cost of providing a unit next year (in present value terms) is $c/(1+r)$, where r is the annual real rate of interest. If we were to force this model to fit the previous framework (where extraction for next year's market has to occur in the *current* period) what transport cost (t_m) would we have to assume for the monopolist? Is it positive or negative? Explain. It is typically assumed that an intertemporal speculator (arbitrageur) can make a profit if the discounted price next year exceeds the current price. What is being assumed about t? Is it positive or negative? Explain.

2. Competition and Complements in Demand

Two independent firms produce a homogeneous good, coal, at constant marginal costs, c. The two coal mines (a and b) are located in the center of the country and the coal must shipped to a market up the coast. This involves first shipping the coal eastward to the coast and then shipping it northward up the coast to the market.

Assume initially that the only method of transport on either leg of the journey is by rail. The coal must first get to the coast on railroad 1. It must then be shipped up the coast on railroad 2. The two railroads act independently and are assumed to have zero costs. Coal can be transferred from one railroad to the other at zero cost.

Let P_a and P_b denote the prices set by the two coal mines and f_1 and f_2 be the fares set by the two railroads. Assume the four prices (denominated in dollars per unit of coal shipped) are set simultaneously and that consumers choose the cheaper offer (inclusive of transport): Consumers demand $D(m) = 120 - m$ units of coal where m is the final price per unit: $\min(f_1 + f_2 + P_a; f_1 + f_2 + P_b)$.

a. Compute the Nash equilibrium strategy combination of the two mines and two railroads if $c = 60$.

Now suppose a *barge* becomes available as an alternative way to transport coal over the second segment of the journey. Railroad 1 must still be used for the journey east and there is no cost in transferring the coal to the barge. The barge is operated independently and—as far as coal shipment is concerned—is a perfect substitute for the second railroad. Unlike the railroads, however, shipping coal by water is costly: the constant marginal cost of shipping coal is d per unit.

b. Suppose $d = 30$. Compute the quantity of coal shipped, prices, profits, and consumer surplus in the Nash equilibrium if $d = 30$? How did these values changed in comparison to the case when the barge was unavailable.

c. Repeat b but assume instead that $d = 10$.

3. Subgame Perfection and Nash Equilibrium in Undominated Strategies

Consider the following conjecture: every Nash equilibrium in undominated strategies (strategies which are not weakly dominated) is necessarily subgame perfect. We have examined several examples in class which are *consistent* with this conjecture. For instance, we noted in the basic invasion game that the imperfect Nash equilibrium—where the enemy stays out and the islanders would fight if invaded—that the latter strategy is weakly dominated: *if* the enemy does not invade, fighting in response to invasion is no worse than retreating; but if the enemy *does* invade, fighting is strictly inferior to retreating. In addition, we noted in a game with no proper subgames that a subgame perfect equilibrium may be supported by a weakly dominated strategy. So far, you have seen no example inconsistent with the conjecture.

Consider the following three-player game of complete but imperfect information:

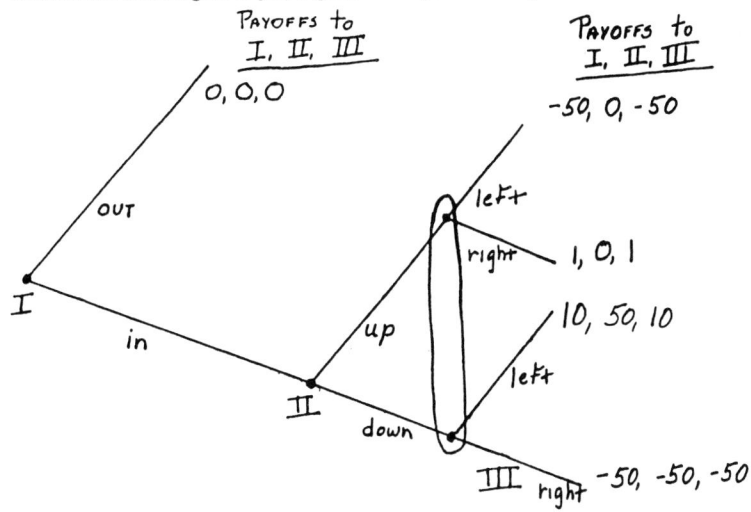

Consider the following strategy combination. Player I:out Player II:down Player III:right.
  a. Is this strategy combination a Nash equilibrium? Explain.
  b. Is this strategy combination subgame perfect? Explain
  c. Is any strategy in this strategy combination weakly dominated? Which one and by what alternative strategy?

4. Nonlinear Pricing and Public Goods

A monopolist owns a highway (see the diagram below) and is trying to maximize profits. He knows that n_l motorists entering his highway work at a local plant b_l miles away while n_h work at a distant plant b_h miles away, where $b_h > b_l > 0$. We refer to members of these two groups as "type l" and "type h" respectively. He cannot determine whether a given motorist is a member of one group or the other.

The monopolist plans to have either one or two exits on his highway (the further exit coincides with the end of the highway) and to charge motorists according to where they exit. A motorist is "free to choose" whether to use the highway and, if he does, which exit to use. A motorist cannot leave the highway at a location without an exit.

The monopolist's costs are independent of the number of motorists using the roadway; but maintenance costs are proportional to the distance to the further exit since that determines the length of his roadway. If the highway has length z, the total cost of operating it is cz.

The monopolist realizes of course that his highway is not the *only* way a motorist can get to his place of employment. A motorist exiting after travelling a distance x can nonetheless reach his place of employment by back roads. The monopolist has concluded that the payoff to a type i motorist who exits x miles from the entrance to the highway is: $U_i = x(2b_i - x)$ for $0 \leq x \leq 2b_i$ and $U_i = 0$ otherwise, where $i = l, h$.

If the motorist selects an alternative to the highway, he receives the reservation utility of zero. a. What is type i's $(i = l, h)$ most preferred location for an exit if he

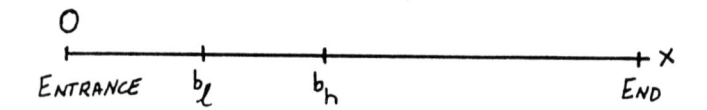

```
O
|————+————+————————————————+ X
ENTRANCE  b_l  b_h              END
```

DISTANCES ARE MEASURED FROM THE ENTRANCE OF THE HIGHWAY.

could locate and utilize an exit at no charge? Assume $b_l = 60$, $b_h = 120$, $n_l = 3000$, and $c = 2000$.

b. Determine the optimal locations for the two exits if $n_h = 1000$.

c. Suppose n_h was larger but no other exogenous variable was different, how would the optimal locations for the two exits change?

d. For what number of type h motorists is it optimal to have *no* intermediate exit before the end of the road.

University of Michigan
Prof. Salant
Fall, 1988

631 Mid-term

1. Assume that all buyers of automobiles are located in the United States. Assume that 3 firms in the United States produce automobiles for the home market and 4 firms in Japan export into the U.S. market. There are no other producers. Assume automobiles are homogeneous, can be produced at each firm at the same constant marginal cost (and zero fixed cost), and sell for a common price indicated by an inverse demand curve which is linear in industry output.

Suppose the Japanese government now imposes an export quota on each of its own firms. The quotas are identical and irreversible. All firms in the industry observe these quotas before simultaneously choosing their outputs. Each quota is marginally smaller than the output of each Japanese firm in the previous equilibrium and so the old equilibrium is marginally displaced.

a. Using the comparative-static result in Gaudet-Salant (equation 9)–i.e. no derivation necessary–will the aggregate profits of the Japanese firms increase or decrease? Explain.

b. Maintaining the assumptions about costs, how would your answer change if the inverse demand curve were instead strictly concave?

2. In the standard (assuming an interior optimum and continuous derivatives) 2-good case of consumer theory, the most preferred consumption bundle can be characterized by two equations. One equation indicates that the optimal bundle lies on the budget constraint and the second equation indicates that the slope of the "iso–utility contour" at that point is exactly equal to the slope of the constraint.

In this question, you are asked to characterize in similar terms the pair of actions that arise in the subgame perfect equilibrium of a two-stage duopoly game.

In particular, suppose firm 1 selects action a_1 and—after observing it—firm 2 selects action a_2. Firm 1 has payoff $\Pi(a_1, a_2)$ and firm 2 has payoff $F(a_1, a_2)$.

a. What first-order condition must hold if firm 2 best replies to firm 1's choice (assume the best reply is strictly positive). Why must this equation hold in a subgame perfect equilibrium?

b. At any interior point $(a_1 > 0, a_2 > 0)$, what is the slope of firm 1's isoprofit contour? At any point, what is the slope of firm 2's best reply? Why must these two slopes (marginal rates of substitution) be equal in a subgame perfect Nash equilibrium? These two equations jointly determine the actions (a_1, a_2) which will arise in the perfect Nash equilibrium.

3. In a finite game of imperfect information, Player 1 owns 6 information sets.

He has 3 choices at one of them and 4 choices at each of the other 5.

   a. A single strategy for him has how many components?

   b. How many strategies does Player 1 have?

   c. Suppose Player 1 has x strategies, Player 2 has y strategies, and Player 3 has z strategies. You have devised a computer program which searches for pure-strategy Nash equilibria by exhaustively examining each strategy combination of players. How many such combinations are there?

   4. In his OP-ED piece in the Sunday New York Times (August 28, 1988), Jay Anoff— a former antitrust lawyer with the Federal Trade Commission—reported that to fly from Washington D.C. to St. Louis (denoted below as route 1) costs $305, to fly from St. Louis to Los Angeles (denoted below as route 2) costs $395, but to fly from D.C. to L.A. with a stop in St. Louis (denoted below as route 3) costs a traveller only $400. He observed that "there is an obvious solution" and proposed that people buy tickets from D.C. to L.A., unpackage them and sell their respective segments. Suppose in the question below that such arbitrage was legal, could not be prevented institutionally and was costless. To simplify further, assume that TWA has a monopoly on each route and operates its planes at zero cost.

   Suppose the demand by travellers on the three routes are respectively:

$$Q_1 = 610 - P_1 \qquad (1)$$
$$Q_2 = 790 - P_2 \qquad (2)$$
$$Q_3 = 800 - P_3 \qquad (3)$$

   a. Compute the prices on the three routes which maximize TWA's profits in the absence of arbitrage.

   b. Suppose there would be arbitrage unless TWA set prices in the three markets to satisfy the following constraint: $P_1 + P_2 = P_3$. Verify that at a profit maximum TWA would want to eliminate arbitrage and compute the new profit-maximizing prices subject to the foregoing equality constraint.

   c. Compute the surplus gain (or loss) to consumers in markets 1, 2, and 3 and to TWA from the threat of competitive arbitrage. Who wins and who loses from the elimination of arbitrage opportunities? Does aggregate output increase? Does aggregate surplus increase?

   d. Construct an example with *different* demand curves where in the absence of arbitrage, the optimal prices are the same as in part a but in the presence of arbitrage TWA's constrained optimum involves increasing the coast-to-coast fare while leaving the other two fares unchanged. (Hint: one approach is to replace the demand curves in markets 1 and 2 with piecewise linear or step functions.) Who would win and lose from Angoff's "obvious solution?" Would aggregate output increase? Would aggregate surplus increase?

MIDTERM

University of Michigan
Economics 631
Professor Salant
October 27, 1987

Instructions: There are seven (multi-part) questions on this exam. They will take some time and thought--so look the exam over carefully at an early opportunity and decide how long it will take you.

In answering the questions, you are free to consult books, notes and articles but not other people. To get credit, you must turn your answers in at the beginning of class on Tuesday, November 3.

1. Consider the following two-player game of imperfect information in extensive form. This game has multiple Nash equilibria only one of which is subgame perfect.

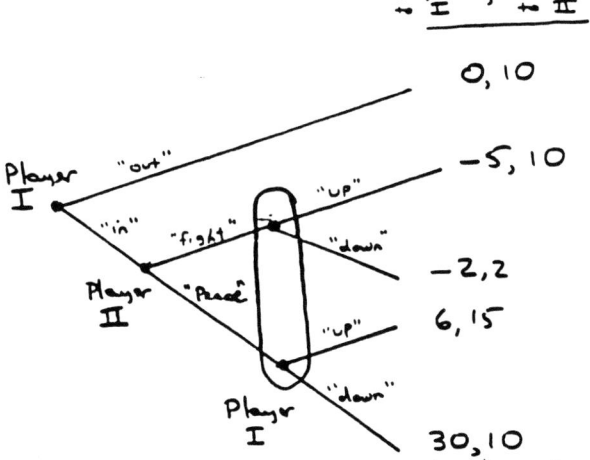

Payoff to I, Payoff to II

- "out" → 0, 10
- "in", "fight", "up" → −5, 10
- "in", "fight", "down" → −2, 2
- "in", "Peace", "up" → 6, 15
- "in", "Peace", "down" → 30, 10

a. Find a strategy combination which not only forms a Nash equilibrium in the whole game but also in the subgame beginning with Player II's move.

b. Reduce the full game to normal form.

c. Identify each of its Nash equilibria.

d. Which of these Nash equilibria are supported by weakly dominated strategies?

2. Consider the following pair of games:

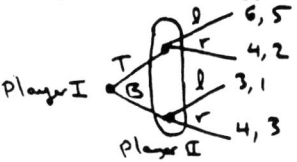

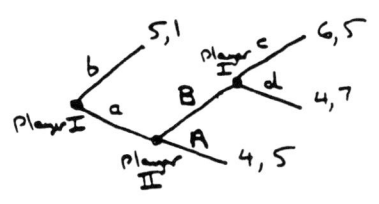

Game 1 (Player I: T/B; Player II: ℓ/r):
- T, ℓ: 6, 5
- T, r: 4, 2
- B, ℓ: 3, 1
- B, r: 4, 3

Game 2 (extensive form): Player I chooses a or b; if b, payoff 5,1 then Player I chooses c/d giving 6,5 or 4,7; if a, Player II chooses A giving 4,5 or B leading to Player I's c/d.

241

The first is a game of perfect information and the second is a game of imperfect information. To each of the following statements, respond True or False:

a. Each game has exactly two Nash equilibria in pure strategies. T or F?

b. Each game has exactly two subgame perfect Nash equilibria in pure strategies. T or F?

c. In the game of imperfect information, successive elimination of weakly dominated strategies in the normal form eliminates no subgame perfect equilibria. T or F?

d. In the game of perfect information, successive elimination of weakly dominated strategies in the normal form eliminates no subgame perfect equilibria. T or F?

3. A monopolist faces the inverse demand curve P=200-2X, where P is the price charged and X is the quantity sold. Assume that the monopolist cannot price discriminate, and charges the same price for each unit, with no access fee. The monopolist has a constant marginal cost of production : C=40. There are no fixed costs and the monopolist maximizes profits.

a. Suppose that the monopolist is unregulated. What price will he charge?

b. Calculate the monopolist's profit and the consumer's surplus at this price.

c. Suppose you are a regulator. You know the demand curve but have no information about the firm's marginal cost. Find a total subsidy as a function of the price charged which you could offer to pay with the property that it would induce the monopolist to set his price equal to the marginal cost.

d. If the monopolist maximizes profits (inclusive of subsidy payments), calculate the new price he will charge, his resulting profits, the consumer's surplus, and the regulator's payment.

4. Two firms sell a homogeneous product in the U.S. market. The market-clearing price paid by consumers depends as follows on the sales of the two firms: $P=120-X_1-X_2$, where X_1 is the output of firm 1 and X_2 is the output of firm 2. Firm 1 is located in the U.S. and firm 2 in Japan. Each firm has the identical constant marginal production cost ($C_1=C_2=30$), zero fixed costs, zero transport costs, and produces goods of identical appearance.

Suppose firm 2 selects X_2 knowing that firm 1 will observe firm 2's choice and then select his own output X_1. A strategy for firm 2 is therefore an output X_2; a strategy for firm 1 is his output as a function of the observed output of the leader, firm 2: $X_1(X_2)$.

a. Compute the pair of strategies which form a subgame perfect equilibrium in this game. Compute the profit to the Japanese firm in this equilibrium.

b. Find some other strategy combination which forms a Nash equilibrium (albeit an imperfect equilibrium) in this game?

c. Characterize the *set* of strategies which form Nash equilibria.

5. Suppose instead the two firms choose their outputs simultaneously. In this case, the strategy of each firm is its output X_i--since neither can observe the other's strategy before selecting its own strategy.

a. Compute the Nash equilibrium in this game. Compute the profit to the Japanese firm in the equilibrium.

b. Suppose--due to a publicly-announced subsidy of S per unit to be paid by the Japanese Government to Japanese exporting firms--that the Japanese firm's constant marginal cost shifts down to $C_2^* = 30-S$. The U.S. firm's marginal cost remains $C_1=30$. Compute the new equilibrium outputs for each firm as a function of S. Compute the profit of the Japanese firm (inclusive of the subsidy payments) as a function of S.

c. Calculate the export subsidy which maximizes the excess of the Japanese firm's profits over its Government's subsidy payments. How much does each firm sell in this equilibrium?
 → maximize joint profits

6. Consider three firms with identical, constant marginal costs and zero fixed costs selling a homogeneous good in a market with linear demand. Suppose that the three firms play a quantity game and move simultaneously. Suppose instead that two of the three firms act together as a Stackelberg leader and anticipate the reaction of the remaining firm to their joint quantity choice. By how much does the joint output of two firms change in the new situation (relative to the initial situation)? By how much do joint profits change?

7. A monopolist (the local telephone company) sells to two types of consumers whose demand curves he knows. Type 1 has an inverse demand curve of $P=20-X$. Type 2 has an inverse demand curve of $P=16-X$, where P is the price of a local phone call and X is the number of calls per month. For simplicity assume there is only one consumer of each type and that the company has zero costs. The company is prevented by law from offering one type of customer a fee schedule unavailable to the other type.

a. Suppose it charges a monthly fee A and price per call P to maximize profits (the solution proposed by Oi). Find the optimal P and A and the induced profits. Note: For completeness, you should consider both the possibility that only one type is served and the possibility that both are served.

b. Suppose instead the company offers (to all consumers) a *pair* of two-part tariffs--P_1, A_1 and P_2, A_2-- structured so that the type one buyer will prefer the first offering and the type 2 buyer will prefer the second. Find the optimal pair of two-part tariffs and the profits achieved under it.

c. In fact, neither (a) nor (b) is optimal. Characterize the strategy proposed by Spence (and widely regarded as optimal) and the profits it can achieve.

d. Suppose, finally, that the monopolist offers a menu with two choices: 16 units for $127 or 20 units for $199. However, the monopolist's offer is only good if each customer expresses an interest in purchasing a different one of the two offerings; otherwise, the monopolist sells nothing.

Consider the simultaneous move game between the two customers. Each can accept either the first offering, the second offering, or neither offering. Verify that it is a Nash equilibrium for the type-one customer to purchase the 20 units and the type-two customer to purchase the 16 units. Calculate the monopolist's profit in this equilibrium. Verify that there are other Nash equilibria in which the monopolist sells nothing and earns nothing.

Professor Salant
Fall, 1987

ANSWERS TO 631 MIDTERM

1. a. First note that (peace) and (down) is the unique Nash equilibrium in the subgame--indeed, each strategy is strictly dominant. The strategy combination (in, down) and (peace) is the unique spe in pure strategies.

b.

	fight	peace
out, up	0,10	0,10
out, down	0,10	0,10
in, up	-5,10	6,15
in, down	-2,2	30,10

c.
There are three Nash equilibria: (in, down) and (peace), (out, up) and (fight) and (out, down) and (fight).

d. The last two are supported by weakly dominated strategies since (fight) is weakly dominated by (peace) for player II.

2.
a. F. The perfect information game has three pure strategy equilibria: (b,c) and (A), (b,d) and (A), and (a,c) and (B).

b. T. The game with imperfect information has no proper subgames; hence both its Nash equilibria are spe. As for the game of perfect information, (b,d) and (A) is not spe but the other two are.

c. F. It eliminated the spe strategy combination (B) for player I and (r) for player II.

d. F. It eliminated the spe (b,c) and (A).

3. a. P=120.
b. Profit=3200; Consumer surplus=1600.
c. Subsidy= $(100-.5P)^2$. = ...
d. P=40, Profit=Subsidy=consumer surplus=6400.

4. a. Firm two (Japanese firm) is the leader and maximizes subject to one's reaction function: $x_1=45-.5x_2$. The equilibrium strategies are $x_2=45$ and $x_1(x_2)=45-.5x_2$. The profit to the Japanese leader is 45(22.5).

b. See c.

c. Let us denote a strategy combination as x_2^* and $x_1^*(x_2)$. Any strategy combination of the following form is a Nash equilibrium:

244

x_2^* is in $[0,90]$
$x_1(x_2)$

a) lies in the worse set of 1's isoprofit contour through the point $45-.5x_2^*, x_2^*$ and
b) passes through that point as depicted below.

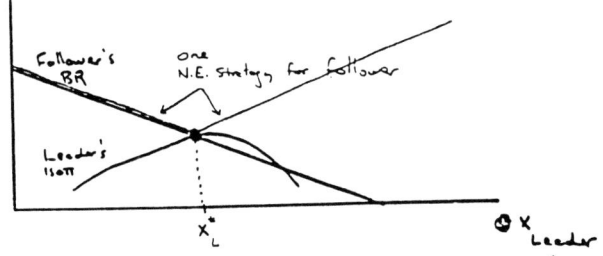

[Figure: Follower's BR and Leader's isoprofit curves intersecting at one N.E. strategy for follower at x_L^*; axes labeled x follower and x Leader]

If the leader selects x_L^* and the follower best replies $x_F = 45 - \frac{1}{2} x_L^*$ then the leader's profit is $x_L^* [120 - x_L^* - 45 - \frac{1}{2}x_L^* - 30] = x_L^*[45 - \frac{1}{2}x_L^*]$.

Hence any $x_L^*, x_F^*(x_L)$ such that $x_L^* \in [0, 90]$ and $x_F^*(x_L)$ as below is an equilibrium.

$x_F^*(x_L)$ s.t. $x_L^* \{ 90 - x_L - x_F^*(x_L) \} \leq x_L^* \{ 45 - \frac{1}{2}x_L^* \}$ for $x_L \neq x_L^*$ and $x_F^*(x_L^*) = 45 - \frac{1}{2}x_L^*$

That is, $x_F^*(x_L) \begin{cases} = 45 - \frac{1}{2}x_L^* & \text{if } x_L = x_L^* \\ \geq 90 - x_L - \frac{x_L^*}{x_L}[45 - \frac{1}{2}x_L^*] & \text{otherwise} \end{cases}$

5. a. $x_1 = x_2 = 30$. Profit of the Japanese firm = 900.
b. $x_1 = (90-s)/3$; $x_2 = 30 + 2s/3$. Profit of the Japanese = $(30 + 2s/3)^2$.
c. The optimal subsidy = 22.5. $x_1 = 22.5$; $x_2 = 45$. The Japanese governement must pay 22.5(45) to the Japanese firm. Hence the subsidy enables the Japanese firm to garner the same profits (excluding the government's subsidy) as if it could precommit to the Stackelberg leader's output.

6. Let $p = f - by$ be the inverse demand curve. Denote the constant marginal cost of each firm by c. Then in a 3-firm symmetric Cournot equilibrium, $x_1 = x_2 = x_3 = (f-c)/4b$. Hence any two firms produce $(f-c)/2b$. The reaction function of any one firm (i) as a function of the joint output of the other two firms is $x_i = (f - bX_{-i} - c)/2b$. If two firms merge and act as a Stackelberg leader, then they will maximize $z(f - bz - b[f - bz - c]/2b - c)$, where z is the joint output. The optimal solution is $z^* = (f-c)/2b$. Hence the joint profits of the two firms are already maximized at the Cournot equilibrium and acting as a merged Stackelberg leader does not strictly increase the profits of the firms.

As discussed in class, this example has implications both for the profitability of horizontal mergers and optimal trade policy.

Since an exogenous horizontal merger among two firms in a three-firm industry operating under Cournot competition leads to a reduction in the joint output of the merged firms, their joint profits must decline if marginal costs and demand are linear.

Moreover, if the two firms are regarded as exporting from one country and the single firm as exporting from another country and if all consumers are located in a third country then the analysis implies that the optimal trade policy is free trade. An export tax (respectively, subsidy) would induce the joint output of the two firms to decrease (resp. increase) and in either case joint profits would decline. Indeed, if we generalize this example slightly so that there are n firms in the home export sector and one abroad, then unless there is a single firm in the home country (as Brander-Spencer assumed) a subsidy (the standard Brander-Spencer conclusion) is suboptimal.

For three or more firms in the home country and one in the foreign country the optimal trade policy is an export tax. Such cases have implications for the effects of an exogenous strike on the profitability of struck firms. In particular, if the optimal trade policy is a tax, then a strike on the export sector of the home firms (which exogenously reduces their joint output) may increase their profits.

7.
a. If one party is served, it should be type I. In that case it is optimal to set P=0 and A=200. The profit earned would then be 200. More could be earned by serving both parties. The best A,p combination would:

maximize $p[20-p+16-p] + 2\{[16-p]^2/2\}$, where the term in curly braces is the maximum access charge that type II would be willing to pay. At an optimum p=2, A=98, and profit=260.

b.
The optimal menu of two-part tariffs p_1,A_1 and p_2,A_2 maximizes $p_1[20-p_1]+p_2[16-p_2]+A_1+A_2$ subject to two participation constraints:
$.5(20-p_1)^2-A_1>0$ and
$.5(16-p_2)^2-A_2>0$ and
subject to two self-selection (incentive compatibility) constraints:

$.5(20-p_1)^2-A_1>.5(20-p_2)^2-A_2$ and
$.5(16-p_2)^2-A_2>.5(16-p_1)^2-A_1$.
In any optimal solution, the type II consumer gets no surplus. For suppose the contrary. If he got surplus, we could remove it by increasing A_2; since this would make the second offering even less attractive to the type I consumer, no other constraint would be violated. In any optimal solution, the type I consumer must be indifferent between the two offerings. For suppose the contrary. Then we could raise A_1 marginally and increase profit without violating any constraint.

We can then simplify the foregoing constrained optimization problem by writing A_1 and A_2 as functions of the two prices:
$A_2=.5(16-p)^2$ and $A_1=.5(20-p_1)^2-.5(20-p_2)^2+.5(16-p_2)^2$.
The profit function can now be written entirely in terms of the two prices

It can be verified that the optimal solution is $p_1=0$
$p_2=4$
$A_1=144$
$A_2=72$
and the resulting profit is 264.

Note that this is less than the profit in the Spence solution (part c). We cannot support the Spence solution with a menu of two-part tariffs for the following reason: to induce the type I player to consume 12 units would require a price of 4; but at a price of 4 the type II player would want to purchase 16 units not 12 units and would get higher utility from doing so than he would if he purchased 12 units. Since his surplus from selecting the offer intended for type II is higher than in the Spence solution, the surplus type I enjoys at the offer actually intended for type I must also be higher--which means that we can extract less surplus from him at the offer we intend for him. That is, although we can induce the type I to consume 20 units with a price of 0, the surplus we can now extract from him is reduced relative to the Spence solution.

c. Offer x_1 units at outlay O_1 and x_2 units at outlay O_2 with the property that O_2 extracts all the surplus from the type II and O_1 leaves type I indifferent between the two offers. It turns out that: $x_2=12$, $x_1=20$, $O_2=120$ and $O_1=152$. Total profit is then 272.

d.

	type II		
	accept 16	accept 20	accept neither
type I accept 16	0,0	65,-71*	0,0$^\lambda$
accept 20	1,1$^\lambda$	0,0	0,0
accept neither	0,0	0,0	0,0$^\lambda$

The (0,0) pairs arise because no transaction occurs unless both offerings are accepted. If type I accepts 20 and type II accepts 16, then type I receives something worth 200 to him and pays 199--for a surplus of 1. Type II receives something worth 128 to him and pays 127--for a surplus of 1.

If instead type II accepts 16 and type I accepts 20, then type I receives something worth 192 and pays only 127 for a surplus of 65. On the other hand, type II receives something worth 128* but must pay 199 for a surplus of -71.

It is a Nash equilibrium for the type I player to accept 20 and the type II player to accept 16; but there are two other equilibria:1) type I and II accept neither offer or 2) type I accepts 16 but type two accepts neither offer. However, since accepting neither is weakly dominated for type II by accepting 16, the latter two equilibria involve a weakly dominated strategy.

In the first Nash equilibrium the monopolist extracts nearly all the surplus: 326 of the 328; in the second, he extracts nothing.

*I assume that the type II consumer can avoid consuming the last four units of the acquired 20 units since that gives him negative marginal utility. His payoff in this instance would be even more negative otherwise.

FINAL EXAM--631

Professor Salant
December 15, 1988
University of Michigan

1. Consider the following game between a waiter and his customer. Once each week, the customer comes to the restaurant for dinner and is served by the same waiter. The waiter can give good or bad service. The customer observes the service and decides whether to tip.

The waiter likes tips but would prefer not to work hard. The customer likes good service but would prefer not to tip. Each party maximizes the expected sum of its payoffs; neither party discounts future payoffs.

For concreteness, assume that the customer tips either $5 or nothing. Good service is worth $10 to him and bad service is worth $0. A tip is worth $5 to the waiter. Rendering good service costs the waiter $2 and giving bad service costs the waiter $0.

The following matrix characterizes the payoffs resulting from each possible pure strategy combination in any given weekly meal.

	tip always	tip if and only if good service	tip if and only if bad service	tip never
good serv.	3,5	3,5	-2,10	-2,10
bad serv.	5,-5	0,0	5,-5	0,0

a. If it is common knowledge from the outset that the customer will be transferred by his employer on a specific future date and will have no further contact with the waiter, what pair of strategies will be adopted in their weekly encounters?

Suppose instead that the transfer will occur at an unknown date. In particular, assume that it is commonly understood at the conclusion of each meal that the customer will return the next week with exogenous probability p; with complementary probability (1-p) the customer will cease coming to the restaurant thereafter (he will be reassigned to another city by his employer).

Consider the following agreement:

*The **waiter** gives good service initially. In each subsequent period, the waiter gives good service provided he has always given good service in the past and has always been tipped. If in the past the waiter gave bad service or the customer failed to tip, the waiter gives him bad service thereafter (until the game terminates).*

*Initially, the **customer** tips if service is good and leaves no tip if that day's service is bad. On subsequent weeks, he adheres to this policy provided he has always received good service and has always previously tipped. Otherwise, he leaves no tip each week until the game terminates.*

248

b. Verify that this agreement is self-enforcing (forms a subgame perfect equilibrium) if the odds the customer will return the following week with 60% probability.

c. Another "regular" patron hears of this self-enforcing scheme and proposes to the waiter a similar verbal agreement. The probability that this patron will be re-assigned to a job in another town is also 40% per week. But he has one meal at the restaurant once every two weeks instead of every week and cannot adjust this frequency. What service and tipping behavior should occur at this table?

d. Suppose the waiter is also responsible for another table. It is frequented by a succession of customers--indeed, a *different* customer every night. What service and tipping behavior should be observed at that table?

2. Krazy Kinko's and Demented Dollar Bill both produce xerox copies at the common constant marginal cost of 2 cents a page. There are N identical consumers. Each customer regards copies from the two stores as identical (i.e. perfect substitutes). Denote by q_b (respectively, q_k) the number of copies the representative individual purchases from Bill (respectively, Kinko). If a consumer buys a total of q $(=q_b+q_k)$ copies from the two stores and spends S cents on other things he gets utility $u(q,S) = 50q - .5q^2 + S$. For this quasilinear utility function, the demand for copies will be independent of income as long as income is large enough that the chosen S is strictly positive (assume income is sufficiently large throughout this question). Denote Kinko's per page price as p_k and Bill's as p_b. Then the representative consumer's total demand for copies is simply $q = 50 - \min(p_k, p_b)$.

Suppose Kinko's publicly announces the following rebate policy: *I will charge you p_k per copy. If you purchase from me and Bill would charge you strictly less, I will rebate to you the difference $(p_k - p_b)$ on each unit you purchased--and I will give you a $1 bonus.* It is common knowledge that the consumers would force Kinko to honor this agreement.

The two firms then engage in a three-stage game. First, Kinko's selects a price. After hearing Kinko's price, Bill announces his price. In the third and final stage, consumers select the better of the two offers. Assume a consumer patronizes one store or the other--but not both. If the offers are equally attractive assume that half of the consumers (N is even) patronize each store.

a. Graph the demand at Bill's as a function of the price he selects (holding constant the prior price selected by Kinko).

b. Deduce the subgame perfect equilibrium strategy combination of this three-stage game.

c. What prices will the two firms charge?

3. Consider the game depicted below. It is claimed that a particular assessment (a particular behavioral strategy combination and particular beliefs) forms a sequential equilibrium. The proposed strategies for each player are represented in the diagram by arrows and the conditional probabilities next to the nodes in each information set indicate the proposed beliefs. Note: in the proposed equilibrium, player II mixes between left and right with equal probability (i.e. probability 1/2); each of the other proposed strategies is a pure strategy.

a. Is the strategy combination sequentially rational for each player given the assessment?

b. What other conditions must be satisfied to show that the assessment is a sequential equilibrium? Is the assessment a sequential equilibrium?

c. Does the strategy combination depicted by the arrows form a Nash equilibrium?

d. Does the strategy combination depicted by the arrows form a subgame perfect equilibrium?

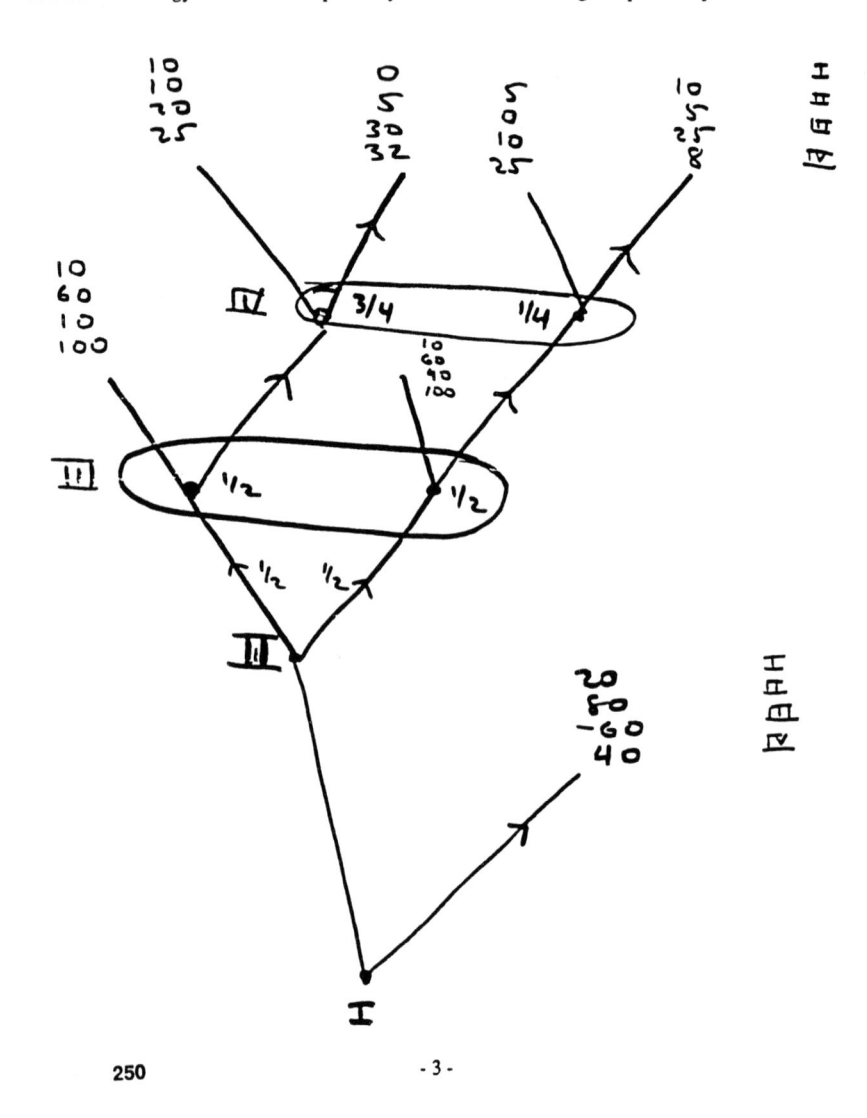

4. The Federal Government wishes to transfer G units of something (pollution permits, wheat, etc.) to the private market and proposes to auction the entire amount.

Under the rules of the auction, a person bids a *per-unit price*, b_i. If his bid is *strictly* higher than that of the other bidders, he is awarded the *entire amount*, G units, and must pay his per-unit bid multiplied times the amount acquired, $b_i G$. If there is a *tie* among the highest bidders, each winner receives an equal share and must pay the common bid times the amount he receives.

On the day after the G units are acquired, the highest bidders can sell simultaneously in a Cournot quantity game some or all of their acquisitions to the private market for the price P=200-Q, where Q is the aggregate liquidation (Q<or=G) and P is the price paid per unit sold. There is no other opportunity to sell to the market and the good is of no value to the original bidders other than at this sale.

Suppose there are four bidders at the auction and the government puts up for sale *80* units.

a. At the final stage, the 80 units will be divided equally among 1, 2, 3, or 4 bidders. What will be the payoffs to the four players in each type of simultaneous-sales subgame?

b. Now consider the prior stage where bids are simultaneously selected. Verify that in one type of subgame perfect equilibrium (there are other types), each of the four bidders receives a quarter of the stock.

c. Determine in that equilibrium the amount of the common winning bid, the subsequent market price, and the profits of each winning bidder net of the bid.

Suppose instead that the government puts up for sale 120 units. Once again, assume there are four bidders.

d. Verify that in this situation it is a subgame perfect equilibrium for one of the bidders to purchase the entire stock initially. Verify that there are no subgame perfect equilibria with multiple winners at the auction. Hence subgame perfect equilibrium play always involves cornering of the auction by some one of the four firms. Hint: analyze the problem as you did in (a) and (b) but assume that 120 units is auctioned.

e. In this subgame perfect equilibrium, determine the amount of the winning bid, the subsequent market price, and the profits of the lone winning bidder net of the bid.

f. To remedy this "cornering" of the auction, it is proposed that the number of bidders be expanded from four to one hundred. Will this eliminate cornering? How many bidders will win the auction in the subgame perfect equilibrium?

g. To raise more revenue, it is proposed that the amount auctioned be raised from 120 units to 240 units. In the new equilibrium, will auction revenues increase? By how much? Explain. [Assume that there are four bidders at the auction].

Answers to Final Exam in Economics 631

1a. Since the stage game has a unique Nash equilibrium, the subgame perfect equilibrium of this finite horizon game of complete information is to play that strategy combination at each stage: Hence, the waiter should give bad service and the customer should never tip.

b. If there has been a *history* of bad service and/or no tipping should the waiter adhere to the agreement? Assuming the customer follows his part of the agreement (i.e. doesn't tip), then the waiter would get 0 per period by giving bad service but only -2 by giving good service. Hence the waiter has no incentive to deviate unilaterally from the agreement following such a history. Following such a history, does the customer have any incentive to deviate unilaterally? Assuming the waiter follows the strategy of giving bad service, the customer would get 0 per period from not tipping and less from alternative strategies.

If there has so far been a *history* of good service and tipping, does the waiter have an incentive to unilaterally deviate from his strategy of continuing to give good service? Assuming that the customer plays his strategy, the waiter will get a sequence of 5's if he adheres to the agreement. If the waiter deviates by rendering bad service, then his deviation will immediately be detected and the customer--again assuming that he follows his part of the strategy--will tip no more. In response, the waiter should thereafter render bad service. Such a deviation generates a sequence of 0's and is therefore inferior at every stage (even the stage of initial cheating). Hence, the waiter will adhere to the agreement regardless of the discount factor.

Given a history of good service and tipping, should the customer unilaterally deviate from the agreement? Assuming that the waiter will adhere to the agreement (i.e. will render good service as long as there has been good service and tipping in past meals but will otherwise give bad service), then the customer could get a sequence of 5's (the "cooperation payoff") until the game terminates randomly if he adheres to his strategy; alternatively, if he deviates optimally, he could get a 10 (the "best cheat payoff") by not tipping after good service but would then get a sequence of 0's (the "punishment payoff") thereafter (until the game terminates) since the waiter would respond by rendering bad service. Plugging these numbers into the formula derived in class, we conclude that the customer will not have an incentive to deviate provided the continuation probability exceeds 50%.

Since 60%>50%, the agreement is self-enforcing.

Note: If the waiter deviated by giving bad service following a history of tipping and good service and the customer followed his "proposed strategy," what would the customer do? As I read the question (and certainly as I intended it), the customer would respond to the bad service in the current meal by not tipping. Hence, there would be no benefit to the waiter from this strategy and--as analyzed above--the agreement is self-enforcing for a sufficiently large continuation probability.

Others read the strategy proposed for the consumer differently--as calling for the consumer to tip unless on a *previous* meal there had been bad service or no tipping. In that case, he would tip following the first meal with bad service and would fail to tip only on succeeding meals.

This is indeed a proposed agreement but it is easy to see that it is not self-enforcing for any discount factor. For the customer observing the first incident of bad service would get -5 if he adhered to this strategy and tipped (getting 0 thereafter) whereas if he deviated by withholding his tip in the current period he would get 0 (and then 0 thereafter).

Although this misreading was common, few if anyone noted that under this interpretation the agreement would not be self-enforcing.

I was quite lenient in the grading of this particular error. I was less lenient on failures to plug the correct numbers into the formula in class and least lenient on failures to identify the unique Nash equilibrium of the stage game!

c. The agreement would be self-enforcing for the patron who comes every other week if and only if the probability of continuing for two weeks (to the next encounter) exceeds 50%. If the probability is 60% the businessman stays one more week, it is 36% (p^2) he will stay two more weeks and have another meal. Since 36%<50%, the agreement would not be self-enforcing. What would occur would be some other Nash equilibrium--for example, the waiter would render bad service and the patron would not tip.

d. Bad service and no tipping.

2a. If Bill charges strictly more than Kinkos, the rebate policy is not activated but everyone will gravitate to Kinkos since the price is less. If Bill charges strictly less than Kinkos, the rebate policy will be activated. In this case, everyone will gravitate to Kinkos since--in the presence of the rebate--it offers better terms: a price per unit (inclusive of the rebate) equal to Bill's and a $1 rebate. In either case, the demand at Bill's is zero. Finally, if he matches Kinko's price *exactly*, the rebate policy is not activated and Bill gets half the demand forthcoming at the common price: q_b=50-p, where p is the common price.

b. In the first stage, Kinko will charge 26 cents (see below). In the second stage, Bill will match whatever price Kinko charges (as long as it is above the marginal cost of 2 cents); if Kinko were to charge below 2 cents, Bill would not match it and would get no customers. In the final stage, the consumers would review the two prices. If the prices differ, the customers would purchase exclusively from Kinkos and would pay the lower of the two prices. That is, if Kinko charged the lower price, they would pay that per unit; if Bill charged the lower price, they would pay Kinko's higher price but then get rebated the difference (and would collect the $1 bonus as well).

c. Foreseeing this response, Kinko will set his price, p, to maximize (p-2)(25-.5p)--where the first of these factors is the price net of the per unit cost and the second factor is the demand forthcoming at Kinkos if both charge the common price p. Hence the optimal price for Kinko to set is 26 cents.

3a. The depicted strategy is sequentially rational given the depicted beliefs. Player I gets 20 from the proposed strategy and 10 from deviating. If II's information set were reached he would get 5 from his mixed strategy and 5 from any alternative strategy. If III's information set were reached he would get .5(30)+.5(25) from the proposed strategy but only .5(40)+.5(10) from deviating. Finally--*given the proposed assessment*--it is sequentially rational for player IV to play to the right since: .75(32)+.25(8)>25.

b. The assessment is not a sequential equilibrium because the beliefs are not consistent. There exist no trembles which generate the beliefs that half the time one is at each of the two nodes in III's information set but 3/4 of the time one is in the left-hand node of IV's information set.

c. The strategy combination is a Nash equilibrium. If Player I deviates he gets 10 instead of 20; if anyone else deviates his payoff is unchanged (from 80, -60, 40 respectively) since no one else gets the opportunity to play.

d. There are two subgames: the whole game and the proper subgame commencing at II's singleton information set. We have verified that the strategy combination is a Nash equilibrium in the whole game. We now show, however, that the strategy combination is not a Nash equilibrium in the proper subgame.

Beginning at II's singleton information set and assuming player II and III play their proposed strategies, then player IV will be at the left node in his information set 1/2 the time and at the right node the rest of the time. If IV plays right, he will get .5(32)+.5(8)=20. If he deviates he will get 25. Hence the proposed strategy does not form a Nash equilibrium in the subgame and the proposed equilibrium is not subgame perfect.

4a. If the 80 units are held by one player, he will want to sell them all (since MR=200-2Q, which is positive for Q=80). It is straightforward to verify that when the 80 units is divided equally among 2,3,or 4 of the bidders, they will likewise wish to sell it all in the resulting Cournot equilibrium sales subgame. Hence in every case the price will be P=200-80=120 per unit and the payoff from the second stage sales (gross of the bid) will be 120(80)/m where m is the number of winning bidders.

b. It is a subgame perfect equilibrium strategy combination for each of the four bidders to bid exactly 120 per unit and to market 120(80)/m in the second stage depending on the number of winners in the auction. Since in (a) you verified that the second stage strategy combination formed a Nash equilibrium, it remains to check whether any bidder would be strictly better off deviating than adhering to his strategy given that the other players adhered to their part of the proposed strategy combination. The profit from the proposed bid equilibrium is zero since each of the four winners must pay 120(80/4) at the auction and then receives 120(80/4) from the sales. If one bidder were to raise his bid marginally, he could corner the stock at a cost of $120^+(80)$ but would then earn only 120(80) which is strictly inferior. Alternatively, if one bidder were to reduce his bid he would lose the auction and would receive a payoff of zero, which is not strictly superior to what his proposed strategy yields.

c. In the play of the game, each bidder bids 120, receives 20 units, sells at price 120 and earns a net profit of 0.

d. If 120 units were held by *one* player at the start of the second stage, he would wish to sell only 100 units since MR=200-2Q and to sell more than 100 units would result in negative marginal revenue. It is straightforward to verify that if two or more bidders had won at the first stage, they would sell more than the monopolist (indeed, given the particular numbers in the example, each would market all 120 units and would obtain 80 per unit). Since the monopolist's strategy maximizes revenue, the industry revenue generated in these other structures must be strictly less. This has implications for the first stage.

Suppose more than one person won the auction in the first stage. If this is to be an equilibrium, each must earn zero profits. For if they earned negative profits, they could do better by not bidding at all. And if they earned strictly positive profits, any one of the winners could always bid epsilon more, corner the stock and by selling only 100 units next period could increase his profits.

Hence, the only possibility is that exactly one person wins the auction in the first stage. If he were to make strictly negative profits, he would have better strategies. If here were to make strictly positive profits, one of the other three would do better to beat his bid. Hence net of his bid he must make no profits.

e. Since in the second period, he sells 100 units at 100 per unit and in the first period he bids b and purchases 120 units, b=10000/120 and profits net of the bid are zero.

f. The argument that cornering will occur with 4 bidders is unchanged if there are 100 bidders. A monopolist would still sell only 100 of the 120 units and oligopolists (m>1,2,...100) would still sell it all at a price of 80.

g. If 240 units were sold, the bidding would still be cornered, 100 units would still be sold in the second period at the price P=100. The only difference would be that the monopolist would withhold from the market 140 (240-100) units instead of 20 units.

Since the monopolist would still win at the second stage and would sell the same amount at the same price as before and since the monopolist would still make no profits net of his bid in the first period (because of the competition for who will be the monopolist) the auction revenues are unchanged.

FINAL EXAM University of Michigan
Economics 631
Professor Salant

There are four multi-part questions on this exam. There is no choice. You may answer the questions in any order. Each question will be counted equally. The midterm and final will receive equal weight.

Refinements of Subgame Perfection

1. a. You are asked to verify for a finite game that a particular assessment (μ, σ) (the first component is beliefs and the second component is strategies) is a sequential equilibrium. What must you show?

b. You are asked to verify for a finite game that a particular strategy combination (σ) is trembling hand perfect (in the agent-normal form). What must you show?

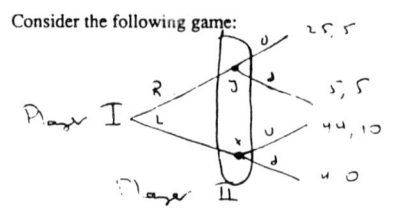

Consider the following game:

c. Following the steps you outlined in (a), verify that the following assessment is a sequential equilibrium:

$$\mu(y) = 1 \qquad \pi = \{1, 0; 0, 1\}$$

d. Following the steps you outlined in (b), verify that the following Nash-equilibrium strategy combination cannot be trembling hand perfect (in the agent-normal form).

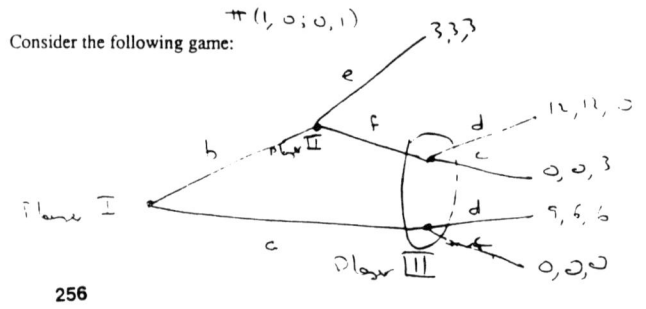

Consider the following game:

$$\pi(1, 0; 0, 1)$$

256

e. Verify that the strategy combination *a;d;e* forms a subgame perfect equilibrium but there exist no beliefs which can rationalize it as a perfect Bayesian equilibrium.

Cost-reducing R and D in a Two-Stage Game with Cournot Competition

2. An industry produces a homogeneous good. The inverse demand curve for the good is p=a-x where p is the industry price, x is the total amount sold, and a is the exogenous vertical intercept. Initially, any firm can produce the good at a constant marginal cost c (and zero fixed costs). Then, an inventor discovers and patents a new technique which can lower the marginal cost of producing the good to c_{new}<c. *For simplicity, let a=140, c=50, and c_{new}=20.*

a. How much would a social planner (a maximizer of consumer plus producer surplus) be willing to pay for the right to use the technology *relative (i.e. the ratio) to the payment of a monopolist*?

b. Suppose instead the industry is a duopoly and the inventor makes a take-it-or-leave-it offer of the following form to the firms: in exchange for z dollars in cash (specified by the inventor), the inventor will transfer to *one and only one* firm the *exclusive* right to use the invention. The duopolists must respond simultaneously to this offer. If both duopolists accept the offer, the right is awarded to only one of them on the basis of flipping a fair coin. If neither accepts the inventor's offer, neither gets the right to use the invention. No one pays the inventor anything unless he gets the right to use the invention. What is the maximum revenue which the inventor can earn from such a scheme?

c. Suppose instead the industry is a duopoly and the inventor makes a take-it-or-leave-it offer of the following form: in exchange for y dollars (specified by the inventor) from a single firm, the inventor is willing to let that firm use the technology; in exchange for y from each firm (a total of 2y), he is willing to let *both* use the technology. The duopolists must respond simultaneously to this offer. Again, no one pays the inventor anything unless he purchases the right to use the invention. What is the maximum revenue which the inventor can earn from such a scheme?

Cournot Equilibrium in a One-Shot Game

3. Suppose a duopoly of firms sells a homogeneous good in a simultaneous move one-shot game in pure strategies. Each firm has a constant marginal cost and no fixed cost. The marginal costs are respectively c_1=5 and c_2=10. The inverse demand curve is as follows: if aggregate supply strictly exceeds 120, then the p=0; if aggregate supply is in (0,120] then p=120; and if aggregate supply is exactly 0, p=1000. In each case, answer "yes" or "no" and explain the basis for your answer.

a. Does a Cournot equilibrium exist?

b. Is the Cournot equilibrium unique? (If your answer to a. was "no," write "not applicable since no Cournot equilibrium exists.")

c. Does any Cournot equilibrium have the property that the firm with the higher marginal cost earns a higher profit than the firm with the lower marginal cost? (If your answer to a. was "no," write "not applicable since no Cournot equilibrium exists.")

Potential Competition in Prices as a Check on Monopoly Power

4. Consider the following three-period game of complete information. Firms sell a homogeneous good, compete in prices and use pure strategies. In the first period, a lone incumbent sells to consumers. At the start of the second period, one entrant can enter or not. If the entrant does not enter, he receives a payoff of zero. If entry occurs, the entrant must pay a one-time entry fee, f>0. Payment of the entry fee is publicly observed. If no entry occurs, the incumbent sells to the consumers for the remaining two periods without threat of further entry. If entry does occur, the two firms set prices simultaneously in the two remaining periods without threat of further entry. There is no discounting. Suppose the industry demand curve (demand correspondence) in each period is as follows:
if p>100, d(p)=0;
if p=100, d(p) is in [0,120];
if 100>p>0, d(p)=120;
if p=0, d(p) is in [120, infinity). Firms compete in prices (Bertrand competition).

a. Suppose firms have identical constant marginal costs. Will the second firm enter? What price will the incumbent charge in each period in the play of the subgame perfect equilibrium ? Does potential competition in this case reduce prices and benefit the consumer relative to what would occur in its absence?

b. Suppose instead the incumbent has marginal cost of *11* and the potential entrant is "breaking-in" a new technology with marginal cost of *6*. Will entry occur if the entry fee is *1000*? Recall that if he enters, the entrant and incumbent set price simultaneously in each of two periods and face no threat of further entry. What price will the incumbent charge in each period in the play of the subgame perfect equilibrium?

Suppose finally that there are instead two potential entrants, A and B. In period two, A can pay an entry fee and compete with the incumbent as a duopolist. In period three, B can pay an entry fee and compete with the incumbent and perhaps A (if A entered). Again, the game terminates after the third period. "Breaking-in" the new technology has spillover effects. Whichever (firm A or B) is the first entrant to use the new technology has entry fee *1000* and marginal cost of *6*. But if it has the benefit of the prior experience of A, firm B has reduced entry fee *300* and reduced marginal cost of *2*.

c. What price will the incumbent charge in each period in the play of the subgame perfect equilibrium? Does the addition of a second potential competitor with even lower marginal costs and a lower entry fee reduce prices and benefit the consumer relative to what would occur in its absence?

Kennedy School of Government, Harvard

Economics 24
Taught at Swarthmore College
THE ECONOMICS OF INDUSTRY

F. M. Scherer
Spring Semester 1989

This course proceeds on an industry case study basis. Recommended purchases, in declining benefit/cost ratio order, are Walter Adams, ed., The Structure of American Industry (seventh edition, Macmillan paperback); David Halberstam, The Reckoning (Morrow paperback, $5.50); Henry Grabowski and John Vernon, The Regulation of Pharmaceuticals (paperback, $4.95); and Robert Crandall, The U.S. Steel Industry in Recurrent Crisis (paperback, $9.95). Backup copies of these plus all other readings are on reserve. Items marked R are on reserve under their own title; items marked 24 are on reserve in the Economics 24 loose-leaf binders.

Readings marked with two asterisks (**) are optional; those with one asterisk are optional but strongly recommended; those with no asterisk comprise the core of the assignments. To help keep the main themes in perspective, the principal issues are stated after the heading for each industry caption.

There will be a mid-term examination weighted one-third. A term paper can be substituted for it.

Week beginning:

Jan. 23   Introduction.

           Issues: Overview of industrial organization analysis.

           F. M. Scherer, Industrial Market Structure and Economic
             Performance, 2nd ed. (hereafter, IMSEP), Chapter 1,
             pp. 9-29 and 41-44, and Chapter 3.
           Adams, Chapter 12.

Jan. 30   The Economics of Agriculture.

           Issues: Purely competitive markets, technogical change, price stabilization, government price supports.

           Adams, Chapter 1.
           L. W. Weiss, Case Studies in American Industry,
             3rd edition, Chapter 2.
           Organization for Econ. Cooperation and Development,
             National Policies and Agricultural Trade, pp. 7-25
             and 50-73.

Symposium on "Agriculture in Transition," in *Issues in Science and Technology*, pp. 97-143.

T. M. Lenard and M. P. Mazur, "Harvest of Waste: The Marketing Order Program," *Regulation*, May/June 1985, pp. 19-26.

Feb. 6 Complete Agriculture. Crude Oil.

Issues: Cartel behavior, government regulation of prices, the windfall profits tax, energy supply.

Adams, Chapter 2.
IMSEP, pp. 169-176.
James Griffin and David Teece, *OPEC Behavior and World Oil Prices*, Chapters 1, 2, and *3.
James Griffin, "OPEC Behavior: A Test of Alternative Hypotheses," *American Economic Review*, December 1985, pp. 954-963.

Feb. 13 Complete Crude Oil. Petroleum Refining and Marketing.

Issues: Mergers, economies of scale, vertical integration, oligopoly pricing, predatory pricing.

L. W. Weiss, *Case Studies in American Industry* (3rd ed.), pp. 270-281.
IMSEP, pp. 118-122, 335-337, 527-530, and **81-118.

Feb. 20 Steel I.

Issues: Mergers, price leadership, limit pricing, technological innovation.

Adams, Chapter 3.
IMSEP, pp. 176-184, 232-242, and 349-352.
Robert Crandall, *The U.S. Steel Industry in Recurrent Crisis*, Introduction plus Chapters 1-4.
**George Stigler, "The Dominant Firm and the Inverted Umbrella," *Journal of Law and Economics*, October 1965.

Feb. 27 Steel II.

Issues: Oligopoly pricing, wage determination, "dumping," import restrictions, "industrial policy."

Crandall, *The U.S. Steel Industry in Recurrent Crisis*, Chapters 5-7.
IMSEP, pp. 349-352.

March 6   Semiconductors. Midterm exam March 8 or 10.

   Issues: Pricing with learning-by-doing, innovation competition, government support of innovation, Japanese industrial policy.

   *Richard Levin, "Innovation and Public Policy in the Semiconductor Industry," in R. Nelson, ed., Government and Technical Progress, pp. 9-95.
   IMSEP, pp. 250-252 and Chapter 15.
   "Selling Business a Theory of Economics," Business Week, Sept. 8, 1973, pp. 85-90.
   Clyde Prestowitz, Trading Places: How We Allowed Japan To Take the Lead, Chapter 2.
   Larry Sumney and Robert Burger, "Revitalizing the U.S. Semiconductor Industry," Issues In Science and Technology, Summer 1987, pp. 32-41.

Mar. 13   Vacation.

Mar. 20   Complete Semiconductors. Computers.

   Issues: Dominant firm pricing, limit pricing, economies of scale, competition in innovation.

   Adams, Chapter 7.
   R. T. DeLamarter, Big Blue, Chapters 3,4,5,6, 12, and 13.
   Franklin Fisher et al., Folded, Spindled, and Mutilated, Chapters 5 and 8.

Mar. 27   Automobiles.

   Issues: Economies of scale, vertical integration, price discrimination, import competition, product innovation.

   Adams, Chapter 4.
   John Kwoka, "Market Power and Market Change in the U.S. Automobile Industry," Journal of Industrial Economics, June 1984, pp. 509-522.
   David Halberstam, The Reckoning (all).
   Arthur Denzau, "The Japanese Auto Cartel," Regulation, 1988, no. 1, pp. 11-16.
   **J. Patrick Wright (for John de Lorean), On a Clear Day You Can See General Motors, Chapters 4, 7-9, and 10-16.

April 3   Complete Automobiles.

    Issues: External diseconomies, government regulation
    of product standards.

    Lester Lave, "Conflicting Objectives in Regulating
      the Automobile," *Science*, May 22, 1981.
    Richard Arnould and Henry Grabowski, "Auto Safety
      Regulation: An Analysis of Market Failure," *Bell
      Journal of Economics*, Spring 1981, pp. 27-48.

April 10   Pharmaceuticals.

    Issues: Technological innovation and the patent
    system, government regulation of product efficacy
    and safety.

    Henry Grabowski and John Vernon, *The Regulation of
      Pharmaceuticals* (all).
    IMSEP, pp. 190-193 and Chapter 16.
    J. J. McRae and F. Tapon, "Some Empirical Evidence on
      Post-Patent Barriers to Entry in the Canadian Pharma-
      ceutical Industry," *Journal of Health Economics*,
      March 1985, pp. 43-61.
    **Peter Temin, "Technology, Regulation, and Market
      Structure in the Modern Pharmaceutical Industry,"
      Bell Journal of Economics, Autumn 1979.

April 17   Complete Pharmaceuticals.   Thanksgiving Break.

    Issues: Entry barriers, government regulation,
    the economics of retailing.

    Sam Peltzman, "By Prescription Only ... or Occas-
      ionally," *Regulation*, 1987, no. 3/4, pp. 23-28.
    Edmund Kitch, "The Vaccine Dilemma," *Issues in Science
      and Technology*, Winter 1986, pp. 108-121.
    Weiss, *Case Studies in American Industry*, pp. 282-290.

April 24   Brewing.

    Issues: Structural change, mergers, advertising and
    image differentiation, economies of scale.

    Adams, Chapter 6.
    IMSEP, Chapter 14.

May 1   Catch-up. Reading period.

    Adams, Chapter 8 (on telecommunications).
    Complete Halberstam, *The Reckoning*.

AUSTRALIAN GRADUATE SCHOOL OF MANAGEMENT
University of New South Wales
ECONOMICS OF REGULATION

85.0301	Term 3, 1989	Peter Swan Gerald Garvey

Laws and regulations both empower and restrict private and public sector managers. This course provides basic tools with which to understand and to utilize the current legal framework, and stresses a wide range of applications. We first analyze how and why restrictive laws andregulations take the forms they do, and the forms they are likely to take in the future using what is known as Public Choice Theory. Even more attention is devoted to the ways in which individuals and organizations can make use of the legal system to supporttheir endeavours. This section will stress laws of commercial contract, liability, and incorporation, using tools from the relatively new fields of Law and Economics and the Economics of Organizations and Institutions.

The course design involves extensive student participation. We intend to have at least half of the air-time allocated to class members.

Evaluation

20% of the course mark will be determined by performance in the student-led discussions.

15% of the course mark will be determined by the presentation of a major project.

65% of the course mark will be determined by the written version of the major project.

Course Outline

The first two weeks will present the analytical framework. The first meeting in each of weeks 3\-9 will be a participative lecture, and the second will be a discussion headed by selected members of the class. Each student will be responsible for preparing materials for and leading one of these discussions, either individually or as part of a group.

Suggested readings for each class are provided. P1 denotes the first reading in the course notes package, and R1 denotes the first reading on reserve.

Week I
1. Overview and Introduction (R1, R11, R12)
2. Theories of Regulation (P1, R11, R12)

Week II
1. Property Rights and the Coase Theorem (P2, P3, R4)
2. Contracts, Constitutions, and Corporate Charters (P4, P5, R7, R10)

Week III
1. Products Liability: Issues of life and death in quality control (P6, P7, P8, P9, R2, R3, R11)
2. Student-led Discussion: Directors' Liability

Week IV
1. Executive Compensation and Incentives (P10, P11, R5, R6)
2. Student Exercise: Structuring an Executive Compensation Package

Week V
1. Labour Market Regulation and Social Welfare Systems (P12, P13, R8)
2. Student-led Discussion: Enterprise Unions

Week VI
1. Make-or-Buy Decisions, Vertical Restraints, and the Trade Practices Commission (TPC) (P14, P15, P16, R9)
2. Student-led Discussion: The TPC *Queensland Wire* Decision

Week VII
1. Management Buy-Outs and Takeovers (P17, P18, P19, P20, R5, R13)
2. Student-led Discussion: John Eliott's acquisition of Elders

Week VIII
1. Franchising vs. Centralised Control (P21, P22, P23, R4, R9)
2. Student Exercise: Design a Franchise Contract/Agreement

Week IX
1. Contract Design: Air Traffic Controllers and "near-misses". (P24, P25, R8)
2. Student Exercise: Managing Sydney Airport

Week X
1. Student Presentations
2. Student Presentations

Reserve Reading

1. Posner, Richard. "The Law and Economics Movement".
2. Manley, Marisa. "Product Liability: You're more exposed than you think".
3. "Product Safety Laws". *Choice*, August 1989.
4. "Hertz Rigged Repair Costs: Investigations. *Financial Review*, January 27, 1988.
5. "Bid for Elders 'Not Fair or Reasonable'". *Financial Review*, August 15, 1989.
6. Dodd, E. Merrick. "For Whom are Corporate Managers Trustees"?
7. Ordover, J., and A. Weiss. "Information and the Law: Evaluating Legal Restrictions on Competitive Contracts".
8. "Wage Decision Where Both Sides Stand to Win". *Financial Review*, August 7, 1989.
9. McMillan, John. "Managing Suppliers: Incentive Systems in Japanese and U.S. Industry".
10. *Government Regulation of Industry: Issues for Australia.* Bureau of Industry Economics Occasional Paper 1, 1986.
11. Landes, W., and R. Posner. *The Economic Structure of Tort Law.*
12. Posner, R. *Economic Analysis of Law*, 2nd edition.
13. Posner, R., and K. Scott. *Economics of Corporation Law and Securities Regulations.*

ECONOMICS OF REGULATION

85.0301   Term 3, 1989   Peter Swan
                                                                                         Gerald Garvey

LIST OF CONTENTS

1. P. Swan, Public and Private Interest Theories of Regulation, (Key 2450).

2. P. Swan, The Economics of Law, (Key 2451).

3. H. Demsetz, "A Framework for the Study of Ownership", in *Ownership, Control, and the Firm*, pp.12–27.

4. R. Posner, and K. Scott, "Economics of Corporation Law and Securities Regulation", pp.90–99.

5. B. Klein, "Transaction Cost Determinants of 'Unfair' Contractual Arrangements", *American Economic Review* 70 (2), May 1980.

6. R. Posner, "Strict Liability: A Comment" in Manne, ed., *The Economics of Legal Relationships*, pp.241–257.

7. P. Swan, "Common Law Rights vs 'No-Fault'", *CIS*.

8. "Product Liability: A New Approach". *Business Council Bulletin*, June 1989 pp.20–25.

9. (i) "Features", *Australian Financial Review*, Thursday, July 27 and Friday, July 29.
   (ii) "Product Liability Draft Altered", *AFR*, August 7, 1989.

10. "A Roundtable Discussion of Management Compensation", *Midland Corporate Finance Journal*, Spring, 1985, pp.23–55.

11. R.S. Kaplan and A.A. Atkinson, *Advanced Management Accounting*, 1989, pp.741–778.

12. P. Swan, and M. Bernstam. "The Political Economy of the Symbiosis between Labour Market Regulation and the Social Welfare System".

13. A Better Way of Working". EPAC Paper 89/02 by F. Hilmer and P. McLaughlin.

14. A. Alchian and S. Woodward: "The Firm is Dead; Long Live the Firm. A Review of Oliver E. Williamson's The Economic Instiitutions of Capitalism", *Journal of Economic Literature*, 1988.

15. S. Masten, "A Legal Basis for the Firm". *Journal of Law, Economics and Organization*, 1988.

16. "The High Court Decision in Queensland Wire". *Business Council Bulletin*, April 1989 pp.12–15.

17. L.E. Browne and E.S. Rosengren, "The Merger Boom: An Overview", *New England Economic Review*, March/April 1989. Also "Discussion", John C. Coffee Jnr., same edition.

18. L. Lowenstein, "No More Cozy Management Buy-outs, *Harvard Business Review*, 1986.

19. "Independents Show Stubborn Streak". *Business Review Weekly*, July 7 1989, pp.38–41.

20. "Banks Yield to Elliott's Charm". *Financial Review*, July 28, 1989.

21. P. Rubin, "The Theory of the Firm and the Structure of the Franchise Contract", *Journal of Law and Economics*, 1978.

22. "Call for Voluntary Code of Ethics" and "Study Sheds Light on Franchising". Both *Australian Financial Review*, May 31, 1989.

23. "Bennetton Denies Allegations of Unfair Business Practices". *Financial Review*, Friday October 21 1988.

24. M. Statern and J. Umbeck, "Close Encounters in the Skies". *Regulation*, AEI, March/April 1983. (Key number 2473).

25. R. Hahn and R.S. Kroszner, "The Mismanagement of Air Transport: A Supply-Side Analysis", *The Public Interest*, Spring 1989.

G

AUSTRALIAN GRADUATE SCHOOL OF MANAGEMENT
University of New South Wales
Industrial Organisation: 85.0201

Peter Swan

1st Term, 1990

Assessment

A test worth 33% of the overall grade in about week 6 and a "hands-on" project due at the end of week 10 worth 60% of the overall grade. There will be brief student presentations of projects in weeks 9 and 10 worth 7%. The project can be done individually or as part of a self-selected group with a maximum size of three/four. As part of the project, participants are encouraged to evaluate actual market situations and industries and to make the project as "hands-on" as possible by getting out and talking to/meeting with the appropriate people.

Brief Course Description

The issues and ideas to be discussed in this course include:

1. An assessment of different approaches to the economics of strategic management.
2. How to go about earning monopoly profits! The relevance of market shares, rates of return and the nature and extent of entry barriers, including strategies of pre-commitment and product differentiation.
3. Natural monopolies and contestable markets with applications to such industries as airlines and Australia's Two Airline Policy. Fortunately the Policy has only a few months to run.
4. Strategic and collusive behaviour including cartel formation and stability. Is OPEC a cartel?
5. Protection, economies of scale and regulation: the automobile and banking industries.

Textbooks

Set Text:

Clarkson, Kenneth W. and Miller, Roger L., *Industrial Organization Theory, Evidence and Public Policy*, McGraw Hill, 1983. A readable non-technical treatment.

Major Supplementary Texts:

Clarke, R., *Industrial Economics*, Blackwell, 1985. This text is English rather than United States in orientation. It is also a little more technical than Clarkson and Miller.

Waterson, M., *Economic Theory of the Industry*, Cambridge University Press, 1984.

> A useful book applying a more rigorous and hence more technical approach than Clarkson and Miller. Those who feel they can cope may prefer to use this text as a supplement to

Clarkson and Miller.

Reekie, W.D., *Industry, Prices and Markets*, Philip Adam, 1979.

Sherer, F.M., *Industrial Market Structure and Economic Performance*, Rand McNally.

George, K.D. and Joll, C., *Industrial Organisation: Competition, Growth and Structural Change*, Allen and Unwin, Sydney, 3rd ed. 1981.

Webb, L.R. and Allan, R.H., *Industrial Economics: Australian Studies*.

Parry, T.G. (ed.), *Australian Industry Policy*, Longman Cheshire, 1982.

Davidson, F.G. and Stewardson, B.R., *Economics and Australian Industry*.

Shepherd, William G., *The Economics of Industrial Organization*, Prentice Hall, 1979.

Stigler, G., *The Organisation of Industry*.

Aoki, M., *The Cooperative Game Theory of the Firm*, Clarendon Press, 1984.

> A good up-to-date survey of different approaches to the theory of the firm with some extensions.

Tirole, Jean, *The Theory of Industrial Organization*, MIT Press, Cambridge, 1989.

> A more rigorous and difficult text but excellent for those more advanced students who can cope with it.

Putterman, L. (ed.), *The Economic Nature of the Firm: A Reader*, CUP, 1986.

> A useful collection of readings on the nature of the firm.

Clarke, R. and McGuinness, T. (eds.), *The Economics of the Firm*, Blackwell, 1987.

Approach

The aim is to provide a balance between an analysis of how firms compete in different industry environments and particular topical case studies. Students are encouraged to participate in all sessions but particularly in applied sessions.

Outline

1. A. The Economics of Strategic Planning: The BCG and Harvard Approaches and the Chicago Critique.

   B. Structure-Conduct-Performance Paradigm: assessment and critique.

2. A. Rivalrous behavior between firms, cartels and price wars.

   B. OPEC: what can account for the massive rise in the price of oil and its precipitous decline?

3. A. Barriers to entry: what factors are responsible and can they be effective? Exit barriers and contestable markets.

   B. The Rise and Demise of Australia's Two Airline Policy and U.S. Airline Deregulation; 1989 saw the failure of the pilot's strike, 1990 ushers in a massive shake-up with the demise of the Two-Airline Policy.

4. A. Imports as potential entry: tariffs, quotas, protection and scale economies.

B. The high cost Australian automobile industry. Is it purely the consequences of mismanaged industry policy?

   Honda and Nissan as successful new entrants into the world automobile industry.

5. A. Advertising and product differentiation: is advertising effective in creating entry barriers or does it encourage competition?

   B. Service competition in the Australian Banking Industry and deregulation.

6. A. Prisoner's dilemma games, tit for tat and all that

   B. In-class test (open book) on material already covered in class.

7. A. Quality and durability: some aspects of product competition under competition and monopoly.

   B. The life of the humble electric light bulb.

8. A. Incentive structures and the organisation–vertical integration

   B. Privatisation and corporatisation–Telecommunications

9. A. Technological innovation and patents–profiting from technological innovation.

   B. Student presentations.

10. Student presentations.

Reading Guide

1. A. Thomas, L.G., "The Economics of Strategic Planning: A Survey of the Issues", in L.G. Thomas (ed.) *The Economics of Strategic Planning*, Lexington, 1986. (This chapter is on Reserve).

   Wernerfelt, B., "From Critical Resources to Corporate Strategy", *Journal of General Management*, 14(3) Spring 1989 (on Reserve).

   B. Clarkson and Miller, chs. 2, 3 and 4; Waterson, ch.1; Clarke, ch.1 and 2; Reekie, ch.3 (Package): Philip L. Williams, in Webb and Allen (Package); D.K. Round, "Concentration in Australian Markets", in T.G. Parry (ed.) (Package); R.R. Officer, "Trade Practices Act", in Webb and Allen (Package); Franklin M. Fisher, "Diagnosing Monopoly", *Quarterly Review of Economics and Business*, 1979(2) (Package).

2. A. Clarkson and Miller, ch.6 and 14; Waterson, ch.2; Clarke, ch.3; Sherer, chs. 5, 6; Shepherd, chs. 15, 16; Stigler, ch.5; Reekie, ch. 5 (Package).

   B. Geroski, P.A., L. Phlips and A. Ulph, "Oligopoly, Competition and Welfare", *Journal of Industrial Economics*, June 1985 (on reserve).

   Marks, R.E. and P.L. Swan, "The Irrelevance of OPEC: Property Rights and Implicit Discount Rates in the World Oil Market", mimeo, AGSM (Package).

   Johany, A.D., *The Myth of the OPEC Cartel*, Wiley, 1980 (see Package).

   Griffin, James M., "OPEC Behavior: A Test of Alternative Hypotheses", *American Economic Review*, December 1985, pp.954–63 (on reserve).

   Graphs on world oil market (see Package).

3. A. Clarkson and Miller, ch. 16; Waterson, ch. 4; Clarke, ch. 4.

   W.J. Baumol, "Contestible Markets, Antitrust and Regulation", *The Wharton Magazine*, Vol.7, No.1, Fall 1982, 23–20 (Package).

   B. Kirby, M.G., *Domestic Airlines Regulation, the Australian Debate*, Centre for Independent Studies, Sydney.

   Albon, R. and Kirby, M.G. "Property Rights, Regulation and Efficiency: A Further Comment on Australia's Two-Airline Policy, *Economic Record*, June 1985 (Package).

   Bailey, E., Graham, D.R. and Kaplan, D., *Deregulating the Airlines*, MIT, 1985.

4. A. Corden, W.M., *Trade Policy and Economic Welfare*, OUP, ch. 8 (Package).

   B. Swan, P.L., Ph.D. Thesis, ch. 7, 8, 14 (see Package for some extracts); Davidson and Stewardson, ch. 5.

   Halberstam, D., *The Reckoning*, Morrow, New York., 1986.

   Shook, R.L., *Honda: An American Success Story*, Prentice Hall, New York, 1988.

5. A. Clarkson and Miller, ch.5; Waterson, ch. 7 (and 6); Clarke, ch. 6.

   Tom T. Nagle, "Do Advertising-Profitability Studies Really Show that Advertising Creates a Barrier to Entry?", *Journal of Law and Economics*, October 1981 (Package).

   B. Swan, P.L. and Harper, I., "The Welfare Gains from Bank Deregulation", *Australian Financial System Inquiry, Commissioned Studies*, Part 1, AGPS, 475–512, 1982.

   Swan, P.L. and Harper, I., "Financial Intermediation under the Microscope", in Juttner and Valentine (eds.), *The Economics and Management of Financial Institutions*, Longman Cheshire, 1987, 50–59 (package).

6. A. Clarkson and Miller, ch. 14; Waterson, ch. 3; Reekie, ch. 5;

   Robert Axelrod, *The Evolution of Co-operation*, Basic Books (see Package for extracts);

   P.A. Geroski, L. Phlips and A. Ulph, "Oligopoly, Competition and Welfare: Some Recent Developments", *Journal of Industrial Economics*, June 1985 (Package).

7. A. Clarkson and Miller, ch. 9; Waterson, ch. 6;

   Peter L. Swan, "Durability of Consumption Goods", *American Economic Review*, December 1970 (on Reserve).

   B. Peter L. Swan, "Less than Optimum Life of the Electric Light Bulb: A Producer Conspiracy?", AGSM Working Paper No. 82–022, 1982 (Package).

   Avenger, R.L., "Product Durability and Market Structure: Some Evidence", *Journal of Industrial Economics*, 19(4) (June 1981) (on Reserve).

8. A. Clarkson and Miller, ch. 15; Waterson, ch. 5; Clarke, ch. 8; Clarke and McGuinness, ch. 5.

   T. Kumpe and P.T. Bolwijn, "Manufacturing: The New Case for Vertical Integration", *Harvard Business Review*, March-April 1988 (Package).

271

C.H. Ferguson, "From the People Who Brought you Voodoo Economics", *Harvard Business Review*, May-June 1988 (Package).

G. Garvey and P.L. Swan, "The Fable of the Barge: Why Workers Don't Hire the Boss, AGSM Working Paper 89–028, 1989 (on Reserve).

H. Demsetz, "Structure of Ownership and the Theory of the Firm" (Package).

Alchian, A., and Demsetz H., "Production, Information Costs and Economic Organization", in Putterman, ch. 9.

B. C. Veljanovski, *Selling the State*, Weidenfeld and Nicolson, London, 1987 (chapter 9 particularly, on Reserve).

P. Abelson (ed.), *Privatisation: An Australian Perspective*, Australian Professional Publications, Sydney 1987, particularly chapter 7 (on Reserve).

Wenders, J.T., *The Economics of Telecommunications: Theory and Policy*, Ballinger, 1987, particularly chapters 3, 4, 10, 11.

Temin, P., *The Fall of the Bell System*, CUP, 1987.

9. A. D.J. Teece, "Profiting from Technological Innovation", in Teece (ed.) *The Competitive Challenge*, Ballinger, pp.184–219 (on Reserve, Package).

AUSTRALIAN GRADUATE SCHOOL OF MANAGEMENT

Industrial Organisation; 85.0201

Peter Swan

1st Term, 1990

I would like an outline of your proposed topic and approach to be adopted by no later than March 26th (2 page maximum please).

Suggestions for Project

(You are welcome to invent your own subject to my approval).

1. Evaluate an industry (preferably Australian) from an industrial organization perspective. In particular, assess its concentration, economies of scale in production at the plant and firm level, distribution and marketing, the nature of the costs—sunk or variable—and barriers entry including regulatory barriers. Do it from the perspective of you as a consultant to a client considering investing in the industry or acquiring a firm already in the industry. To what extent are entry barriers and excess returns capitalised into the acquisition price?

2. There has been an enormous spate of mergers and acquisitions in recent years. Assess whether a sample of these can be explained predominantly in industrial organizational terms. For example, where firm size is small relative to the attainable scale economies mergers are more likely to be "successful" and give gains to both consumers and producers (as well as shareholders). In particular you may wish to attempt to build a model which predicts (or attempts to predict) merger and acquisition activity.

3. Present a mock case on industrial organizational grounds to the Trade Practices Commission on some significant topic, such as, for example, Coles acquisition of Myers, in relation to the Section 50(1) and anti-merger provisions or other relevant provisions of the Trade Practices Act. The Queensland Wire case is another interesting one, but there are many others such as the Murdoch acquisitions and "media monopoly" questions. The Queensland Wire decision to require BHP to sell steel fence posts to its competitors is a recent controversial decision with potentially important implications for vertical integration as a strategy.

4. Assess the measures, both legal and ethical, that some successful cartel such as the doctors, or lawyers engaged in conveyancing, use to preserve their monopoly. What lessons can be learned from these measures about acquiring and retaining high returns in other activities?

5. Assess the likely development of the Australian banking industry from an industrial organizational viewpoint if one of the major private banks acquires the Commonwealth Bank or if the major private banks are permitted to merge again. Assess the strategy of both Westpac and ANZ of attempting to grow large on a world scale by overseas acquisitions.

6. Can you provide an explanation for the massive waves of price competition in the Sydney retail petrol market. Why does (or did) the price oscillate between 46 cents and 58 cents per litre every fortnight or so with all service stations raising their prices by up to 14 cents per litre or more within an hour or so of each other? The industry is now introducing "rack pricing" in an attempt to prevent discounters gaining access to "cheap petrol". All petrol

stations will be required to pay the same price. What effect is this strategy likely to have on oil majors and petrol stations.

7. Examine the nature of price and non-price competition in an industry of your choice.

8. A mythical business school, MSGA, offering the MBA Degree in Sydney is considering entering a new market, namely the market for "full-cost" fee paying overseas students in competition with the new Management School at Sydney University and the proposed Rochester School in the Western Suburbs at Camden, initially to be established at South Head in Sydney, potentially a number of other management schools in Australia, and of course schools in the U.S. (Harvard, Stanford, Chicago, etc.) and in the U.K. Consider the advisability of this entry from an industrial organizational perspective. Take into account such factors as "sunk costs" and "downside" risk as well as pricing strategies, the target market of students, (country of origin) student academic entry requirements, the feasibility of combining fee-paying and tax-subsidised students, etc.

9. Consider, from an industrial organizational perspective the nature of competition between unions in the building industry, in particular the tactics which were employed by the BWIU and other unions competing for members in this area. Consider the implications of the resort by employers to common law and Trade Practices Law to impose heavy penalties on striking unions for the strategies of unions and employers.

10. Privatisation and deregulation are issues very much to the fore: consider the industrial organization effects of either the corporatisation/privatisation/deregulation of Telecom, Australian Airlines, Qantas, Commonwealth Bank, NSW Electricity Authority or Australia Post. Since the existing management generally has some veto power over such changes how would you prevent all the monopoly rents accruing to the managements of the newly privatised organisaion?

11. A new hi-tech firm is considering entering some long-established industry employing more conventional technology. Preferably basing your study on a real case, consider the nature of entry barriers and possible responses from the incumbents to the threat of entry.

12. Examine the policies of the bank clearing house towards the non-banks and the new banks. Have the major banks been successful in imposing significant early barriers on their rivals? Look carefully at the arrangements over electronic funds transfer. What are the implications for competition in the financial sector?

13. Consider from an industrial organisation perspective the 'appropriate' charge for the mythical business school MSGA to place on entering Australian students. Assume that unless fees are charged that students will be liable for the HEX graduate tax. Consider questions such as reputations, the quality of competing schools, the likely pricing policies of other business schools such as Sydney and Macquarie and the proposed Rochester School.

14. See if you can explain the ownership and organisational structure of one or two major businesses. Thus why for example is BHP owned by its capital suppliers (shareholders) while McKinsey and Co. and most professional organisations are partnerships? How is performance monitored in such diverse types of organisation? What factors are likely to determine the hierarchical structure and the degree of vertical integration?

15. You are the corporate advisor to one of the about to be corporatised/privatised government trading enterprises and you are asked to provide advice on possible divestment of assets, splitting up of the organisation, hierarchical structure, vertical integration and degree of contracting out. Come up with a proposal which you can justify for an actual organisation. You may also consider a restructuring proposal for an existing private sector organisation.

16. The VFT (Very Fast Train) Consortium plan to build a $5 billion fast train travelling at 350 km/h between Sydney and Melbourne. The operating costs on the fast train will be lower than on the airlines. Model the pricing and service competition between the airlines and the

VFT so as to predict the likely equilibrium set of train and plane fares. What effect is airline deregulation likely to have on your proposed solution.

17. The formal end of the Two Airline Policy occurs in October of this year. Develop a business plan for your new airline, New Entrant Airways, setting out the likely reactions of the existing airlines and other possible new entrants.

18. In the light of recent theories about debt and leverage as devices to discipline managers and thus ensure toughness and honesty, examine empirically the relationship between leverage, bankruptcy risk and organisational performance.

19. Provide an economic analysis of the causes, management and consequences of the pilot's dispute. To what extent was it engineered by Ansett and Australian Airlines to (1), dramatically lower their costs and half the number of pilots prior to airline deregulation in October of this year and (2), to reduce profitability in the airline industry for some time thus making it virtually impossible for the proposed new airlines to get off the ground.

20. The same mythical business school, MSGA, is contemplating a series of mergers and acquisitions in its drive to be the number 1 school in the Southern Hemisphere (if it is not already). Analyse such a corporate strategy from an IO perspective. Should the Trade Practices Commission step in to preserve competition?

21. Analyse a strategy of high debt and leverage as a managerial devise to encourage the honesty and toughness of managers. Why has it or hasn't such a strategy worked for some of Australia's high-flying entrepreneurs?

AUSTRALIAN GRADUATE SCHOOL OF MANAGEMENT

INDUSTRIAL ORGANISATION : 85.0201

Peter Swan   1989 T2

Mid Term Test

Attempt any two questions.

Open Book In-Class Test.

Question 1 *True* or *False*. Attempt any three of the five parts. Keep your explanations brief and to the point.

    a. "Because a cartel maximizes joint profit but not the individual profits of members, there is an incentive for a member to violate the rules of the cartel. However, this is not applicable to OPEC as oil is an exhaustible resource."

    b. "The Cournot model assumes that each firm believes that every other firm will hold its price fixed when the firm's price is varied. Each firm's behaviour is optimal given the strategy of its rivals."

    c. "Local content schemes operate by effectively paying what would otherwise be tariff revenue to subsidise high cost local production for the domestic market. Export facilitation schemes effectively redirect the tariff revenue to subsidise production for export markets."

    d. "The large advertising budgets of the branded detergent manufacturers are better explained by the nature of the product than they are by the extent of monopoly power."

    e. "An incumbent firm need only acquire market share and 'act tough' to deter would-be entrants."

Question 2 Explain how you might use some of your tools from Industrial Organisation to value an organisation. For example, suppose you are the merchant bank, Whitlam Turnbull, and you are to be paid X million dollars to value Alan Bond's brewing interests or to value Australian Airlines as part of a privatisation deal, what concepts would be most valuable and how would you use them? Feel free to choose other examples or applications.

Question 3 Bain believes that entry barriers include capital market imperfections, scale economies, advertising and product differentiation, while Stigler would reject any factor as an entry barrier unless it is a cost borne by new entrant firms which is not borne by the incumbent firm(s). Suppose it is unprofitable to enter an industry in which the incumbent firm or firms is selling a complex durable product at a price in excess of marginal costs. The new entrant's product is regarded as being different (and inferior) to the incumbent, who in the past has incurred substantial R and D and selling costs. Briefly apply the analysis of each author to this situation and if there is a difference explain which one you think is correct. How might Stigler and Bain view the contestable market approach to entry barriers? What might this approach have to say about the case in hand?

AUSTRALIAN GRADUATE SCHOOL OF MANAGEMENT

Peter Swan   Industrial Organisation   85.0201

2nd Term, 1988

In-Class Test

Closed Book
Monday 18th July

Attempt Any Two (2) out of the Three (3) Questions

1. In recent weeks there have been a number of reports attributing the falling price of oil on world markets to "above quota" production and hence "cheating" by OPEC member nations.

    Why do cartel members "cheat" when it is in their collective interest not to do so? Explain some of the factors that would either encourage or discourage "cheating". What factors other than cheating might you wish to address if you are an oil industry executive attempting to explain past oil price movements and predict future movements?

2. You are a consultant to a company wishing to enter the MBA market with a facility in Sydney. With or without links to Fairfax, Greiner and a foreign business school, assess the likely entry barriers and the means by which they can be overcome. Try and predict also the likely counter-strategies to be employed by encumbent firms (such as AGSM). Do not ignore factors such as scale capital requirements, sunk costs and credible strategies.

3. You are setting the strategy for General Motors-Holdens, or another of the major motor manufacturers, in Australia in the late 1960's. Discuss the relative merits of and likely results of the following courses of action given the growing threat from the Japanese auto manufacturers:

i. lobby for local content plans and increased protection so that other manufacturers will have to meet the high costs of tooling up for 95 per cent local content; or

ii. lobby for lower protection so that the smaller manufacturers go bankrupt and their assets can be acquired cheaply; or

iii. institute a program of product and scale improvement so that most of the limited Australian market can be captured at existing levels of protection; or

iv. lobby for a market-sharing quota scheme on imports so that imported Japanese cars cannot compete. Buy off the importers' opposition by granting them the value of the scarce quota rights or enter into a "Voluntary" Export Restraint agreement with Japan to limit their exports to Australia; or

v. make takeover offers for the other major Australian manufacturers and rationalise the industry by limiting production to one or two large-scale models with common components which can be exported as well.

PETER SWAN, University of New South Wales

Industrial Organization
Mid-Term Test

10 July 1987

It is In-Class and Open Book.

Attempt Question 1 and either Question 2 or Question 3 but not both.

Question 1

Attempt any 3 of the 5 parts. Keep your answers brief and limited to a page or two.

a. Explain the possible relevance of the Von Stackleberg Price Leadership model to Saudi Arabia's behaviour in reducing oil production in the late 1970's and early 1980's.

b. Would you expect to see many "successful" examples of cartels operating in Australia without either strong "professional ethics" (if it is a profession) or a high degree of government involvement? Why or why not? Explain briefly.

c. Explain what is meant by a "credible threat" or "credible deterrence". How is it related to sunk costs?

d. Assess critically the statement: "Most of Australian manufacturing industry involves significant economies of scale and sizeable sunk costs. Hence Baumol's "contestable markets" approach can never be relevant to such Australian industry".

e. Assess the statement: "The Dorfman-Steiner model of optimal advertising states that the marginal value of advertising will be high when the firm is in a competitive situation with a high demand elasticity. Hence on the basis of this model we would expect competitive firms to advertise more than monopolies".

2nd Term 1987   85.0201   Peter Swan

Do either *Question 2* or *Question 3* but not both.

Question 2

Assess the relevance of the Structure-Conduct-Performance paradigm for an Australian industry of your choice.

Question 3

It is sometimes claimed that Industrial Organization is a form of analysis directed at improving public policy towards and increasing competition in industry but that its tools are often used in an effort to raise entry barriers and generate economic rents. Comment on and illustrate this statement in relation to a particular industry of your choice, e.g. the Australian Airline Industry or Automobile Industry.

University of New South Wales
INDUSTRIAL ORGANIZATION 85.0201

Peter Swan   1986 T2.

Mid Term Test

Due Wednesday 20th August, 1986.

Attempt any four questions.

Q.1 **True** or **False**, attempt any five questions giving a two or three line explanation.

   a. Because a cartel maximizes joint profit but not the profit of an individual member, there is an incentive for a member to violate the rules of the cartel.

   b. The basic purpose of advertising is to shift the demand curve to the right and to make it steeper.

   c. Cartels tend to stable so long as the members and not the taxpayer meet the costs of enforcement.

   d. A contestable market is one in which there are no barriers to entry or to exit but economies of scale involving costs which are not sunk are impossible.

   e. The Cournot model assumes that each firm believes that every other firm will hold its output fixed when price is varied.

   f. In an oligopoly, unlike monopoly and perfect competition, each firm generally makes conjectures about the possible responses of rival firms.

Q.2 You are advising an oil speculator who owns one million litres of oil in storage tanks for which he paid $50,000. He had forecast correctly the rise in oil prices so that today's value is $125,000. Due to a growing oil glut you estimate that the value of the oil will increase to only $137,500 in a year's time in future dollar terms which is a nominal rise of 10% p.a. The firm has the opportunity to put funds into securities paying 11 per cent nominal interest p.a. You estimate that inflation over the next year will be of the order of 7 per cent.

   a. Would you advise the firm to market its oil or maintain its stocks? Why?

   b. What effect does the purchase price of $50,000 have on the recommendation? Would it make any difference if the purchase price was $140,000?

   c. You now pay some credence to a rumour that oil companies including their storage tanks are about to be nationalized with compensation which is at most $100,000 per million litres. How does this news affect the discount rate the company uses to evaluate its future profit stream from oil?

    d. Is there a parallel between your answer to (c) and the property rights explanation for the 1960's decline in the real price of oil and the subsequent 1974 "OPEC" oil price hike of about 400%?

Q.3 Bain believes that entry barriers include capital market imperfections, scale economies, advertising and product differentiation, while Stigler would reject any factor as an entry barrier unless it is a cost borne by new entrant firms which is not borne by the incumbent firm(s). Suppose it is unprofitable to enter an industry in which the incumbent firm or firms is selling a complex durable product at a price in excess of marginal costs. The new entrant's product is regarded as being different (and inferior) to the incumbent, who in the past has incurred substantial R and D and selling costs. Briefly apply the analysis of each author to this situation and if there is a difference explain which one you think is correct. How might Stigler and Bain view the contestable market approach to entry barriers? What might this approach have to say about the case in hand?

Q.4 The payoff from co-operating in an industry is $12 while the temptation for cheating and defection is $20 so long as you are the only one to cheat. If you all cheat the return is $5.00. The 'sucker' payment if you co-operate and others cheat is $1.

    a. Set out the payoff matrix in this industry for two players.

    b. Given that no formal collusion is possible, what is your optimal strategy if this game is played only once? Is it a Nash equilibrium? Why or why not?

    c. Suppose the game is to be repeated a known and finite number of times. How does repetition affect your optimal strategy in this case? Suppose that there is no fixed number of plays but there is a probability that the game will end on each play. How is your strategy affected?

    d. Suppose the incumbent firms are playing a tit-for-tat strategy, which is 'nice' and a 'nasty' alternates between 'defect' and 'co-operate'. Given that all players have the same discount factor, how would you go about computing the discount factor below which the nasties would invade the nice population? What is it?

Q.5 Suppose that there are ten identical producers of spring water, that each of these firms has zero costs of production, so long as it produces less than (or equal to) 9 gallons of water per hour, and that it is impossible for each to produce more than 9 gallons per hour. Suppose that the market demand curve for this water is as follows:

Price (dollars per gallon)	Number of gallons demanded per hour	Price (dollars per gallon)	Number of gallons demanded per hour
11	0	5	60
10	10	4	70
9	20	3	80
8	30	2	90
7	40	1	100
6	50	1/2	105

a. If the firms take the price of water as given (as in the case of perfect competition), what will be the price and output of each firm?

b. If the firms form a completely effective cartel, what will be the price and output of each firm?

c. How much money will each firm be willing to pay to achieve and enforce the collusive agreement described in part b?

d. Suppose that one of the firms secretly breaks the terms of the agreement and shades its price. What effect will this have on its profits?

282

G

UNIVERSITY OF CHICAGO
Department of Economics

Professor Lester Telser   Winter, 1989
Econ 382

THEORIES OF COMPETITION AND THEIR APPLICATIONS
Reading List and Course Outline

The most frequently used books for the course are as follows:

Clark, J.M., 1923, <u>Studies in the Economics of Overhead Costs</u>, Chicago: University of Chicago Press.

Gale, David, 1960, <u>Theory of Linear Economic Models</u>, New York: McGraw-Hill.

Luce, R. Duncan and Howard Raiffa, 1957, <u>Games and Decisions</u>, New York: Wiley.

Telser, Lester, 1978, <u>Economic Theory and the Core</u>, Chicago: University of Chicago Press, Midway Reprint 1988.

_____, 1987, <u>A Theory of Efficient Cooperation and Competition</u>, Cambridge University Press.

_____, 1988, <u>Theories of Competition</u>, New York: North-Holland.

Schumpeter, Joseph A., 1954, <u>Capitalism, Socialism and Democracy</u>, London: Unwin Universal Books (4th ed.).

Stigler, George J., 1983, <u>The Organization of Industry</u>, Homewood, IL: Richard D. Irwin Publishers, Chicago: University of Chicago Press reprint - paperback, 1983.

The detailed references are given at the end. An (*) denotes recommended but not required readings.

A. <u>The Classical Heritage</u>

1. Cournot 1838. Chapters 5, 7, 8, 9.
2. Edgeworth 1881. Pp. 37-42, 45-56.
3. Bohm-Bawerk 1891. Book 4, chapters 1-6.
4. Marshall 1920. Book 3, chapters 1-2.
5. Knight 1921. Part 2, chapters 3, 6.
6. Clark, J.M. 1923. Chapters 1-12.
7. Chamberlin 1933. Chapters 2-3.
8. Schumpeter 1954. Part II.
9. Stigler 1968. Chapters 2, 3, and Appendix.
10. Friedman, J. 1977. Chapter 2.
11. Sharkey, William W. 1982. Chapter 2.
12. Telser, 1987, Chapter 1.

Professor Lester Telser
Econ 382 - Winter, 1989
Page 2

B. **Basic Game Theory**

1. Luce and Raiffa 1957. Chapters 1, 4, 5, 8.
2. Gale 1960. Chapter 6.
3. *Gillies. Solutions to General Non-Zero-Sum Games. Chapter 3 in Tucker and Luce, 1959.
4. *von Neumann, On the Theory of Games of Strategy. Chapter 1 in Tucker and Luce, 1959.
5. Friedman, J. 1977. Chapter 7, N-Person Noncooperative Games.
6. *van Damme, 1983. Chapters 1 & 3, Useful material on noncooperative games.

C. **Market Exchange**

1. Telser 1988. Chapters 1-2.
2. Telser 1978. Chapter 7.
3. Gale 1960. Chapters 2, 3, 4, Chapter 5, Section 6.
4. Debreu and Scarf 1963.
5. *Aumann 1964.
6. *Aumann 1966.
7. *Farrell 1959 and 1961.
8. *Rothenberg 1960 and 1961.
9. *Scarf 1973, Chapter 8.

D. **Industry Equilibrium**

1. Viner 1931.
2. Telser 1978. Chapters 1-4; Telser, 1987, Chapters 3-5.
3. Sharkey 1977.
4. Stigler 1968. Chapters 5, 6, 7, 16, 17, 18.
5. *Nash 1950; *Nash 1953.
6. Luce and Raiffa 1957. Chapters 6, 7, 9.
7. Sharkey 1982. Chapters 4-6.
8. Telser, 1987, Chapter 1, 2.

E. **Corporations, Modern Coalitions**

1. Smith, Adam 1776. Book V, Chapter I, Part III, Article 1. Joint-Stock Companies.
2. Marshall 1920. Book II, Chapters 8-9.
3. Marshall 1923. Book II, Chapters II, IV.
4. Bittlingmayer 1982.
5. Bittlingmayer 1984.

F. **Self-Enforcing Agreements**

1. Nash 1951.
2. Telser 1987, Chapter 6.
3. Axelrod 1984, Chapters 1-5.
4. Telser 1988, Chapters 3, 5.
5. Telser 1988, Chapter 5.

Professor Lester Telser
Econ 382 - Winter, 1989
Page 3

REFERENCES

*Aumann, Robert, 1964. "Markets with a Continuum of Traders," *Econometrica* 32: 39-50.

_____, 1966. "Existence of Competitive Equilibria in Markets with a Continuum of Traders," *Econometrica* 34: 1-17.

Bittlingmayer, George, 1982. "Decreasing Average Cost: A New Look at the Addyston Pipe Case," *Journal of Law and Economics* 25: (October): 201-29.

_____, 1985. "Bad Antitrust Policy Caused the Great Merger Wave," *Journal of Law and Economics* 28(1), April: 77-119.

Bohm-Bawerk, Eugene von, 1930. *The Positive Theory of Capital*, translated by William A. Smart, photo-offset of 1891 edition, New York: Stechert.

Chamberlin, E.H., 1933. *The Theory of Monopolistic Competition*, Cambridge, MA: Harvard University Press.

Cournot, Augustin, 1960. *Researches into the Mathematical Principles of the Theory of Wealth*, translated by National Bacan from 1838 french edition, Introductory Essay by Irving Fisher, New York: Kelley.

Damme, Eric van, 1983. *Refinements of the Nash Equilibrium Concept*, Berlin: Springer.

Debreu, G. and H. Scarf, 1963. "A Limit Theorem on the Core of an Economy," *International Economic Review* 4: 235-246.

Edgeworth, Francis Y., 1881. *Mathematical Psychics*, London: Kegan-Paul.

Farrell, M.J., 1959. "The Convexity Assumption in the Theory of Competitive Markets," *Journal of Political Economy* 67: 377-391.

_____, 1961. "A Reply," *Journal of Political Economy* 69: 484-489.

Friedman, J., 1977. *Oligopoly and the Theory of Games*, Amsterdam: North-Holland.

Knight, Frank H., 1921. *Risk, Uncertainty and Profit*, Boston: Houghton-Mifflin.

Marshall, Alfred, 1920. *Industry and Trade*, 3rd edition, London: MacMillan.

Nash, Alfred, 1950. "The Bargaining Problem," *Econometrica* 18: 155-162.

_____, 1951. "Non-Cooperative Games," *Ann. Math.* 54: 286-295.

_____, 1953. "Two-Person Cooperative Games," *Econometrica* 21: 128-140.

Professor Lester Telser
Econ 382 - Winter, 1989
Page 4

*Neumann, John von and Oskar Morgenstern, 1947. *Theory of Games and Economic Behavior*, 2nd edition, Princeton, NJ: Princeton University Press.

*Rothenberg, Jerome, 1960. "Non-Convexity, Aggregation, and Pareto Optimality," *Journal of Political Economy* 58: 435-468.

_____, 1961. "Comments on Non-Convexity," *Journal of Political Economy* 69: 490-492.

Scarf, Herbert E., 1971. "On the Existence of a Cooperative Solution for a General Class of N-Person Games," *Journal of Economic Theory* 3: 169-181.

_____, 1973. *Computation of Economic Equilibria*, New Haven, CT: Yale University Press.

Shapley, L.S. and Martin Shubik, 1969. "On the Core of an Economic System with Externalities," *American Economic Review* 59: 678-684.

Sharkey, William W., 1977. "Efficient Production When Demand is Uncertain," *Journal of Public Economics* 8: 369-84.

_____, 1982. *The Theory of Natural Monopoly*, Cambridge: Cambridge University Press.

*Shubik, Martin, 1959a. "Edgeworth Market Games," *Contributions to the Theory of Games*, (eds., A. W. Tucker and R.D. Luce), Vol. 4, Princeton, NJ: Princeton University Press.

Smith, Adam, 1776. *Wealth of Nations*, Modern Library Edition.

Stigler, George J., 1963. *Capital and Rates of Return in Manufacturing Industries*, Princeton NJ: Princeton University Press. Chicago: University of Chicago reprint - paperback, 1983.

Telser, L.G., 1980. "A Theory of Self-Enforcing Agreements," *Journal of Business* 53: 27-44.

Viner, Jacob, 1931. "Cost Curves and Supply Curves," (reprinted in *AEA* Readings in Price Theory, eds., G. Stigler and K. Boulding).

October 1989

M. A. UTTON
MICHAEL WATERSON

U&G

UNIVERSITY OF READING
DEPARTMENT OF ECONOMICS

BUSINESS ECONOMICS (E8)

The course will consist of 28 lectures and approximately 8 seminars. One lecture a week will be given in the Autumn Term and two lectures a week in the Lent Term. Seminars will be held fortnightly. One test paper will be written at the beginning of the Lent Term and one essay handed in each term.

The continuous assessment work for the course will be based on the two essays, the Lent Term test paper and the second year Departmental Examination (held at the beginning of the Summer Term).

Course Outline

Topic

I. **The Business Environment**

   External and internal constraints on the efficiency and growth of firms: risk and uncertainty; finance; competition and government policies; internal co-ordination problems.

   Types of efficiency.

   A preliminary framework for the analysis of business.

II **Some economics of the Firm**

   Constraints on the firm's management discretion. Internal organisation and management structure.

III **Enterprise growth**

   The economics of vertical integration and the relative efficiency of market and internal transactions.

   Diversifying an enterprise's product range

   Internal expansion vs. growth by merger.

IV **Concentration and Market Structure**

   Factors shaping market structure : economies of scale and scope;

   learning effects; mergers; stochastic factors; government policies

   Aggregate and market concentration and their measurement

   Concentration in the UK

V Pricing Decisions

The problem of pricing in imperfect markets

i) Pricing by a dominant firm : the limits of discretion

Theories of limit pricing

The economics of vertical restraints

Predatory pricing and competition

ii) Pricing problems in oligopoly

The central features of oligopolistic markets

Formal and informal methods of price co-ordination

Barriers to entry and strategic behaviour

VI Non-price competition

Product differentiation - modelling and inferences

Optimal advertising strategy

The economic effects of advertising

Product innovation, technological change and the spread of innovation

VII Profitability and enterprise performance

Measures of profitability. The interpretation of inter and intra-industry differences in profitability.

VIII Government and business

The rationale of competition policy

The control of dominant firms, mergers and restrictive practices

REFERENCES

The following book is recommended as the basic text for the course, but it will need to be supplemented by extensive reading from the list below:

R. CLARKE - *Industrial Economics* (paperback), 1985, Blackwell.

The following texts will be referred to frequently throughout the course:

P.J. Devine, N. Lee, R.M. Jones, W.J. Tyson - *An Introduction to Industrial Economics*, Allen and Unwin, 3rd edition, 1979.

D.Hay and D.J. Morris - *Industrial Economics*, CUP, 1979.

F.M. Scherer - *Industrial Market Structure and Economic Performance*, 2nd edition, 1980, Rand McNally.

J.V. Koch - *Industrial Organisation and Prices*, Prentice Hall, 2nd edition, 1980.

The following references relate to the topics numbered I-VII in the course outline and to the accompanying discussion topics and essay titles.

Topic I
R. Clarke, *Industrial Economics* chapters 1 & 2.
D.A. Hay and D.J. Morris, *Industrial Economics*, chapter I.
J.V. Koch, *Industrial Organisation and Prices*, Prentice Hall, 2nd edition, 1980, chapters 2 and 5.
F.M. Scherer, *Industrial Market Structure and EconomicPerformance*, chapters 1 and 2.
S. Davies and B. Lyons *Economics of Industrial Organisations*, Longman, 1989, chapter 3
M. Waterson, *Economic Theory of the Industry*, CUP, 1984, chapter 1.

Topic II
R. Clarke and T. McGuiness, *The economics of the Firm*, Basil Blackwell, 1987, chapters 2 and 3.
M. Ricketts, *The Economics of Business Enterprise*, Wheatsheaf, 1987.
A. Chandler, *Strategy and Structure*, MIT press, 1962, Chapter 7.
J. Stiglitz, *Credit Markets and the Control of Capital, Journal of Money, Credit and Banking*, 1985

Topic III
R. Clarke, *Industrial Economics*, chapters 8 and 9.
O. Williamson, *Markets and Hierarchies*, Free Press, 1975, chapters 1 and 2.
J.V. Koch, *Industrial Organisations and Prices*, Prentice Hall, 1980, chapter 10.
F.M. Scherer, *Industrial Market Structure and Economic Performance*, chapters 9 and 12.
A. Koutsoyiannis, *Non-Price Decisions*, chapter 5, especially sections 1-3 and chapter 6, especially sections 1,2 and 5.
M.A. Utton, *The Political Economy of Big Business*, chapter 5.

D. Needham, *The Economics of Industrial Structure, Conduct and Performance*, Holt, Rinehart and Winston, 1978, chapters 8 and 9.
P.J. Devine, N. Lee, R.M. Jones and W.J. Tyson, *Introduction to Industrial Economics*, chapter 5.
G. Hay, *Vertical Restraints*, Fiscal Studies, 1985.
M.A. Utton, *Diversification and Competition*, CUP, 1979.

Topic IV

R. Clarke, *Industrial Economics*, Chapter 2
F.M. Scherer, *Industrial Market Structure and Economic Performance*, Chapter 4
C.F. Pratten, *Economies of Scale in Manufacturing Industry* Books 1 and 3, CUP, 1971.
M.C. Sawyer, *The Economics of Industries and Firms*, Chaps. 3 & 4 Croom Helm.
J.V. Koch, *Industrial Organisation and Prices*, Prentice Hall, 1980, Chaps 6-8.
M.A. Utton, *The Political Economy of Big Business*, Martin Robertson, 1982, Chapter 3.
S.J. Prais, *The Growth of Giant Enterprises in Britain* CUP, 1976, Chapts. 1 & 2.

Topic V

R. Clarke, *Industrial Economics*, chapter 3.
S. Davies and B. Lyons, *Economics of Industrial Organisation*, Longman, Chapter 2, 1989.
J.V. Koch, *Industrial Organisation and Prices*, Prentice Hall, 1980, chapts 12 and 13.
A. Koutsoyiannis, *Modern Microeconomics*, chapters 10, 13 and 14.
F. Scherer, *Industrial Market Structure and Economic Performance*, chapters 5, 6 and 11.
P.J. Devine, N. Lee, R.M. Jones and W.J. Tyson, *An Introduction to Industrial Economics*, Allen and Unwin, 1979, pp.235-252.
R.D. Blair and L.W. Kenny, *Microeconomics for Managerial Decision Making*, chapter 12.
J.S. McGee, Predatory Pricing Revisited, *Journal of Law and Economics*, 1980.
J.F. Brodley and G.A. Hay, Predatory Pricing: Competing Economic Theories and the Evolution of Legal Standards, *Cornell Law Review* (SSRR).
J. Vickers, The Economics of Predatory Practices, *Fiscal Studies*, 1985.
J. Vickers, Strategic Competition Among the Few - Some Recent Developments in the Economics of Industry, *Oxford Review of Economic Policy*, 1985, (SSRR).
B.S. Yamey, Predatory Price Cutting: Notes and Comments, *Journal of Law and Economics*, 1972.
M.C. Sawyer, *The Economics of Industries and Firms*, 1981, chapter 9.
M.A. Utton, *Diversification and Competition*, chapter 5, CUP, 1979.

Topic VI

R. Clarke, *Industrial Economics*, chapters 6 and 7.
P.J. Devine, N. Lee, R.M. Jones, H.J. Tyson, *An Introduction to Industrial Economics*, pp.252-264.
F.M. Scherer, *Industrial Market Structure and Economic Performance*, chapters 14 and 15.
H. Goldschmid, H.K. Mann and J.F. Weston, eds., *Industrial Concentration: The New Learning*, chapters by Mann, Brozen and Markham.
M.C. Sawyer, *The Economics of Industries and Firms*, chapter 7.
M.A. Utton, *The Political Economy of Big Business*, chapter 4.
R.D. Blair and L.W. Kenny, *Microeconomics for Managerial Decision Making*, chapter 13.

M. Waterson, <u>Economic Theory of the Industry</u>, CUP, 1984, Chapter 7.
J. V. Koch, <u>Industrial Organization and Prices</u>, Chapters 9 and 11.
M. Waterson, "Models of Product Differentiation", <u>Bulletin of Economic Research</u>, 1989.

TOPIC VII
R. Clarke, <u>Industrial Economics</u>, Chapter 5.
F. M. Scherer, <u>Industrial Market Structure and Economic Performance</u>, Chapter 9.
P. J. Devine, N. Lee, R. M. Jones and W. J. Tyson, <u>Introduction to Industrial Economics</u>, Chapter 8 (except section 8.3).
D. A. Hay and D. J. Morris, <u>Industrial Economics</u>, Chapter 7.
H. Demsetz, "Two Systems of Belief About Monopoly" in H. J. Goldschmid et al. (eds), <u>Industrial Concentration: The New Learning</u>, Little Brown, 1974.
F. M. Fisher and J. J. McGowan, "On the Misuse of Accounting Rates of Return to Infer Monopoly Profits", <u>American Economic Review</u>, 1983.

TOPIC VIII
R. Clarke, <u>Industrial Economics</u>, Chapters 11 and 12.
P. J. Devine, N. Lee, R. M. Jones and W. J. Tyson, <u>Introduction to Industrial Economics</u>, Chapter 9 (pp. 330-369).
M. C. Sawyer, <u>The Economics of Industries and Firms</u>, Chapter 15.
HMSO, <u>Mergers Policy</u>, 1988.
HMSO, <u>Restrictive Practices Policy</u>, 1988.
HMSO, <u>Opening Markets: New Policy on Restrictive Trade Practices</u>, 1989.
M. A. Utton, <u>The Political Economy of Big Business</u>, Chapter 7.
F. M. Scherer, <u>Industrial Market Structure and Economic Performance</u>, Chapter 18.
G. Hay, "Competition Policy", <u>Oxford Review of Economic Policy</u>, 1985, SSRR.
M. A. Utton, <u>The Economics of Regulating Industry</u>, Blackwell, 1986, Chapters 6-8.
R. Shaw and P. Simpson, "The Monopolies Commission and the Process of Competition", <u>Fiscal Studies</u>, 1985, SSRR.
J. Fairburn, "British Merger Policy", <u>Fiscal Studies</u>, 1985, SSRR.
K. George, "Monopoly and Merger Policy", <u>Fiscal Studies</u>, 1985, SSRR.
D. Hay and J. Vickers, <u>The Economics of Market Dominance</u>, Blackwell, 1987, Chapters 1 and 2.

SSRR - Photocopies available in the Social Sciences Reading Room, 2nd floor of the Tower Block.

M. A. UTTON
M. WATERSON

UNIVERSITY OF CALIFORNIA
Department of Economics
School of Business Administration

G

Course Outline
Fall, 1989

Econ 224 - The Economics of Institutions
Oliver Williamson

Texts:

Putterman, L., editor (1966). *The Economic Nature of the Firm: A Reader*. New York: Cambridge University Press.

Williamson, O.E. (1985). *The Economic Institutions of Capitalism*. New York: The Free Press.

*denotes optional in readings listed below.

I. Background

*Hayek, F. (1945). "The Use of Knowledge in Society," *American Economic Review*, 35 (September): 519-30.

*Llewellyn, Karl N. (1931). "What Price Contract? An Essay in Perspective," *Yale Law Journal*, 40 (May): 704-51.

*Commons, J. R. (1924). "Law and Economics," *Yale Law Journal*, 34: 371-82.

*Davis, L. E. and D. C. North (1971). *Institutional Change and American Economic Growth*. New York: Cambridge University Press, pp. 3-25.

Coase, R. H. (1988). *The Firm, the Market and the Law*. Chicago: University of Chicago Press, Chapters 2-3.

Arrow, Kenneth J. (1963). "Uncertainty and the Welfare Economics of Medical Care," *American Economic Review*, 53 (December): 941-73.

Simon, Herbert A. (1962). "The Architecture of Complexity," *Proceedings of the American Philosophical Society*, 106 (December): 467-82.

Dalton, Melville (1959). *Men Who Manage*. New York: John Wiley and Sons, pp. 194-215.

II. The New Institutional Economics

1. general

Mathews, R. C. O. (1986). "The Economics of Institutions and the Sources of Economic Growth," *Economic Journal*, 96 (December): 903-18.

2. transaction cost economics

   Williamson (1985): Prologue and Chapters 1-3.

   Klein, Benjamin, R. A. Crawford, and A. A. Alchian. "Vertical Integration, Appropriable Rents, and the Competitive Contracting Process," Chapter 18 in Putterman (1986).

   *Alchian, A. A. (1984). "Specificity, Specialization, and Coalitions," Journal of Economic Theory and Institutions, 140 (March): 34-49.

   Alchian, A. A. and S. Woodward (1987). "Reflections on the Theory of the Firm," Journal of Institutional and Theoretical Economics, 143 (March): 110-37.

3. agency theory

   Alchian, A. and H. Demsetz, "Production, Information Costs, and Economic Organization," Chapter 9 in Putterman (1986).

   Jensen, M. and W. Meckling, "Theory of the Firm," Chapter 17 in Putterman (1986).

   Pratt, John, and Richard Zeckhauser (1985). "An Overview" in Pratt and Zeckhauser, eds., Principals and Agents. Cambridge: Harvard University Press, pp. 15-22.

   *Holmstrom, B. (1979). "Moral Hazard and Observability," Bell Journal of Economics, 10 (Spring): 74-91.

   Tirole, Jean (1986). "Hierarchies and Bureaucracies: On the Role of Collusion in Organizations," Journal of Law, Economics, and Organization, 2 (Fall): 181-214.

4. property rights

   Demsetz, H. (1967). "Toward a Theory of Property Rights," American Economic Review, 57 (May): 347-59.

   Coase, Ronald H. (1959). "The Federal Communications Commission," The Journal of Law and Economics, 2 (October): 1-40.

5. other

   Kreps, David (1984). "Corporate Culture and Economic Theory," unpublished manuscript.

   Akerlof, George (1983). "Loyalty Filters," American Economic Review, 73 (March): 54-63.

   Milgrom, Paul and John Roberts (1988). "An Economic Approach to Influence Activities in Organizations," American Journal of Sociology (Supplement), 94: S154-S179.

Crew, Michael and Charlotte Twight (1989). "On the Efficiency of the Law: A Public Choice Perspective," (unpublished manuscript).

*Milgrom, Paul and John Roberts (1988). "Bargaining Costs, Influence Costs, and the Organization of Economic Activity," Research Paper No. 934 (GSB).

*Hirschman, Albert O. (1970). <u>Exit, Voice and Loyalty</u>. Cambridge, MA: Harvard University Press.

Leibenstein, H. "Allocative Efficiency and X-Efficiency," Chapter 12 in Putterman (1986).

III. Applications

1. vertical integration

Grossman, S., and O. Hart (1986). "The Costs and Benefits of Ownership: A Theory of Vertical and Lateral Integration," <u>Journal of Political Economy</u>, 94 (August): 691-719.

Williamson (1985): Chapters 4-6.

Williamson, O. E. (1988). "The Logic of Economic Organization," <u>Journal of Law, Economics, and Organization</u>, 3 (Spring): 65-93.

*Riordan, M. and O. Williamson (1985). "Asset Specificity and Economic Organization," <u>International Journal of Industrial Organization</u>, 3: 365-78.

Joskow, P. (1988). "Asset Specificity and the Structure of Vertical Relationships: Empirical Evidence," <u>Journal of Law, Economics, and Organization</u>, 3 (Spring): 95-117.

2. complex contracting

*Klein, B. (1980). "Transaction Cost Determinants of 'Unfair' Contractual Arrangements," <u>American Economic Review</u>, 70 (May): 356-62.

Klein, B. and K. B. Leffler (1981). "The Role of Market Forces in Assuring Contractual Performance," <u>Journal of Political Economy</u>, 89 (August): 615-41.

Williamson (1985): Chapters 7-8.

Greif, A. (1989). "Reputation and Coalitions in Medieval Trade: Evidence from the Geniza Documents," unpublished manuscript.

Leitzel, J. (1989). "The New Institutional Economics and a Model of Contract," <u>Journal of Economic Behavior and Organization</u>, 11 (February): 75-89.

Masten, Scott (1984). "The Organization of Production: Evidence from the Aerospace Industry," *Journal of Law and Economics*, 27 (October): 403-18.

3. finance

Fama, E., "Agency Problems and the Theory of the Firm," Chapter 16 in Putterman (1986).

*Fama, E. F. and M. C. Jensen (1983). "Separation of Ownership and Control," *Journal of Law and Economics*, 26 (June): 301-26.

Williamson, O. E. (1988). "Corporate Finance and Corporate Governance," *Journal of Finance*, (July): 567-91.

4. labor

Marglin, S. "What Do Bosses Do?" Chapter 20 in Putterman (1986).

Williamson (1985): Chapters 9-10.

Bowles, S. "The Production Process in a Competitive Economy," Chapter 24 in Putterman (1986).

5. business strategy

Teece, D. (1986). "Profiting from Technological Innovation," *Research Policy*, 15 (December): 285-305.

Aghion, P. and P. Bolton (1987). "Contracts as a Barrier to Entry," *American Economic Review*, 77 (June): 388-402.

6. regulation

Demsetz, H. (1968b). "Why Regulate Utilities?" *Journal of Law and Economics*, 11 (April): 55-66.

Williamson (1985): Chapter 13.

Laffont, Jean-Jacques and Jean Tirole (1989). "The Politics of Government Decision Making: Regulatory Institutions," (unpublished manuscript).

7. socialist enterprise reform

(to be completed following October conference at UCLA)

8. politics

*Stigler, G. J. (1971). "The Theory of Economic Regulation," *Bell Journal of Economics and Management Science*, 2 (Spring): 3-21.

*Yarborough, B. and R. Yarborough (1987). "Institutions for the Governance of Opportunism in International Trade," *Journal of Law, Economics, and Organization*, 3 (Spring): 129-39.

*Moe, T. (1989). "The Politics of Structural Choice: Toward a Theory of Public Bureaucracy," unpublished manuscript.

*Weingast, Barry and William Marshall (1988): The Industrial Organization of Congress; or Why Legislatures, Like Firms, Are Not Organized as Markets," *Journal of Political Economy*, 96: 132-63.

IV. Critiques

1. general

    Winship, Christopher and Sherwin Rosen (1988). "Introduction: Sociological and Economic Approaches to the Analysis of Social Structure," *Supplement to the American Journal of Sociology*, 94: S1-S16.

    Coase, Ronald (1978). "Economics and Contiguous Disciplines," *Journal of Legal Studies*, 7: 201-11.

2. embeddedness

    Granovetter, Mark (1985). "Economic Action and Social Structure: The Problem of Embeddedness," *American Journal of Sociology*, 91 (November): 481-510.

    David, Paul (1985). "Clio and the Economics of QWERTY", *American Economic Review*. 75 (May): 332-37.

    *Hamilton, Gary and Nicole Woolsey Biggert (1988). "Market, Culture, and Authority," *American Journal of Sociology* (Supplement), 94: S52-S94.

3. social structuralism

    *Dimaggio, Paul and Walter Powell (1983). "The Iron Cage Revisited: Institutional Isomorphism and Collective Rationality in Organizational Fields," *American Sociological Review*, 48 (April): 147-60.

    Eccles, Robert and Harrison White (1988). "Price and Authority in Inter-Profit Center Transactions," *American Journal of Sociology* (Supplement), 94: S17-S51.

4. power

    *Emerson, Richard (1962). "Power Dependence Relations," *American Sociological Review*, 27: 31-41.

    Cook, K. and R. Emerson (1984). "Exchange Networks and the Analysis of Complex Organizations," *Research in the Sociology of Organizations*, 3: 1-30.

5. responses

   Williamson, Oliver (1988). "Economics and Sociology," in George Farkas and Paula England, eds., <u>Industries, Firms, and Jobs</u>, New York: Plenum Press, pp. 159-86.

   Williamson, Oliver (1989). "Chester Barnard and the Incipient Science of Organization," unpublished manuscript.

V. Some Surveys (all optional)

   Tirole, Jean (1988). "The Theory of the Firm," Chapter 1 in <u>The Theory of Industrial Organization</u>. Cambridge, MA: MIT Press.

   August 1988 issue of <u>Canadian Journal of Economics</u> (articles by Milgrom and Roberts, by Tirole, and by Hart).

   Stiglitz, J. (1987). "The Causes and Consequences of the Dependence of Quality and Price," <u>Journal of Economic Literature</u>, <u>25</u> (March): 1-48.

   Williamson, O. (1989). "Transaction Cost Economics," in R. Schmalensee and R. Willig, eds., <u>Handbook of Industrial Organization</u>, Cambridge, MA: MIT Press.

ECONOMICS READING LISTS, COURSE OUTLINES, EXAMS, PUZZLES & PROBLEMS
Compiled by Edward Tower, Duke University, August 1990

VOLUME 1 MICROECONOMICS READING LISTS, 227pp.
Including Experimental, Games, Information, Growth, Distribution, Search, Technology, Uncertainty.
de Alessi, Allen, Aron, Baumol, Benabou, Carlton, Cass, Cox, Diamond, Dixit, Ericson, Forster, Frech, Friedman, Green, Grossman, Kuenne, Lazear, Lovell, Mandler, Marglin, Mas-Colell, Newbery, O'Brien, Palmquist, Pencavel, Polemarchakis, Pollak, Randall, Rosen, Scherer, Silberberg, Sunder, Waterson, Weymark, Winter.

VOLUME 2 MICROECONOMICS EXAMS, PUZZLES & PROBLEMS, 283pp.
Cox, Elmendorf, Ingersoll, Nalebuff, Segerson, UCLA, Chic., Col., MI, MN, Penn, Princ., VA, WA, WO, WI.

VOLUME 3 MACRO, MONETARY & FINANCIAL ECONOMICS READING LISTS, 259pp. Abel, Blanchard, Blinder, Cagan, Cass, Eisner, Feiwel, Friedman, Garber, Gordon, Harcourt, Hester, Maccini, Mankiw, Mayer, Mishkin, Mott, Pissarides, Sawyer, Sheffrin, Shell, Shiller, Stein, Summers.

VOLUME 4 MACROECONOMICS, EXAMS, PUZZLES & PROBLEMS, 264pp.
Corden, UCLA, Chic., Col., Duke, Harvard, MI, MN, Penn, Princ., VA, WA, WO, WI.

VOLUME 5 DEVELOPMENT ECONOMICS READING LISTS, 238pp.
Including Human Resources, Institutions, Macro Policy, Public Choice, Project Evaluation, Public Finance in LDCs.
Alm, Aricanli, Balassa, Bardhan, Behrman, Berry, Brock, Bruce, Case, Deolalikar, Devarajan, Edwards, Harris, Helleiner, Krueger, Leff, Marglin, de Melo, Newbery, Nugent, Perkins, Poulson, Rodrik, Schor, Sicular, Snodgrass, Timmer, Vietorisz, Williamson, Zimbalist.

VOLUME 6 DEVELOPMENT ECONOMICS EXAMS, PUZZLES & PROBLEMS with additional reading lists, 193pp.
Including Cases in Dev. Strategies.
Papanek, Schydlowsky, Stern, Streeten, UCLA, Chic., Col., Duke, MI, Penn, Princ., WA, WO, WI.

VOLUME 7 INDUSTRIAL ORGANIZATION & REGULATION READING LISTS, 297pp. Arnould, Baumol, Borenstein, Carlton, Frech, Gertner, Grabowski, Joskow, Katz, Miller, Peltzman, Pindyck, Polasky, Porter, Postlewaite, Salant, Scherer, Swan, Telser, Utton, Waterson, Williamson, Willig.

VOLUME 8 INDUSTRIAL ORGANIZATION & REGULATION EXAMS, PUZZLES & PROBLEMS, 253pp.
Salant, Stegemann, UCLA, Chic., Col., MI, MN, Penn, Princ., VA, WA, WO, WI.

VOLUME 9 INTERNATIONAL ECONOMICS READING LISTS, 292pp.
Anderson, Bardhan, Black, Cohen, Connolly, Copeland, Corden, Dixit, Dominguez, Dornbusch, Edwards, Engel, Ethier, Grossman, Grubel, Helleiner, Kreinin, Krishna, Krueger, Maskus, Matusz, Neary, Obstfeld, Roubini, Snape, Stein, Stern, Vousden, Wigle, Willett.

VOLUME 10 INTERNATIONAL ECONOMICS EXAMS, PUZZLES & PROBLEMS
with additional reading lists, 283pp.
Connolly, Deardorff, Dixit, Dutton, Kenen, Stegemann, Vousden, BC, UCLA, Chic., Col., MI, Penn, Princ., VA, WA, WI.

VOLUME 11 PUBLIC FINANCE READING LISTS, 280pp.
Alm, Anderson, Bishop, Blomquist, Conrad, Ehrenberg, Elmendorf, Feldstein, Fullerton, Gordon, Groenewegen, Hausman, Haveman, Katz, Kesselman, Newbery, Poterba, Quigley, Samuels, Sandler, Schmid, Skinner, Slemrod, Strick, Summers, Viscusi, Wagner, Wildasin.

VOLUME 12 PUBLIC FINANCE EXAMS, PUZZLES & PROBLEMS, 258pp.
Summers, UCLA, Chic., Col., MI, MN, Penn, Princ., VA, WA,WI.

VOLUME 13 ECONOMETRICS READING LISTS, 222pp.
Ashenfelter, Bodkin, Conrad, Hajivassiliou, Kennedy, Kmenta, Maasoumi, Mariano, Mishkin, Mount, Nerlove, Ogaki, Phillips, Porter, Sawyer, Small, Tomek, Witte, Yohe.

VOLUME 14 ECONOMETRICS EXAMS, PUZZLES & PROBLEMS, 298pp.
Gallant, Hajivassiliou, Leung, UCLA, Chic., Col., MI, MN, Penn, Princ., VA, WI.

VOLUME 15 LABOR ECONOMICS READING LISTS, 208pp.
Including Demography, Women, Individuals & Families, Population & Development.
Ashenfelter, Borjas, Brown, Card, Ehrenberg, Gibbons, Gunderson, Hamermesh, Krueger, Lalonde, Lazear, Lee, Marglin, Murphy, Pencavel, Perlman, Polachek, Pollak, Reid, Rosen, Rosenberg, Schor, Stafford, Topel, Yotopoulos.

VOLUME 16 LABOR ECONOMICS EXAMS, PUZZLES & PROBLEMS with additional reading lists, 204 pp.
Including Demography.
Allen, Kniesner, UCLA, Chic., Col., Indiana, MI, MN, Penn, Princ., WI.

VOLUME 17 COMPARATIVE SYSTEMS & PLANNING, 244pp.
Bunce, Bushnell, Connolly, Delgado, Ericson, Garnaut, Goldstein, Marrese, Naylor, Panayotou, Patrick, Putterman, Reynolds, Sicular, Snodgrass, Spechler, Stern, Weitzman, Zimbalist, Col., MI, Penn, WI.

VOLUME 18 MONETARY & FINANCIAL ECONOMICS EXAMS, PUZZLES & PROBLEMS, 264pp.
UCLA, Chic., MI, MN, Penn, Princ., VA, WO, WI.

VOLUME 19 MATHEMATICAL ECONOMICS & APPLIED GENERAL EQUILIBRIUM MODELLING, 242pp.
Including Analytics of Econ. Dev. & Planning, Microcomputer Applications, Control Theory.
Adelman, Dixon, Ericson, Fried, Fullerton, Hertel, Hsiao, Kendrick, Langham, Parmenter, Powell, Robinson, Welford, Wilcoxen, UCLA, Chic., Col., MN, Princ., WI.

VOLUME 20 PUBLIC CHOICE, POLITICAL ECONOMY, LAW & WAR, 266pp.
Including Property Rights, Modernization & Westernization, Non-Neoclassical Theory, Policy Development, Social Institutions, Social Choice, Ec. of Legal Rules and Institutions, Wartime Economies, Vice.

de Alessi, Banuri, Buchanan, Cohen, Cook, Coughlin, Eckert, Feiwel, Fried, Garber, Goodwin, Harper, Harris, Havrilesky, Hirsch, Inman, Katz, Kuenne, Marglin, Mayer, Melendez, Milgate, Mueller, Olson, Polinsky, Postlewaite, Rose-Ackerman, Russell, Samuels, Sandler, Schmid, Schor, Stigler, Vanberg, Viscusi, Weymark, Witte, MI.

VOLUME 21 ENVIRONMENTAL & NATURAL RESOURCE ECONOMICS, 253pp.
Berck, Bishop, Blomquist, Braden, Copes, Dewees, Fisher, Freeman, Kramer, Munro, Polasky, Porter, Randall, Russell, Salant, Seneca, Smith, Stavins, Tietenberg, Toman, Zilberman, IL, MI, WA.

VOLUME 22 AGRICULTURAL ECONOMICS & AGRICULTURE IN ECONOMIC DEVELOPMENT, 200pp.
Including Polit. Ec. of Ag. Dev., World Food System, Real Estate Markets, Rural Dev., Ag. Regulation, Technology, Land Economics.
Anderson, Bates, Berck, de Janvry, Langham, Perloff, Rausser, Ruttan, Sadoulet, Smith, Stevens, Timmer, Wohlgenant, Zilberman, Zusman, Chic.

VOLUME 23 ECONOMIC HISTORY, 240pp.
Cameron, Coats, David, Engerman, English, Goldin, Harley, Jackson, McClelland, Moggridge, Reid, J-L Rosenthal, Sokoloff, Sylla, Temin, Williamson, Wright, UCLA, Chic., MI.

VOLUME 24 HISTORY OF ECONOMIC THOUGHT, 269pp.
Including Methodology, Economics as Literature, Kniesner's Guide to Writing Doctoral Dissertations.
Aspromourgos, Barber, Baumol, Bodkin, Borcherding, Caldwell, Ekelund, Glahe, Gift, Goodwin, Groenewegen, Hands, Harcourt, Kniesner, Lodewijks, Mayer, Mott, Perlman, Putterman, Rochon, Rossetti, Samuels, Spechler, Stigler, Chic., MI, Princ.

VOLUME 25 URBAN, REGIONAL, HEALTH, EDUCATION & TRANSPORT ECONOMICS, 222pp.
Including State & Local Pub. Fin., Econ. of the University.
Arnould, Blomquist, Clotfelter, Ehrenberg, Feldman, Heaver, Hirsch, Inman, Kain, Leonard, Newhouse, Peteraf, Sindelar, Small, Sullivan, Waters, Weisbrod, Wildasin, Wolfe, Wolkoff, Chic., Princ.

The price of each volume is $20. The discount price for the complete set of 25 Economics volumes is $350. A special offer for individuals buying economics volumes: Buy 2 volumes at the regular price, and get additional volumes for $15 each when ordering directly from Eno River Press. These prices include postage and handling for domestic orders only. Other postage charges are: foreign surface @ $1 per volume; Canada air @ $3 per volume; Europe & Latin America air @ $4 per volume; and Asia, Africa & Pacific air @ $10 per volume. U.S. funds only please.

Eno River Press
Box 4900, Duke Station
Durham, N.C. 27706-4900
U.S.A.

BUSINESS ADMINISTRATION READING LISTS AND COURSE OUTLINES
1990

Compiled by Richard Schwindt, *Simon Fraser University*

Volume 1   ACCOUNTING, 229 pages

Contributors: Ashiq Ali, V. Bernard, W.L. Ferrara, G.T. Gilbert, Robert Hagerman, S. Hamlen, Charles Horngren, Young K. Kwon, Herman Leonard, Laureen Maines, G. Mueller, R.D. Nair, Paul Newman, Pekin Ogan, Alan J. Richardson, Byung T. Ro, H.M. Schoenfeld, Gordon Shillinglaw, Brett Trueman, Ross L. Watts, Roman L. Weil, J.J. Williams, Dave Wright, William F. Wright

Volume 2   MARKETING, 315 pages

Contributors: Erin Anderson, I.E. Berger, Thomas Bonoma, Noel Capon, Douglas J. Dalrymple, Wayne DeSarbo, Jehoshua Eliashberg, Pete Fader, Bruce Fauman, Neil M. Ford, Morris B. Holbrook, Stanley C. Hollander, Wayne Hoyer, Ajay Kohli, Philip Kotler, K. Sridhar Moorthy, K.S. Palda, Gordon Patzer, Vithala Rao, Thomas S. Robertson, D. Sexton, John Sherry, Louis W. Stern, Vern Terpstra, Charles B. Weinberg, Jerry Wind, Russell S. Winer, Ugur Yucelt, Youjae Yi

Volume 3   CORPORATE FINANCE AND INVESTMENTS, 206 pages

Contributors: Franklin Allen, S. Bhattacharyya, L.D. Booth, Peter Carr, Michael Fishman, Steve Foerster, Virginia G. France, N. Bulent Gultekin, Robert L. Hagerman, Milton Harris, Campbell R. Harvey, Michael L. Hemler, Roger Ibbotson, Kose John, Jonathan M. Karpoff, Allan W. Kleidon, Robert Korajczyk, Claudio Loderer, James H. Lorie, John D. Martin, M.P. Narayanan, Andrew Postelwaite, Asani Sarkar, G. William Schwert, Lemma W. Senbet, S.Smidt, Stephen P. Zeldes

Volume 4   FINANCIAL THEORY, INSTITUTIONS AND MONEY MARKETS, 202 pages

Contributors: George P. Baker, George Constantinides, Yoon Dokko, Mark R. Eaker, Robert A. Eisenbeis, Edwin J. Elton, Joel Hasbrouck, Chi-fu Huang, Michael Jensen, Avraham Kamara, Robert Kauffman, Robert Korajczyk, Robert E. Krainer, John D. Martin, Frederic S. Mishkin, I.G. Morgan, Carol Osler, James V. Poapst, Arnold Sametz, Anthony Saunders, G. William Schwert, Jay Shanken, S. Smidt, Lewis Spellman, Hal R. Varian, P. Wachtel, Jerry Warner, S. Wheatley, James A. Wilcox, Ralph Winter

Volume 5   INTERNATIONAL BUSINESS, 268 pages

Contributors: Yair Aharoni, Schon Beechler, Earl Cheit, Kang Rae Cho, Jose de la Torre, Steven Globerman, Leslie E. Grayson, Richard Locke, Richard Lyons, Richard W. Moxon, Thomas P. Murtha, Thomas Pugel, Pierre Regibeau, Tom Roehl, Alan Rugman, J.A. Sawyer, Vern Terpstra, J. Frederick Truitt, Stephen Weiss, David Yoffie

Volume 6   INTERNATIONAL BANKING AND FINANCE, 153 pages

Contributors: Robert Aubey, Catherine Bonser-Neal, Laurence D. Booth, Bhagwan Chowdhry, Gunther Dufey, Bernard Dumas, Mark Eaker, David Eiteman, Holger Engberg, Jack Glen, R.J. Herring, Robert Higgins, Robert J. Hodrick, Philippe Jorion, K. Kasa, Richard Levich, Antonio Mello, Carol Osler, Raman Uppal, Ingo Walter, S. Wheatley, Josef Zechner

Volume 7   ORGAIZATIONAL BEHAVIOR, 265 pages

Contributors: Hugh J. Arnold, Susan Ashford, Ellen Auster, Douglas Austrom, Fred Dansereau, Daniel R. Denison, Randall B. Dunham, Peter Frost, Barrie Gibbs, William Glick, Mary Ann Glynn, John Godard, Dev Jennings, Todd Jick, H. Leblebici, Larry Moore, Trond Petersen, Karlene Roberts, Ben Rosen, James P. Walsh, Ross A. Webber

Volume 8   INDUSTRIAL RELATIONS AND HUMAN RESOURCES MANAGEMENT 266 pages

Contributors: William J. Bigoness, Francine Blau, Mario Bognanno, James G. Clawson, William Cooke, John Crispo, Gerald Ferris, John H. Godard, Wallace Hendricks, Archie Kleingartner, Thomas Kochan, Robert LaLonde, John Lawler, David Levine, David McPhillips, Daniel Mitchell, Larry Moore, Raymond A. Noe, Oscar A. Ornati, Robert Rogow, Denise Rousseau, Richard Rowan, James G. Scoville, K. Taira, Harry Triandis, Anil Verma, James P. Walsh

Volume 9   QUANTITATIVE METHODS, RESEARCH DESIGN AND COMPUTER APPLICATIONS IN BUSINESS, 286 pages

Contributors: Charles Blair, David Blair, Norman L. Chervany, Thomas Cooley, Joseph G. Davis, Sid Deshmukh, Al Dexter, Jehoshua Eliashberg, Gordon C. Everest, Gerald Ferris, Robert M. Freund, William Glick, Terry Harrison, Michael Hottenstein, Ted D. Klastorin, M.R. Leenders, Ting-peng Liang, Henry Lucas, Alan W. Neebe, L. Orman, E.R. Petersen, Trond K. Petersen, Donald Richter, Larry Robinson, Paul Rubin, John Sviokla, Clinton White, Carson Woo, W.T. Ziemba

Volume 10   BUSINESS, GOVERNMENT AND SOCIETY, 252 pages

Contributors: Mitchel Abolafia, James A. Brander, R. Chatov, Earl Cheit, Edwin M. Epstein, Gerald Faulhaber, Murray Frank, Thomas Kerr, George C. Lodge, Alfred A. Marcus, David D. Martin, D. Nickerson, Eli Noam, Seth Norton, O. Ornati, Kurt Parkum, Bohumir Pazderka, Sam Peltzman, William A. Sax, Walter D. Scott, William Stanbury, George J. Stigler, Richard S. Tedlow, Richard Vietor, A. Vining, David Vogel, Murray L. Weidenbaum, L.J. White

Volume 11   BUSINESS POLICY AND STRATEGY, 242 pages

Contributors: David A. Aaker, Anthony Boardman, Bala Chakravarthy, Joseph D'Cruz, Gerald Faulhaber, James Fitzsimmons, Murray Frank, Michael Geringer, Arnoldo C. Hax, R.M. Jalland, Alton C. Johnson, Aneel Karnani, Kenneth MacCrimmon, Will Mitchell, K.S. Palda, Margaret A. Peteraf, Robert S. Pindyck, Michael Porter, Katharine Rockett, T.W. Ruefli, Edward Snyder, Howard H. Stevenson, Valerie Suslow, F. Brian Talbot, David J. Teece, Andrew Van de Ven, R.E. White

Volume 12   RISK, DECISION MAKING AND BARGAINING, 271 pages
Compiled by Richard Schwindt & Tim McDaniels

Contributors: R.J. Aldag, Robert Ashton, Max Bazerman, Lee Roy Beach, David Bell, James H. Berson, Philip Bromiley, Peter Carnevale, Peter Cramton, J. David Cummins, Jose de la Torre, James S. Dyer, Baruch Fischhoff, Leonard Greenhalgh, Robin Gregory, Milton Harris, Terry Harrison, Aron Katsenelinboigen, Gordon Kaufman, L. Robin Keller, Peter Kempthorne, Craig W. Kirkwood, Howard Kunreuther, James D. Laing, Kenneth MacCrimmon, Theodore Marmor, John W. Minton, Barry Nalebuff, John W. Payne, J. Edward Russo, Rakesh K. Sarin, George Strauss, A. J. Taylor, Dean Tjosvold, Larry Tomassini, Paul Vatter, Thomas S. Wallsten, Elke Weber, Robert Witt